EVIDENCE OF BAD CHAR

The rule excluding evidence of the defendant's general bad character and disposition to commit the offence has been described as one of the most hallowed rules of evidence. In *Maxwell v DPP*, Lord Sankey described it as 'one of the most deeply rooted and jealously guarded principles of our criminal law.' In reality, it is not particularly ancient, and in recent years it has been increasingly attacked. On technical grounds, the body of law surrounding it has been criticised as over-complicated and inconsistent, and more radical critics have condemned it as unduly favourable to the guilty. In response to this, it was completely recast in Part II of the Criminal Justice Act 2003. This book offers a thorough analysis of the new provisions. The author, an acknowledged expert on the law of evidence, has been engaged in training lawyers and judges on the effect and scope of the new provisions.

Volume 2 in the Criminal Law Library series

Evidence of Bad Character

JR SPENCER

·H A R T·
PUBLISHING

OXFORD AND PORTLAND, OREGON
2006

Published in North America (US and Canada) by
Hart Publishing
c/o International Specialized Book Services
920 NE 58th Avenue, Suite 300
Portland, OR 97213-3786
USA

Tel: +1 503 287 3093 or toll-free: (1) 800 944 6190
Fax: +1 503 280 8832
E-mail: orders@isbs.com
Website: www.isbs.com

Hart Publishing, 16C Worcester Place, Oxford, OX1 2JW
Telephone: +44 (0)1865 517530 Fax: +44 (0) 1865 510710
E-mail: mail@hartpub.co.uk
Website: http//:www.hartpub.co.uk

British Library Cataloguing in Publication Data
Data Available
ISBN-13: 978-1-84113-648-6 (paperback)
ISBN-10: 1-84113-648-4 (paperback)

Typeset by Hope Services Ltd, Abingdon, Oxon
Printed and bound in Great Britain by
TJ International, Padstow, Cornwall

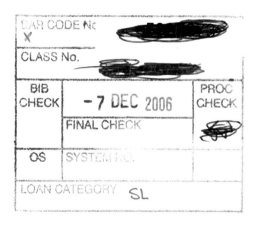

PREFACE

When the Criminal Justice Act 2003 was passed, the Judicial Studies Board organised what the popular press would have called a 'training marathon' to ensure that, when the new legislation was brought into force, the judiciary responsible for criminal work—some 2,000 professional judges and 30,000 lay justices—would (in another journalistic cliché) 'hit the ground running.' For the professional judiciary, this involved putting every judge involved in criminal cases through a short residential training course: courses that ran continuously between mid-January and mid-March 2005, to be ready for when the key provisions of the Act came into force, which was expected to be in April or in May. To help with all this, a team of trainers was recruited and various people were commissioned to write commentaries explaining the main points of the new legislation.

The Judicial Studies Board did me the honour of asking me to join this programme by providing a commentary on the Criminal Justice Act provisions dealing with bad character evidence, which was distributed to all the judges before the training began, and then by acting as one of the instructors at the courses. The three months during which these courses ran were intellectually strenuous: at each session, some new point of difficulty arising from the provisions would come to light, and new challenges were made to my initial solutions to the more obvious ones. As the training progressed, the existence of my commentary became widely known and practitioners began to ask the Judicial Studies Board for access to it. In response to this, it was revised in the light of the input from the judges at the seminars, and a new and improved version was made publicly available on the Judicial Studies Board website. This in turn led to yet more people contacting me with questions and comments about the provisions, and how they are likely to operate in practice.

As the year wore on, written comments on the new provisions began to appear in the legal press, and the Court of Appeal began to hear the first appeals brought by defendants convicted in cases in which they had been applied. Faced with these appeals, the Court of Appeal adopted a co-ordinated approach. Cases raising similar issues were collected into batches, for hearing before courts presided over by senior and experienced judges, who produced wide-ranging judgments specifically intended to provide guidance to the courts below. By December 2005, the Court of Appeal had decided seven of these leading cases, in which no less than

30 defendants were involved.[1] Thanks mainly to these decisions, the law has now become much clearer, and in one of the most recent cases, *Renda and others* [2005] EWCA Crim 2826, the Court of Appeal said, 'This legislation has now been in force for nearly a year. The principles have been considered by this Court on a number of occasions. The responsibility for their application is not for this Court but for trial judges.'

With many of the problems posed by the drafting of the provisions now answered by the courts, the end of December 2005 seemed a good time to produce yet a further new version of the commentary, this time expanded to take account of the case law, and made more widely available as a little book. As readers will discover, this text consists of the expanded commentary plus, as a series of appendices, a collection of basic texts: Criminal Justice Act 2003 Part 11, Chapter 1; Criminal Justice Act 2003 (Categories of Offences) Order 2004, SI 2004/3346; the relevant provisions of the Criminal Procedure Rules 2005, SI 2005/384; the relevant Judicial Studies Board specimen directions, and the text of the seven leading cases.

My grateful thanks are due to a number of people, and groups of people, without whom this book would not have seen the light of day. These include the Judicial Studies Board, who hold the copyright in the original version of the commentary, and who not only allowed but actually encouraged me to publish this expanded version; Richard Hart of Hart Publishing Ltd, who agreed to publish it; and my son Andrew Spencer, of counsel, whose idea it originally was to turn the commentary into a book.

I am also indebted to a range of people who discussed the provisions with me, so providing me with new ideas and challenging my own. These include my friend and colleague Dr Roderick Munday, who shared with me the task of lecturing on bad character evidence at the seminars; although I do not always agree with them, his views are always stimulating. They also include Judge John Phillips, who commissioned the text on behalf of the Judicial Studies Board, and who kindly read and commented both on the original draft and on parts of the revised commentary; and Judge David Radford, who with his brethren at Snaresbrook Crown Court told me how the new law is working out in practice. But above all, my thanks are due to the judges and practitioners whose comments at the seminars and in correspondence afterwards raised new questions and helped me to refine my own ideas.

---

[1] *Hanson, Gilmore and P* [2005] EWCA Crim 824, [2005] 1 WLR 3169 (22 March); *Bovell and Dowds* [2005] EWCA Crim 1091, [2005] 2 CrAppR 27 (401) (25 April); *Edwards, Fysh, Duggan and Chohan* [2005] EWCA Crim 1813, [2006] 1 CrAppR 3 (31) (29 June); *Highton, Van Nguyen and Carp* [2005] EWCA Crim 1985, [2005] 1 WLR 3472 (28 July); *Renda, Ball, Akram, Osborurne, Razaq and Razaq* [2005] EWCA Crim 2826 (10 November); *Weir, Somanathan, Yaxley-Lennon, Manister, Hong and De* [2005] EWCA Crim 2866 [2006] 1 CrAppR 19 (303) (11 November); and *Edwards and Rowlands, McLean, Smith, and Enright and Gray* [2005] EWCA Crim 3244 (21 December).

As previously mentioned, the government's original plan was that the bad character evidence provisions of the Criminal Justice Act 2003 should come into force in April 2005, at the same time as the other provisions about evidence, and the training programme for judges was constructed on that basis. This being so, there was consternation in the legal world when, in October 2004, the government announced that it now proposed to bring the bad character evidence provisions into force on 15 December 2004—before the training programme had begun. In Parliament, and in the press, the government was accused of advancing the implementation date for the sole purpose of ensuring favourable headlines in the press about being 'tough on crime' at a politically convenient time. Unabashed, it still brought the provisions into force early, and in consequence the judges were, in effect, thrown in at the deep end without having yet been taught to swim. Fortunately, they seem to have coped with the new provisions relatively easily, and it is to their credit that they did so. However, when wrestling untrained with the new provisions, they must have seen the irony of the situation when on 15 December 2004 the main item in the news was not the Home Office press release announcing 'Evidence of bad character to be disclosed to juries,' but the personal problems of the Home Secretary, who on that day resigned in unfortunate circumstances.

The bad character evidence provisions of the Criminal Justice Act 2003 were enacted amid bitter controversy. In seeking to make evidence of the defendant's bad character more readily admissible, the government stressed the need (as they saw it) to increase the proportion of convictions. In opposing this, lawyers in both Houses of Parliament accused the government of throwing away a vital safeguard against the wrongful conviction of the innocent. Tempers rose, and at times the government and its proposals were denounced in the strongest terms. At one point, Lord Thomas of Gresford, QC, likened the Home Secretary to Robespierre, and drew a parallel between the justice system he foresaw as evolving after these reforms and the one that France knew during the Reign of Terror.[2] Much of the discussion of the provisions that has taken place in the legal press has been equally gloomy, and some of it almost as apocalyptic.

Unlike most of my fellow academics, I am in favour of these provisions, as those who read the rest of this book will discover.

In my view, admitting evidence of the defendant's previous misconduct is neither dangerous nor unjust, provided there is other solid evidence that links him to the offence. The danger arises where such evidence is allowed to be used as a substitute for more convincing evidence where the case against him is otherwise weak. The risk, as has been widely pointed out by those opposed to these provisions, is that the police will go out and arrest 'all the usual suspects'. But I believe the risk of injustice is only real if, after arrest, 'the usual suspicions' then suffice to see the usual suspects are convicted. This outcome can be avoided by excluding evidence

---

[2] Hansard, HL, vol 667 cols 1257–1258 (14 December 2004).

of the defendant's bad character in any case in which the rest of the evidence is weak. Powers to exclude bad character evidence in certain cases are expressly conferred by sections 101(3) and 103(3) of the Act, and these powers are supplemented, in my view, by the court's general discretion under section 78 of the Police and Criminal Evidence Act 1984 to exclude prosecution evidence that would make the trial unfair. These powers can and should be used to counter this particular risk.

In *Hanson, Gilmore and P*,[3] the first of the leading cases in which the new provisions were interpreted, the Court of Appeal took essentially this line.

> The starting point should be for judges and practitioners to bear in mind that Parliament's purpose in the legislation, as we divine it from the terms of the Act, was to assist in the evidence based conviction of the guilty, without putting those who are not guilty at risk of conviction by prejudice. It is accordingly to be hoped that prosecution applications to adduce such evidence will not be made routinely, simply because a defendant has previous convictions, but will be based on the particular circumstances of each case.

A court, it later added, 'must always consider the strength of the prosecution case. If there is no or very little other evidence against a defendant, it is unlikely to be just to admit his previous convictions, whatever they are . . . Evidence of bad character cannot be used simply to bolster a weak case . . .'

I believe as long as these points are born in mind, the new law on bad character evidence will be a tool that helps the criminal courts achieve their overriding objective: which, as the new Criminal Procedure Rules remind us, is to deal with cases justly—and this means, first and foremost, securing the acquittal of the innocent and the conviction of the guilty.

JR SPENCER
Cambridge, January 2006

---

[3] See n 1 above; p 153 below.

CONTENTS

TABLE OF CASES

*References in **bold** are to the page numbers of the Appendices. Otherwise references are to paragraph numbers in the commentary.*

TABLE OF LEGISLATION

*References in **bold** are to the page numbers of the Appendices. Otherwise references are to paragraph numbers in the commentary.*

Primary Legislation

Statutory Instruments

TABLE OF TREATIES

TABLE OF REFERENCES TO
STATUTES IN CASES

*References in **bold** are to the page numbers of the Appendices. Otherwise references are to paragraph numbers in the commentary.*

1

INTRODUCTION

1.1 In English law, the defendant's character, whether good or bad, has always been considered relevant to sentence, insofar as the court had a discretion as to the sentence to impose.[1] It therefore goes without saying that evidence of the defendant's bad character has always been admissible in evidence at the sentencing stage. Indeed, in the past the legal system has taken considerable trouble to ensure that the sentencing court is made aware of the criminal record of the defendant, if he had one: for several centuries, first-time offenders convicted of theft or manslaughter were branded on the thumb, in order to make absolutely sure that they would be sentenced with the full rigour of the law if they appeared in court again.[2]

1.2 By contrast, the courts have been traditionally reluctant to treat the defendant's bad character as admissible evidence at the earlier stage of the proceedings at which his guilt or innocence is determined. Until the Criminal Justice Act (CJA) 2003, the position at trial was that a defendant with a clean record could adduce his good character as evidence in the hope of persuading the court that he was less likely to have committed the offence charged, or more credible in his evidence, or both;[3] but a defendant whose character was bad could not in general have this used in evidence against him at the trial. The rule excluding evidence of the defendant's general bad character and disposition to commit the offence as evidence at trial has been described as one of the most hallowed rules of evidence. In *Maxwell v DPP*, Lord Sankey described it as 'one of the most deeply rooted and jealously guarded principles of our criminal law.'[4]

1.3 In reality, however, the rule is not particularly ancient,[5] and in recent years it has been increasingly attacked. On technical grounds, the body of law surrounding

---

[1] Although views have differed sharply over the years as to how much weight the sentencing court ought to give to it. For a review, see AJ Ashworth, *Sentencing and Criminal Justice* (4th edn, Cambridge, CUP, 2005) ch 6.

[2] JH Baker, *An Introduction to English Legal History* (4th edn, London, Butterworths, 2002) 515.

[3] *Vye* [1993] 1 WLR 471; *Aziz* [1996] AC 41; and see the Judicial Studies Board Specimen Direction no 23.

[4] [1894] AC 57, at 65.

[5] It dates from the mid-nineteenth century; see J Stone, 'The Rule of Exclusion of Similar Fact Evidence: England' (1933) 46 *Harvard Law Review* 954. An early case was *Cole* (unreported 1810): see *Russell on Crime* (12th edn, London, Stevens, 1964) 737.

it has been criticised as over-complicated and inconsistent, and more radical critics have condemned it as unduly favourable to the guilty. It was in response to this that it was completely recast in Part 11 of the CJA 2003.

Technical Criticisms of the Previous Law

1.4 In broad outline, the basic rule was not difficult to state. The classic formulation was made by Lord Herschell in *Makin v Attorney-General for New South Wales*[6]:

> It is undoubtedly not competent for the prosecution to adduce evidence tending to show that the accused has been guilty of criminal acts other than those covered by the indictment, for the purpose of leading to the conclusion that the accused is a person likely from his criminal conduct or character to have committed the offence for which he is being tried. On the other hand, the mere fact that the evidence adduced tends to show the commission of other crimes does not render it inadmissible if it be relevant to an issue before the jury, and it may be so relevant if it bears upon the question whether the acts alleged to constitute the crime charged in the indictment were designed or accidental, or to rebut a defence which would otherwise be open to the accused.

But, as Lord Herschell admitted, if the principles themselves are clear 'the application of them is by no means free from difficulty.' Around the basic rule, a large body of detailed law grew up. This evolved as three separate groups of rules, governing three situations: the defendant's bad character as evidence in-chief, the defendant's bad character as a topic of cross-examination, and the defendant's bad character as evidence for a co-defendant. One criticism of the resulting body of law was that, in each group, the principle was interpreted in different ways.

1.5 Another technical criticism was the gulf between the rules governing evidence of the defendant's character and disposition, and the rules on evidence of the character and disposition of other people (and in particular, prosecution witnesses). For defendants, the rule was that they could produce evidence of their good character if they had one, but their bad character could not generally be used against them. For witnesses, the position was the reverse: a witness was liable to have his discreditable past brought up against him to undermine his credibility, but his good character could not generally be used to enhance it.[7] A related criticism centred upon what frequently happened in sex cases. Although the defendant's

---

[6] [1894] AC 57.
[7] The law on this point is complex—and distinctly odd. Where the character of a witness is attacked, he can be 'rehabilitated' by evidence of his general reputation for veracity, but not by concrete evidence of his truthful behaviour; see *Beard* [1998] Crim LR 585.

record for sexual misbehaviour (if he had one) was usually suppressed, at common law the defence could use the complainant's irregular sex-life in an attempt to discredit her or her complaint. This led to legislative intervention in 1976 and again in 1999.[8]

Radical Criticism

1.6 The rule was also criticised more radically as counter-intuitive and unduly favourable to the guilty. The radical critics argued that it is not unfair to assume that a person with a demonstrably bad character is more likely to be guilty of the offence charged than a person whose character is demonstrably good. So this is a piece of background information which the tribunal of fact should know—and should be trusted to give the appropriate degree of weight.

1.7 The rule was also said to be unrealistic. In practice, the jury or magistrates sometimes know that the defendant has a criminal record, and where they do not know, may guess (and possibly guess wrong). The point was well illustrated by a letter from a former juror to *The Times* some years ago:

> I see that after a recent trial at the Old Bailey . . . some jurors burst into tears, when having acquitted a defendant of murder they were told that he had previous convictions. I would have thought that it was very easy to know whether a defendant had a murky past, although the jury is not supposed to take this into consideration in their deliberations. It is my experience, having sat on several juries, that if the defendant has a clean past record the defending counsel will make a big thing of this, and even if the defendant has pleaded guilty, counsel will say that the present position of the defendant is due to a temporary lapse of honesty. If, however, the defendant has a bad record, defending counsel keeps very quiet on this point. My experience resulted in only a small sample, but it seemed to work every time.[9]

Because of this, it would be better, it was said, if the matter were brought out into the open and the fact-finders given official information about the defendant's antecedents which is accurate.[10]

---

[8] Sexual Offences Act 1976 s2; Youth Justice and Criminal Evidence Act 1999 s41.

[9] *The Times*, 17 March 1986.

[10] A point eloquently made by Penny Darbyshire, 'Previous Misconduct and Magistrates' Courts: Some Tales from the Real World' [1997] *Crim LR* 105. The psychology of this is disputed: see Sally Lloyd-Bostock, 'The Effect on Lay Magistrates of Hearing that the Defendant is of Good Character, being Left to Speculate, or Hearing that He has a Previous Conviction' [2006] *Crim LR* 189.

1.8 Radical critics also pointed out that in continental Europe, including in countries where as here the system is broadly 'adversarial,' and those where lay people are involved as fact-finders, the court is routinely informed about the defendant's criminal record. In theory, continental courts regard evidence about the defendant's character as mainly relevant to sentence, and hear his antecedents at the start of the proceedings because—unlike in England—the finding of guilt and the sentencing take place at one single session, at which evidence relevant to guilt or innocence and evidence relevant to sentence are heard together. But whatever the theoretical position may be, in practice continental courts are undoubtedly influenced by information about the defendant's character when deciding the issue of his guilt, at least to some extent. And this is not generally criticised as tending to produce injustice.

1.9 Radical criticism of the exclusionary rule was accentuated by various high-profile cases where, following a defendant's acquittal, he was shown to have a record that appeared to put his guilt beyond doubt. One such case was that of Simon Berkowitz, who in 1992 was accused of burgling the offices of Paddy Ashdown's solicitor and stealing papers relating to an embarrassing incident in Mr Ashdown's private life, which he had then tried to sell to the *News of the World* for £30,000. His defence was that he had been given them, for nothing, by a man he had met in a pub, whose identity he did not know, and the jury acquitted him. It then came out that he had a record of 240 previous convictions, 230 of them for burglary.[11] A similar reaction was provoked by the case of William Beggs. In 1987, Beggs was convicted of murdering a man by slashing him with a razor-blade, the court hearing evidence of several earlier incidents in which he had apparently cut men for no intelligible reason. In 1990, the Court of Appeal quashed his conviction, because evidence of the other incidents should not have been admitted.[12] Then in 2001, he was convicted of another and particularly gruesome murder. The detective responsible for his arrest in 1987 told the BBC that when his earlier conviction was quashed he was 'quite aghast at what had happened.'[13]

The Law Commission's Proposals

1.10 In 1994, the Home Secretary referred the rules on evidence of previous misconduct to the Law Commission, which produced a lengthy Consultation

---

[11] *The Times*, 5–13 August 1992.
[12] (1990) 90 CrAppR 430.
[13] BBC news, 12 October 2001.

Paper in 1996,[14] followed in 2001 by a Report.[15] The Law Commission accepted the technical criticisms of the exclusionary rule, but rejected the radical criticism. In this, the Law Commission was influenced by experimental work carried out by Dr Sally Lloyd-Bostock, suggesting that fact-finders are more likely to convict where they know that the defendant has a criminal record.[16] From this the Law Commission deduced that bad character evidence is potentially 'prejudicial', and a broad exclusionary rule is necessary to keep most of it out. However, they were in no doubt that the rules as they then stood were untidy, and put forward a scheme to codify and amend them. Their proposals were designed to rationalise the current rules, and not to make character evidence more readily admissible. As they explained:

> We are unable to say whether, if our scheme were carried into effect, more or less bad character evidence would be presented to fact-finders. . . . Our inability to make such a prediction does not trouble us because . . . we have not started from a position that the admittance of more or less bad character evidence should be the outcome of our recommendations. We have sought, rather, to construct a consistent and balanced process under which the conflicting interests of the various parties may best be advanced and protected, and the fairness of criminal trials generally enhanced.[17]

1.11 To govern the use of bad character evidence by the prosecution, the Law Commission proposed a single rule, applicable to both evidence in-chief and evidence elicited from the defendant in cross-examination. Where such evidence 'had to do with the alleged facts of the offence,' or was 'misconduct in connection with the investigation or prosecution of that offence,' it should be admissible automatically. But in other cases, the prosecution should only be allowed to adduce such evidence by leave, and this should only be given where one of a number of 'gateway' conditions applies: (i) it is background information without which the court would find it difficult or impossible to understand the case; (ii) it has 'substantial probative value' in respect of a matter in issue in the proceedings; (iii) it relates to the defendant's credibility, in a case where the defendant has defended himself by attacking another person's credibility, or (iv) it is given to 'correct a false impression' that the defendant has created.

---

[14] *Evidence in Criminal Proceedings: Previous Misconduct of a Defendant* (Law Commission Consultation Paper no 141, 1996). For academic comment, see Paul Roberts, 'All the Usual Suspects: a Critical Appraisal of the Law Commission Consultation Paper No. 141' [1997] *Crim LR* 75; Jenny McEwan, 'Law Commission Dodges the Nettles in Consultation Paper No. 141' [1997] *Crim LR* 93, and Darbyshire, n 10 above.
[15] *Evidence of Bad Character in Criminal Proceedings* (Law Com no 273, Cm 5257, October 2001). See Jenny McEwan, 'Previous Misconduct at the Crossroads: Which Way Ahead?' [2002] *Crim LR* 180.
[16] For the first study, see Sally Lloyd-Bostock, 'The Effects on Juries of Hearing about the Defendant's Previous Criminal Record: a Simulation Study' [2000] *Crim LR* 734; for the second study, on magistrates, see Appendix A of the Law Commission Report, n 15 above.
[17] Law Commission Report, n 15 above, §§1.10 and §1.11.

1.12 The Law Commission also made two recommendations to strengthen the position of the defence when faced with evidence of bad character. First, it proposed a restriction on the joinder of counts for different offences that are broadly similar, but not similar enough to make the evidence 'cross-admissible'.[18] Secondly, it proposed a new duty on the court to stop the trial where the case consists of 'similar fact' evidence arising from a number of different incidents, and it appears that the evidence may be 'contaminated': ie, the result of fabrication or suggestion.

1.13 As regards evidence of the defendant's bad character when adduced in his defence by a co-defendant, the Law Commission also proposed a requirement of judicial leave, to be granted only where a number of conditions are met. And it proposed a similar leave requirement where any of the parties proposes to adduce evidence of the bad character of a person other than the defendant: whether a witness, or any other person who had allegedly been involved in the events.

1.14 In his *Review of the Criminal Courts*,[19] which appeared shortly before the Law Commission Report, Lord Justice Auld acknowledged his own 'long held resistance' to putting a defendant's previous convictions in evidence, but expressed the view that 'there is much to be said for a more radical view than has so far found favour with the Law Commission, for placing more trust in the fact finders and for introducing some reality in this complex corner of the law.' But, he stressed, in his view a review of the law relating to bad character evidence ought properly to take place in the context of 'a wider review of the law of criminal evidence as a whole.'[20]

The Government's Response: the New Law

1.15 After hinting in two White Papers that it also favoured a more radical reform,[21] in November 2002 the government introduced a Criminal Justice Bill containing clauses about character evidence that were based in part on the Law Commission's proposals, but had been significantly 'bent' to make evidence of the defendant's bad character more readily admissible.

---

[18] As in *Ludlow v Metropolitan Police Commissioner* [1971] AC 29.
[19] The Stationery Office, October 2001.
[20] Chapter 11, §120.
[21] 'Complex, sometimes archaic and ambiguous laws give rise to legal arguments over the admissibility or otherwise of evidence which slow down the process of criminal trials. Reform should have the aim of ensuring that in deciding cases, courts have access to all relevant information': *Criminal Justice, The Way Ahead* (Cm 5074, February 2001). In *Justice for All* (Cm 5563, July 2002) the government announced its intention to 'overhaul the rules of evidence to ensure the widest possible range of relevant material is available for a judgment. This includes making information available to judges and juries on previous convictions and misconduct where it is relevant and put in context.'

1.16 This was done in part by dropping, as regards evidence of the defendant's bad character, the Law Commission's main proposed safeguard: namely, the requirement of judicial leave. The leave requirement was to be retained to control the admission of evidence of bad character of 'non-defendants'—but not the admission of such evidence against the defendant (whether by the prosecution or a co-defendant).

1.17 Like the Law Commission, the government proposed to make evidence of the defendant's misbehaviour automatically admissible if it was closely connected with the facts of the alleged offence, or took place during the investigation or prosecution. Evidence of the defendant's 'bad character' that fell outside this definition would be admissible against him, without any need for judicial leave, where it came within a number of specified 'gateways.' Some of these were similar to those contained in the Law Commission's scheme, but had been enlarged by the removal of qualifying words and phrases. And there was an extra 'gateway' of potentially enormous breadth: where the material 'is evidence of the defendant's conviction for an offence of the same description, or of the same category, as the one with which he is charged.'[22] This extra 'gateway' was criticised in Parliament, and the Bill was eventually amended so as to block it up. But in the course of the reconstruction, one of the other 'gateways' was enlarged, with a view to letting through some of the evidence that the government had hoped would get in through the 'gateway' that Parliament removed.[23]

Scheme in Part 11 of the Criminal Justice Act 2003

1.18 In broad outline, the 'character evidence' provisions that were eventually enacted are as follows.

(i) 'Evidence of bad character' is defined so as to exclude evidence directly connected with the offence with which the defendant is charged, plus any misbehaviour during the course of the investigation or prosecution (section 98).

(ii) The common law rules governing 'the admissibility of evidence of bad character in criminal proceedings' are abolished (section 99), and so are the rules contained in the Criminal Evidence Act 1898 about cross-examining defendants as to character (Schedule 37, Part 5).

(iii) Evidence of the bad character of a person other than the defendant is admissible only with judicial leave, to be granted only on certain stated grounds (section 100).

---

[22] Clause 84(1)(d) in the Bill.
[23] For further details, see §4.18 below.

(iv) Evidence of the defendant's bad character is admissible if any of the follow-
      ing 'gateways' is open, but not otherwise (section 101(1)):

   (a) all parties to the proceedings agree to the evidence being admissible;
   (b) the evidence is adduced by the defendant himself or is given in answer to
        a question asked by him in cross-examination and intended to elicit it;
   (c) it is important explanatory evidence;
   (d) it is relevant to an important matter in issue between the defendant and
        the prosecution;
   (e) it has substantial probative value in relation to an important matter in
        issue between the defendant and a co-defendant;
   (f) it is evidence to correct a false impression given by the defendant; or
   (g) the defendant has made an attack on another person's character.

The meaning of five of these 'gateways' is elaborated in sections 102 to 106. Judicial
leave is not required: but where 'gateway' (d) or (g) is involved, the court has (in
effect) a discretion to exclude (section 101(3)).

1.19 Adopting the Law Commission's proposal (see §1.10 above), the Act
imposes a duty on the court to stop the trial where the evidence of bad character
'is contaminated' (section 107). But the Act did not implement the Law
Commission's recommendation about limiting the joinder of counts for different
offences that are broadly similar, although not similar enough to make the evidence 'cross-admissible.' Nor did it carry out the Law Commission's proposal to
repeal section 27 of the Theft Act 1968, which makes evidence of previous misconduct widely admissible in prosecutions for handling stolen goods; so this
remains in force, as do some other similar provisions.[24]

Scope of the reform

1.20 By section 99(1), 'The common law rules governing the admissibility of evidence of bad character in criminal proceedings are abolished.' The abolition is
limited to the rules relating to *bad* character, and therefore leaves intact the common law rules about the admissibility of evidence of *good* character, and the weight
to be accorded to it. And insofar as this provision abolishes the existing rules on
evidence of bad character, it only applies to those relating to 'bad character' as
restrictively defined in section 98 (see Ch 2 below). One commentator has also

---

[24] eg s1(2) of the Official Secrets Act 1911: see Roderick Munday, 'What Constitutes "Other
Reprehensible Behaviour" under the Bad Character Provisions of the Criminal Justice Act 2003?'
[2005] *Crim LR* 24.

pointed out that section 99 abolishes the common rules on the *admissibility* of evidence of bad character, and not their *inadmissibility*—with the suggestion that it is theoretically possible to argue that the common law exclusionary rules qualify the apparent admissibility of such evidence under the provisions of the Act;[25] but as this interpretation would frustrate the obvious purpose of the Act, the argument seems most unlikely to succeed. The same commentator points out, more plausibly, that section 99 does not abolish the common law rules—such as they are—about the *weight* to be given to evidence of misconduct.

To What Extent does the Court have Power to Exclude Bad Character Evidence that is Prima Facie Admissible under Section 101?

1.21 If the 'gateway' through which it would otherwise go is section 101(1)(d) ('it is relevant to an important matter in issue between the defendant and the prosecution') or section 101(1)(g) ('the defendant has made an attack on another person's character'), then section 101(3) expressly confers on the court a duty to exclude, the terms of which mirror those of the power contained in section 78 of the Police and Criminal Evidence Act (PACE), only expressed in mandatory terms:[26]

> The court must not admit evidence under subsection (1)(d) or (g) if, on an application by the defendant to exclude it, it appears to the court that the admission of the evidence would have such an adverse effect on the fairness of the proceedings that the court ought not to admit it.

And where the prosecution seek to admit evidence of the defendant's previous convictions by attempting to use 'gateway (d)' as enlarged by section 103(2), the duty to exclude evidence is reinforced by section 103(3), which also provides that:

> Subsection (2) does not apply in the case of a particular defendant if the court is satisfied, by reason of the length of time since the conviction or for any other reason, that it would be unjust for it to apply in his case.

But what is the position if the 'gateway' is one of the others? Could the court validly exclude the evidence by virtue of its PACE 1984 section 78 power to exclude

---

[25] Colin Tapper, 'The Criminal Justice Act 2003: Evidence of Bad Character' [2004] *Crim LR* 533, at 540.

[26] In practice, the fact that PACE 1984 s78 says the judge 'may' exclude whereas CJA 2003 s101(4) says the judge 'must' exclude is unlikely to produce different results. It would be a singularly perverse judge who, when applying s78, first found 'the admission of the evidence would have such an adverse effect on the fairness of the proceedings that the court ought not to admit it,' but then decided that, because s78 says 'may' not 'must,' he would exercise his discretion to admit it!

prosecution evidence that would make the trial unfair, or its common law discretion to exclude evidence that is more prejudicial than probative?[27] This is a loose end that the Act does not firmly tie, and the position is left open.

1.22 Section 112(3) provides that 'Nothing in this Chapter affects the exclusion of evidence . . . (c) on grounds other than the fact that it is evidence of a person's bad character.' This obviously allows the court to exclude evidence where it is inadmissible for some reason other than its status as evidence of bad character—for example, where the source of it is hearsay, or it was illegally obtained. But it is not wholly clear that it applies to allow the court to exclude the evidence under either section 78 of PACE 1984, or because it is more prejudicial than probative, where a step in the argument is the proposition that 'this evidence is weak, and/or misleading, because it is evidence of bad character.' And it obviously falls short of section 126(2)(a)—which, in the context of the reform of the hearsay rule, expressly provides that nothing in the relevant provisions prejudices section 78 of PACE 1984.

1.23 One possible view is that the court's general discretionary powers to suppress evidence are excluded in respect of bad character evidence admissible under section 101. On this view, the general power in section 78 of PACE 1984 is impliedly ousted by reason of the fact that section 101(3) confers a power expressed in virtually identical terms, but only in respect of evidence admissible via the 'gateways' mentioned section 1(d) and (g). Similarly, it could be said that the common law power to exclude evidence considered by the court to be more prejudicial than probative is impliedly excluded by section 99, which abolishes the common law rules on the admissibility of evidence of bad character. The common law exclusionary rules, it could be argued, were built on the basic premise that evidence of the defendant's bad character is more prejudicial than probative almost by definition, and therefore to be admitted only in highly exceptional cases. If the courts construed the new rules contained in sections 101 onwards as subject to a general discretion to exclude evidence they consider to be more prejudicial than probative, this would frustrate the evident will of Parliament to replace the common law rules with something else.

1.24 The alternative view is that the new rules on bad character evidence are indeed subject to the courts' general discretionary powers to exclude evidence. These powers, it could be argued, are a fundamental part of the rules of criminal

---

[27] *Christie* [1914] AC 545; the discretion was expressly preserved when PACE 1984 s78 of was enacted; by s82(3), 'Nothing in this Part of this Act shall prejudice any power of a court to exclude evidence (whether by preventing questions being put or otherwise) at its discretion.'

evidence, where they exist to ensure that defendants are fairly tried—so only express words in a statute should be taken to exclude them. When Parliament has previously changed the law to make admissible other forms of evidence that were previously excluded, the courts have always construed the new rules as subject to the discretionary powers to exclude;[28] indeed, they have done so even where the statute in question gave the court some specific discretionary power to do so.[29] So, because Parliament has not expressly stated that the general exclusionary powers are ousted, it must be assumed they still apply.

1.25 In fact, the Court of Appeal has now twice expressed a preference for the view that the court's general powers under section 78 of PACE 1984 do apply here. In *Highton and others*, Lord Woolf said this:

> The question also arises whether reliance can be placed on section 78 of the Police and Criminal Evidence Act 1984. The application of section 78 does not call directly for decision in this case. We, therefore, do not propose to express any concluded view as to the relevance of section 78. However, it is right that we should say that, without having heard full argument, our inclination is to say that section 78 provides an additional protection to a defendant. In the light of this preliminary view as to the effect of section 78, judges may consider that it is a sensible precaution, when making rulings as to the use of evidence of bad character, to apply the provisions of section 78 and exclude evidence where it would be appropriate to do so under section 78, pending a definitive ruling to the contrary. Adopting this course will avoid any risk of injustice to the defendant.
>
> In addition, as section 78 serves a very similar purpose to article 6 of the Convention for the Protection of Human Rights and Fundamental Freedoms, following the course we have recommended should avoid any risk of the court failing to comply with article 6. To apply section 78 should also be consistent with the result to which the court would come if it complied with its obligation under section 3 of the Human Rights Act 1998 to construe sections 101 and 103 of the 2003 Act in accordance with the Convention.[30]

1.26 In *Somanathan*,[31] where the issue was whether evidence of the defendant's bad character was admissible against him *inter alia* through 'gateway (f),' a differently constituted Court of Appeal said:

> We note that the provisions of section 101(3) do not apply to subsection (1)(f), and we see no reason to doubt that section 78 of the 1984 Act should be considered where section 101(1)(f) is relied on (see the judgment of Lord Woolf CJ in *Highton and others*).

---

[28] eg with the evidence of young children; see *DPP v M* [1997] 2 CrAppR 70, at 75.
[29] As with 'documentary hearsay' under the Criminal Justice Act 1988; see *R v D* [2002] 2 CrAppR (36) 601, at 613.
[30] [2005] EWCA Crim 1985, [2005] 1 WLR 3472, **p 183 below**, at §§13 and 14.
[31] See *Weir and others* [2005] EWCA Crim 2866, **p 206 below**, [2006] 1 CrAppR 19 (203), at §44.

It therefore now seems safe to assume that the court's general discretion under section 78 of PACE 1984 does indeed apply to evidence of the defendant's bad character which would otherwise be admissible under the new provisions.

1.27 However, it seems likely that, in practice, the court's general discretion to exclude evidence of the defendant's bad character will not add very much to what is already present in the Act itself. The 'gateways' contained in section 101(1)(d) and (g) are already subject to a discretionary power to exclude set out in section 101(3). Of the other gateways, no issue of discretionary exclusion is likely to arise in respect of the ones contained in section 101(1)(a) (where the parties have agreed to admit the evidence) or (b) (where the bad character evidence came from the defendant). So, in practice, the issue is only relevant to the 'gateways' described in section 101(1)(c) ('important explanatory evidence'), (e) ('it has substantial probative value in relation to an important matter in issue between the defendant and a co-defendant') and (f) ('it is given to correct a false impression given by the defendant').

1.28 As regards 'important explanatory evidence' under section 101(1)(c), the Act provides that 'evidence is important explanatory evidence if (a) without it, the court or jury would find it impossible or difficult properly to understand other evidence in the case, and (b) its value for understanding the case as a whole is substantial.'[32] If a court finds this test is satisfied, it is unlikely to find it appropriate to exclude the evidence under either of its discretionary powers. The same is true of evidence 'given to correct a false impression' under section 101(1)(f). The Act provides that 'evidence is admissible under section 101(1)(f) only if it goes no further than is necessary to correct the false impression.'[33] Again, if a court has found this test to be satisfied, it is hardly likely to view the evidence as either making the trial 'unfair' or being more prejudicial than probative. And it seems even less likely that a court would apply either of the exclusionary discretions to shut out bad character evidence that would otherwise be admissible on behalf of a co-defendant under section 101(1)(e). Section 78 of PACE 1984 is expressly limited to prosecution evidence;[34] and the courts have always treated the common law discretion as limited in this way too, declining to use it to exclude bad character evidence called by co-defendants.[35]

---

[32] CJA 2003 s102.
[33] *Ibid* s105(6).
[34] By PACE 1984 s78(1), 'In any proceedings the court may refuse to allow evidence *on which the prosecution proposes to rely* to be given if . . ..'
[35] *Neale* (1977) 65 CrApp R 304, at 306; IH Dennis, *The Law of Evidence* (2nd edn, London, Sweet & Maxwell, 2002) 650.

On What Basis should the Courts Exercise their Powers to Exclude Otherwise Admissible Evidence of the Defendant's Bad Character?

1.29 What is the real risk with admitting evidence of the defendant's bad character? I believe that the real danger is not so much that the tribunal of fact will be unduly prejudiced by it: instead, it is the risk that it will be used to tip the scales in a case in which the rest of the evidence is weak or non-existent.[36]

1.30 A gruesome illustration of this problem is the famous case of Oscar Slater,[37] who was wrongly convicted and sentenced to death for the murder of Miss Gilchrist in Glasgow in 1908, was reprieved and, after 19 years digging granite in a prison quarry at Peterhead, was released and compensated out of public funds when his conviction was eventually quashed in 1928. At his trial, the prosecutor made much of his general bad character, as a man who lived on the edge of the law, changing wives, surnames and addresses regularly, and existing on the proceeds of gambling and (it seems) of prostitution. In his direction to the jury, the judge famously said:

> He has maintained himself by the ruin of men and the ruin of women, living for years past in a way that many blackguards scorn to live . . . A man of that kind has not the presumption of innocence in his favour which is a form in the case of every man, but a reality in the case of the ordinary man.

1.31 This case is often cited by those who argue that admitting evidence of the defendant's bad character is always unfair and dangerous. But it seems to me that the real problem in that affair was that the bad character evidence was admitted, and made much of, to supplement a case in which the rest of the evidence was completely worthless. The only evidence linking Oscar Slater either directly or indirectly with the victim or the offence were several 'fleeting glance' identifications, all of them highly suspect. As one English commentator, Sir Herbert Stephen, put it, Slater was convicted and sentenced to death on evidence that no English judge would have allowed to go to a jury, and on which 'no bench of magistrates in England would have ordered the destruction of a terrier which was alleged to have bitten somebody.'[38]

---

[36] See §§1.58–1.63 below.
[37] William Roughead, *The Trial of Oscar Slater* (Edinburgh, Hodge, 1929). An abridged account appears in John Mortimer (ed), *Famous Trials* (London, Penguin, 1984).
[38] Quoted by Roughead, *ibid.*

1.32 If this is the real danger, then the first principle that courts should apply when exercising their discretion is that evidence of the defendant's bad character ought to be excluded where the rest of the evidence is weak. This point has already been made judicially, with some force, by the Court of Appeal in *Hanson and others*, in words that have already been quoted in the Preface:

> The starting point should be for judges and practitioners to bear in mind that Parliament's purpose in the legislation, as we divine it from the terms of the Act, was to assist in the evidence based conviction of the guilty, without putting those who are not guilty at risk of conviction by prejudice. It is accordingly to be hoped that prosecution applications to adduce such evidence will not be made routinely, simply because a defendant has previous convictions, but will be based on the particular circumstances of each case.[39]
>
> [The judge] must always consider the strength of the prosecution case. If there is no or very little other evidence against a defendant, it is unlikely to be just to admit his previous convictions, whatever they are . . . Evidence of bad character cannot be used simply to bolster a weak case or to prejudice the minds of a jury against a defendant.[40]

1.33 The second major problem with evidence of bad character is the risk that it will give rise to complicated 'satellite issues' which deflect the attention of the tribunal of fact from the central issues in the case, and from properly examining the core evidence that implicates the defendant in the alleged offence directly. As the Court of Appeal said in *Smith*, 'We do, however, give a word of caution for the future about the general undesirability of the jury being required to explore satellite issues one stage removed from the charges they are trying unless this is really necessary.'[41]

1.34 A striking example of this problem is *Sylvester*.[42] The defendant was prosecuted for assaulting his cohabitee, the prosecution case being that he had deliberately banged her head against the garage door, his defence being that she had bumped it accidentally. At trial, evidence was admitted of a series of earlier incidents in their relationship, all of which were disputed, and the court also heard disputed evidence about an incident related to the defendant's work while he was serving in the police.

1.35 In quashing the resulting conviction, Pill LJ said:

> The danger about letting in peripheral and collateral matters is one thing leading to another, as happened in this case. The trial lasted four days and a great deal of material

---

[39] [2005] EWCA Crim 824, [2005] 1 WLR 3169, **p 153 below**, at §4.
[40] Ibid at §10 and 18.
[41] Reported with *Edwards and Rowlands* [2005] EWCA Crim 3244, **p 230 below**, at §86.
[42] [2005] EWCA Crim 1794. The trial took place before the new law on bad character evidence came into force, but the appeal was heard afterwards.

was admitted the relevance of which to the charge before the jury was at best extremely limited, even if properly admitted. There is a real danger, in our judgment, that the jury were distracted from the central issue in the case. If justice is to be done, trials must be kept within reasonable bounds. The central issue must not be so overlaid with consideration of peripheral matters that the judge and the jury are likely to lose sight of the central issue.

1.36 So the second guiding principle for the courts when exercising their discretion to exclude bad character evidence, surely, is that they should exclude evidence the hearing of which is likely to take up a disproportionate amount of time and distract the attention of the fact-finders from the evidence which bears directly on the central issues.

1.37 Where judges at first instance exercise a discretion, or a duty which is highly 'fact-specific', courts above are usually unwilling to criticise their decision, provided that it was made taking all the relevant factors into account. To a court's decision to admit or reject evidence of bad character this general rule undoubtedly applies.[43]

Are the New Provisions Compatible with the European Convention on Human Rights?

1.38 In this author's view, they are. However, it is likely that—at least initially— some defendants will use Convention arguments to support their applications for evidence of bad character to be excluded. In their weaker form, these arguments will invite the court, where it has a power or duty to exclude the evidence, to use it. In their stronger form, they might even invite the court to 'read down' some of the provisions of the Act—in other words, invite the court to read them in some less-than-natural sense, in order to exclude evidence apparently admissible under the Act. The Convention arguments most likely to be heard are the following.

1.39 'Admitting evidence of the defendant's bad character is by definition incompatible with his right to a fair trial under Article 6 ECHR.'

1.40 This argument was examined by the Law Commission, which was generally opposed to the use of bad character evidence against defendants, and it concluded that it was unobjectionable on this ground. The Strasbourg case law contains no

[43] *Hanson* [2005] EWCA Crim 824, [2005] 1 WLR 3169, **p 153 below** at §15; *Renda* [2005] EWCA Crim 2826, **p 193 below**, at §§3 and 4.

suggestion that admitting evidence of the defendant's bad character is contrary to the notion of a fair trial and, if anything, points in the opposite direction. In one case, the Commission said that, since so many Contracting States provide for the disclosure of previous convictions in their criminal procedure, it was not prepared to hold that such a procedure involved a breach of Article 6.[44]

1.41 'Admitting evidence of the defendant's bad character reverses the burden of proof, and is therefore incompatible with Article 6(2), which provides that "Everyone charged with a criminal offence shall be presumed innocent until proved guilty." '

1.42 This argument was one of many used against the character evidence provisions when the Bill was before Parliament:[45] but it is misconceived. The burden of proof is reversed when the defendant is given the task of proving his innocence and the prosecution, not the defendant, has the benefit of the doubt. Clearly the bad character provisions of the Act do not have this effect. They make evidence admissible against some defendants which was inadmissible before, and to that extent make it easier for the prosecution to discharge the burden of proving the defendant's guilt. But this is not at all the same as requiring the defendant to prove his innocence.[46] (If this argument were valid, it would be impossible to change the existing rules of evidence in any way at all, except to make them more favourable to the defence.)

1.43 'An element in the concept of "fair trial" in Article 6 of the Convention is "equality of arms". Part 11 of the CJA 2003 is incompatible with this, because it makes evidence of the defendant's bad character admissible without judicial leave, whereas if the prosecution witnesses have bad characters, the defendant needs judicial leave to bring this out. So, to preserve the defendant's right to a fair trial, Part 11 of the Act must be 'read down' so that evidence of the defendant's bad character is admissible only where judicial leave is granted.'

1.44 This 'imbalance' argument was raised by the Joint Committee on Human Rights when the Criminal Justice Bill was before Parliament. In reply, the Minister explained the imbalance is not what it seems, because the defendant—unlike a

---

[44] Law Commission Report, n 15 above, §§3.7 and 3.8. The Law Commission also said that 'it is clear from the recital of facts that previous convictions have been before the court, and indeed have influenced the judgment'—as in *Unterpertinger v Austria* (1991) 13 EHRR 175 and in *Kostovski v Netherlands* (1990) 12 EHRR 434.

[45] By Lord Kingsland, Hansard, HL, vol 654 col 729 (4 November 2003), who said the legislation was 'profoundly pernicious, and makes a mockery of the presumption of innocence.'

[46] See the Court of Appeal's answer to the same argument when raised against the provisions of the Criminal Justice and Public Order Act (CJPOA) 1994 attenuating the right of silence: *Cowan* [1996] QBD 373, at 379.

witness—has a right to object to the admission of evidence. The Joint Committee was content to accept this explanation and withdrew its objection.[47]

1.45 'An element in the defendant's right to a fair trial under Article 6 is his right to defend himself effectively. The CJA 2003 scheme—like the previous law—contains a rule that if a defendant attacks the character of another person, his own bad character can be revealed.[48] This undermines his right to defend himself, and hence is incompatible with Article 6. In the light of this, evidence of the defendant's bad character should not be admitted in this situation, irrespective of what the CJA 2003 apparently provides.'

1.46 This argument was examined by the Law Commission and found wanting. As it explained, 'One cannot get away from the [Strasbourg] jurisprudence supporting the fairness of reliance on previous convictions at trial. Although a defendant in the position described is, in a sense, being "forced" to distort the defence, he or she is only doing so to avoid a consequence that the Strasbourg court would not regard as in itself unfair.'

1.47 'Article 4 of Protocol 7 to the Convention provides (inter alia) that the defendant shall not be punished twice for the same offence. Admitting evidence of the defendant's previous convictions offends against this principle.'

1.48 But admitting evidence that the defendant has committed an offence in the past in order to help it to decide whether he has committed an offence in the present is not the same as punishing him a second time for the earlier offence. (And even if it were, the United Kingdom has not yet ratified Protocol 7,[49] and in consequence, the rights that it protects do not count as 'Convention rights' for the purpose of the extra protection accorded to them by the Human Rights Act 1998.[50])

---

[47] House of Lords, House of Commons, Joint Committee on Human Rights, Second Report of Session 2002–3 (Criminal Justice Bill), HL Paper 40, HC 374, §23.

[48] CJA 2003 s101(1)(g) and 106; §4.84–§4.108 below.

[49] Although the government has announced its intention to do so. With that in mind, the Family Law (Property and Maintenance) Bill, before Parliament at the time of writing, is designed to bring UK law into line with Article 5 of the Protocol.

[50] This does not mean, of course, that UK courts are completely free to disregard them. Even where the Human Rights Act 1998 does not apply, 'It is well settled that the Convention may be deployed for the purpose of the resolution of an ambiguity in English primary or secondary legislation': *R v Home Secretary, ex parte Brind* [1991] 1 AC 696, per Lord Ackner at 760.

Does Part 11 of the Criminal Justice Act 2003 Really Change Things? Is it Really 'Business as Before'?

1.49 A view that was sometimes heard when the provisions were first in force was that in reality they would change little: in practice, the courts are left free to conduct 'business as usual' provided they dress their old decisions in the language of the new rules. The former rules on evidence of bad character, it was said, were premised on the notion that admitting such evidence is basically incompatible with giving the defendant a fair trial. One way or another, the new rules leave the courts enough elbow-room to exclude evidence of bad character where they feel that admitting it would be unfair—which means, essentially, where it would have been excluded under the law as it was before the Act. In some cases, the court is overtly given a discretion to exclude; where it is not, the sections of the Act contain vague phrases under the cover of which a discretion to exclude can operate, and the general discretion to exclude 'unfair' evidence under section 78 of PACE 1984 applies. So, in practice, the courts can—and should—exclude bad character evidence in all cases where they would have excluded it before.

1.50 I believe that this approach to the new provisions is wrong in principle. There can be no doubt that when enacting these provisions, Parliament intended to change the law and not just to codify the law as then existing. As the Explanatory Notes clearly stated, 'The intention is that this Part of the Act will provide a new basis for the admissibility of previous convictions and other misconduct.'[51] This being so, the courts have a constitutional duty to respect the legislator's will, and not to frustrate the intended change by interpreting the new law to conform as closely as possible with the old[52]: as the Court of Appeal indicated 10 years ago, when refusing to take this approach in relation to the 'right of silence' provisions of the CJPOA 1994.[53]

1.51 Recognising this, the Court of Appeal in *Edwards and Rowlands*[54] said 'Under the new regime it is apparent that Parliament intended that evidence of bad character would be put before juries more frequently than in the past.' In

---

[51] At §358. Cf §371: 'Section 103(1)(a) makes it clear that evidence that shows that the defendant has a propensity to commit offences of the kind with which he is charged can be admitted under this head.'

[52] See *Bank of England v Vagliano Bros* and §1.64 below.

[53] *Cowan* [1996] QBD 373, at 378–79: 'Mr Mansfield's approach frankly was that section 35 [of the CJPOA 1994] is so at variance with established principle, that its operation should be reduced and marginalised as far as possible. We cannot agree.'

[54] [2005] EWCA Crim 3244, **p 230 below**, at §1.

Hanson, Gilmore and P,[55] the Court of Appeal said that, under the new law, it is no longer true that 'what used to be referred to as striking similarity must be shown before convictions become admissible,' and that evidence of bad character is now admissible on the basis that it shows a tendency to commit offences of this general type. Similarly, in *Weir and others*,[56] the Court of Appeal pointed out that section 99 abolishes the common law rules on the admissibility of evidence of bad character, and said 'The 2003 Act completely reverses the pre-existing general rule. Evidence of bad character is now admissible if it satisfies certain criteria (see section 101(1)), and the approach is no longer one of inadmissibility subject to exceptions . . .'

1.52 That it is not 'business as before', and that evidence of the defendant's bad character is now admissible in many situations in which it would previously have been excluded, is also clear from the outcome of a number of the reported cases.

1.53 Thus, in *Bradley*,[57] the Court of Appeal upheld the defendant's conviction for robbery, to which he was linked by DNA evidence, the trial court having heard evidence of his previous conviction for robbery. In *Hanson*,[58] and again in *Gilmore*,[59] the Court of Appeal upheld the defendants' convictions for theft, returned at trials in which the jury had heard evidence of his previous convictions for offences of dishonesty. In *P*,[60] *Weir*,[61] and again in *Manister*,[62] the Court of Appeal upheld the defendants' convictions for sex offences, following trials at which the jury had heard evidence of their previous behaviour that provided an indication of their particular sexual tastes. And in *Duggan*,[63] the Court of Appeal upheld the defendant's conviction for wounding with intent, arising from an incident in which he claimed he had acted in self defence, the trial judge having admitted evidence of his previous conviction for assault. (These cases are discussed in further detail at §§4.30–4.34 below.)

---

[55] [2005] EWCA Crim 824, [2005] 1 WLR 3169, **p 153 below**.
[56] [2005] EWCA Crim 2866, [2006] 1 CrAppR 19 (303), **p 206 below**, at §35.
[57] [2005] EWCA Crim 20, [2005] 1 CrAppR 24 (397).
[58] [2005] EWCA Crim 824, [2005] 1 WLR 3169, **p 153 below**.
[59] Decided together with *Hanson*, n 58 above.
[60] Decided together with *Hanson*.
[61] [2005] EWCA Crim 2866 [2006] 1 CrAppR 19 (303), **p 206 below**.
[62] Decided together with *Weir*, n 61 above.
[63] Decided together with *Edwards* [2005] EWCA Crim 1813, [2006] 1 CrAppR 3 (31) **p 169 below**.

Should it be 'Business as Before'? Is Admitting Evidence of the Defendant's Bad Character Inherently Unfair?

1.54 There is a school of thought that admitting evidence of the defendant's bad character in a criminal case is inherently dangerous, because it carries with it an unacceptable risk of convicting the innocent. This assumption lay behind the vocal opposition to the new provisions when the Criminal Justice Bill was in Parliament, and it underlies much of the comment about them that has appeared in both the legal and the general press, most of which is hostile. According to this view, the old strict rules that generally excluded such evidence were right, and the attempt in the CJA 2003 to make it more widely admissible is an evil to be resisted. It follows that the courts should be encouraged, so far as possible, to interpret the new law in such a way as to produce the same results as the old.

1.55 The traditional argument against admitting evidence of the defendant's bad character is as follows. Where a court knows that the defendant has a criminal record, or is otherwise of bad character, this makes it significantly more likely to convict him; therefore, such evidence is prejudicial; therefore, it should not normally be admitted. This reasoning is simplistic. In general, evidence is not excluded as 'prejudicial' merely because it makes the court more inclined to convict: if this were so, the prosecution would not be permitted to call any evidence at all! The real question is not whether the evidence is 'prejudicial,' but whether it is unfairly so. Evidence is unfairly prejudicial only (i) where it has the power to influence the court to convict although it is not logically relevant to the defendant's guilt at all, or (ii) where it has some slender logical relevance to the defendant's guilt but its power to persuade the court to convict is out of all proportion.[64]

1.56 Evidence of bad character—which usually means evidence that the defendant has a criminal record—is not unfairly prejudicial in sense (i), because if a person is of bad character, it is reasonable to assume that he is more likely to break the law than a person whose character is good. This is, of course, one of the reasons why in criminal proceedings defendants whose records are clean are permitted to call evidence of good character. It also explains why in civil proceedings a person's 'track-record' may be taken into account in deciding whether he has committed the misconduct of which he is currently accused,[65] or is likely to misconduct

---

[64] The term used by the Law Commission to describe this phenomenon is 'moral prejudice': see their Working Paper, LC Consultation Paper no 141, at §7.2; and Dennis, n 35 above, at 622.

[65] See *O'Brien v Chief Constable of South Wales Police* [2005] UKHL 26, [2005] 2 AC 534, where in an action against the police for misfeasance in office and malicious prosecution, the claimant was entitled to call evidence suggesting that the officer of whose misbehaviour he complained had acted similarly towards other suspects in the past.

himself in future.[66] And it was also recognised by the judges even in some criminal cases decided under the earlier law: as Lord Steyn said in *Randall*:

> It is difficult to support a proposition that evidence of propensity can never be relevant to the issues. Postulate a joint trial involving two accused arising from an assault committed in a pub. The one man has a long list of previous convictions involving assaults in pubs. It shows him to be prone to fighting when he had consumed alcohol. The other man has an unblemished record. Relying on experience and common sense one may rhetorically ask why the propensity to violence of one man should not be deployed by the other man as part of his defence that he did not commit the assault.[67]

If psychological studies make it clear beyond doubt that courts are more likely to convict defendants where they know that they have criminal records, the Criminal Statistics make it equally clear that people with criminal records are more likely to commit offences than those who do not; and the second of these propositions does much to explain the first. Broadly speaking, the Criminal Statistics suggest that those who have criminal records are, in general, more likely to commit criminal offences than those who do not—and those with long criminal records are very much more likely, as too are those whose previous convictions are recent.[68] Taken on its own, the fact that a defendant is of bad character will never be anything more than a piece of inconclusive circumstantial evidence—but it is wrong to regard it as completely irrelevant.

1.57 Is bad character evidence unfairly prejudicial in sense (ii)? The Law Commission assumed that fact-finders were bound to give it disproportionate weight. A body of psychological research shows beyond any doubt at all that where the fact-finder is aware that the defendant has convictions, or is of bad character, this increases his willingness to convict. But to show that fact-finders are influenced by such evidence is not the same as showing that they are influenced by it *disproportionately*: that is to say, that they treat it as increasing the probability of the defendant having committed the offence more than it actually does. A recent study in which a serious attempt was made to relate the psychological evidence on the impact of such evidence on fact-finders to the criminological evidence about the comparative offending rates of those who do and do not have criminal records,

---

[66] For example, when deciding in proceedings relating to children whether to allow a particular person to have contact with a child would involve an unacceptable degree of risk: eg *In Re P (A Minor) (Wardship)* [1987] 2 FLR 467.

[67] [2004] UKHL 69, [2004] 1 WLR 56, at §22.

[68] Mike Redmayne, 'The Relevance of Bad Character' [2002] *Cambridge Law Journal* 684. After examining a range of statistics, including those on reconviction rates, he says, 'Taken at face value, these figures imply that recent same-crime previous convictions have considerable probative value. The burglary figure, for example, suggests that a person with a previous conviction for burglary is 125 times more likely to commit a burglary than a person without such a previous conviction.'(!)

concluded that there is no basis for the assumption that the Law Commission made.[69]

1.58 The real difficulty with bad character evidence, I believe, is not so much the risk that it will inflame the fact-finder, but that it is a form of evidence that is typically weak; and like other forms of weak evidence, it presents a danger where the court is invited to convict on this and little else—as in the case of Oscar Slater, discussed in §1.30 above. From this it follows, I believe, that a key factor in determining whether it is fair to admit evidence of bad character should be the strength of the rest of the evidence. It cannot be a substitute for 'hard evidence' that implicates the defendant more directly—and it should not be admitted to strengthen a case in which the other evidence is slender.[70] On the other hand, I believe there is no unfairness involved in admitting this sort of evidence where the other evidence is strong, and in particular where it may clinch the case.

1.59 Thus, if D is prosecuted for indecently assaulting P in a park, and the entire prosecution evidence is P's testimony that she was assaulted in the dark by a man she is unable to identify and the fact that D was somewhere in the area at the time, it would be risky to admit the fact that D has a criminal record—or even a record of indecent assault. On the other hand, if a man is prosecuted for indecent offences against boys, and it is proved that he had picked them up at a public lavatory and invited them back to his flat for the night, and that one of them had there slept with him in his bed, it seems neither risky nor unjust to admit evidence of his record for similar offences, if he claims in his defence that nothing untoward took place.[71]

1.60 Similarly, to take the facts of two cases decided under the new provisions, if a defendant is charged with a robbery, to which he is linked by the discovery of his DNA on the stocking mask one of the robbers dropped in flight, and he explains the presence of his DNA on it by saying that he might have used the stocking for polishing a car, and having spat on it when doing so, then left it lying around where the robber later found it and picked it up, it does not seem unjust to allow the court to hear that he has a previous conviction for robbery;[72] and when a man is accused of indecently assaulting a 10-year-old girl, and he admits the opportun-

---

[69] Redmayne, *ibid.* After examining the statistics, the author provisionally suggests that 'the presumption that previous convictions are more prejudicial than probative is based on a lack of understanding of offending patterns' (at 700). His final conclusion is as follows: 'In the near future, evidence of previous misconduct may be presented to juries much more often than at present. Our analysis indicates that there is less reason to object to this than has often been supposed. Yet it also suggests that we do not have all that much reason to be confident that this or indeed any other policy gets it right.'

[70] At any rate, where the 'bad character evidence' merely establishes a general propensity to commit this type of offence. If in some way it is more directly relevant—as in *Straffen* [1952] 2 QB 911, for example—then there is no reason for treating it as 'second class evidence.'

[71] *King* [1967] 2 QB 338.

[72] *Bradley* [2005] EWCA Crim 20, [2005] 1 CrAppR 24 (397).

ity and also giving money to her afterwards, but denies that anything untoward took place, it does not seem unjust to admit evidence that, not long before, he was cautioned for taking an indecent photograph of a child.[73]

1.61 The sense that there is no real unfairness in admitting evidence of the defendant's bad character in cases where there is a substantial body of other credible evidence is probably the unspoken thought that lies behind the pre-Act case law in which courts repeatedly said that bad character evidence is admissible when it is 'relevant to an issue before the jury' or when it 'rebuts a defence.' Cases in which this is so are, by definition, cases in which there is a substantial body of other evidence.[74]

1.62 On the other hand, this approach to the matter is contradicted by a different line taken by some courts in the past, which have indicated that bad character evidence should be kept out if the other evidence is strong, but that it is permissible to make use of it where the other evidence is weak:[75] a line of reasoning that, it is suggested, is deeply flawed and dangerous, and should not be followed.

1.63 Because evidence of bad character tends to be inherently weak, it is not only important that judges should exercise their discretion to exclude it in cases where there is not a solid body of evidence that is more compelling. It is also important that, where it is admitted, prosecutors avoid trying to make too much of it. And it is also important that, where necessary, judges give juries appropriate warnings against treating it as stronger than it is. It is with this thought in mind that, in the Judicial Studies Board specimen direction on evidence of bad character, the following sentence is included:

> You must decide to what extent, if at all, his character helps you when you are considering whether or not he is guilty. But bear in mind that his bad character cannot by itself prove that he is guilty. It would therefore be wrong to jump to the conclusion that he is guilty just because of his bad character.

Construing the New Legislation

1.64 Part 11 of the CJA 2003 sets out to codify the law on evidence of bad character. In *Bank of England v Vagliano Bros*,[76] the House of Lords said that the proper course when construing a codifying statute is:

---

[73] *Weir* [2005] EWCA Crim 2866, [2006] 1 CrAppR 19 (303), **p 206 below.**
[74] On this, see DW Elliott, 'Young Person's Guide to Similar Fact Evidence' [1983] *Crim LR* 284.
[75] eg *Britzman* [1983] 1 WLR 350, at 355: 'Finally, there is no need for the prosecution to rely upon section 1(f)(ii) if the evidence against a defendant is overwhelming.'
[76] [1891] AC 107.

to examine the language of the statute and ask what is its natural meaning, uninfluenced by any considerations derived from the previous state of the law, and not to start with inquiring how the law previously stood, and then, assuming that it was probably intended to leave it unaltered, to see if the words of the enactment will bear an interpretation in conformity with this view. If a statute, intended to embody a code in a particular branch of the law, is to be treated in this fashion . . . its utility will be almost entirely destroyed, and the very object with which it was enacted will be frustrated.

This is the approach that the Court of Appeal has taken to the new provisions, as we have already seen. In *Weir*, the Court of Appeal rejected the notion that the statutory provisions should be read in the light of the pre-existing common law.[77] Similarly, in *Renda*, where evidence of the defendant's bad character had been admitted via 'gateway (f)' on the basis that it was needed 'to correct a false impression given by the defendant,' the Court of Appeal said it was unhelpful to cite, in this connection, case law on whether the defendant had 'put his character in issue' under section 1(3)(ii) of the Criminal Evidence Act 1898: the provision which dealt with false impressions given by defendants under the previous law.

Status of Explanatory Notes as an Aid to Construction

1.65 In writing this commentary, I have assumed that it is proper to refer to the Explanatory Notes as an aid to the construction of provisions of the Act. In an article in the *Criminal Law Review*, Dr Munday puts forward arguments of principle against their use.[78] However, that this can properly be done is supported by abundant recent case law which is binding on the lower courts[79]; and when called upon to construe the provisions on bad character in the CJA 2003, the Court of Appeal has already shown its willingness to use them.[80]

1.66 I believe that the courts are right to look at the Explanatory Notes for guidance, and I am not convinced by any principled objections to their use. There is an obvious objection to using as an aid to construction an Explanatory Note that was drafted after the relevant provision has been enacted: but this does not apply where (as in cases discussed in this commentary) a note in identical terms was

---

[77] [2005] EWCA Crim 2866 at §35.

[78] Roderick Munday, 'Bad Character Rules and Riddles: "Explanatory Notes" and True Meanings of s.103(1) of the Criminal Justice Act 2003' [2005] *Crim LR* 337. Roderick Munday, Explanatory Notes and Statutory Interpretation (2006) 170 *JPN* 124.

[79] See *R (Westminster City Council) v National Asylum Support Service* [2002] 1 WLR 2956, per Lord Steyn; *R (Confederation of Passengers etc) v Humber Bridge Board* [2004] QB 310 (CA); *Montila* [2004] 1 WLR 3141 (HL) at §35 and 36, *R(S) v Chief Constable of South Yorks Police* [2004] 1 WLR 2196 (per Lord Steyn at §4). *Attorney-General's Reference (No 5 of 2002)* [2005] 1 AC 167 (per Lord Bingham, at §21).

[80] *Weir*, n 73 above, at §§35 and 36.

before Parliament at the time the provisions were being discussed and voted on. In this discussion, furthermore, a sense of proportion needs to be retained. The point at issue is only whether the courts are allowed to look at the Explanatory Notes for help and inspiration: the suggestion is not that they should be bound to follow them.[81]

Coming into Force—Date from which the New Law Applies

1.67 The commencement date for the 'character evidence' provisions of the CJA 2003 was 15 December 2004.[82] As the changes they contain are procedural, not substantive, they would normally apply in any proceedings taking place after the commencement date, irrespective of when the alleged offence was committed.[83] However, the normal rule is qualified by section 141, which states that none of the evidential provisions in the Act shall apply 'in relation to criminal proceedings begun before the commencement of that provision.'

1.68 At first sight, this suggests that, contrary to the normal rule, the new law on character evidence applies only in respect of prosecutions instituted after 15 December. However, matters are more complicated, because section 141 is preceded by section 140, a definition section, of which the first two sentences are as follows: 'In this Chapter [ie Chapter 3, where section 141 appears] "criminal proceedings" means criminal proceedings in relation to which the strict rules of evidence apply.' 'Criminal proceedings in relation to which the strict rules of evidence apply' means, in effect, 'trials.' So, in section 140, 'criminal proceedings' means 'trials,'[84] and the result appears to be that the new provisions apply in *trials* that began after 15 December 2004, irrespective of when the prosecution was instituted.

1.69 It is questionable whether this result is what the draftsman really intended: if he had really meant to say that the new provisions operate in respect of trials starting after the commencement date, he has found a very convoluted way of doing so. From the press statement issued on the commencement date, it is plain that the

---

[81] Last summer I read an examination paper in which a student, asked to interpret a statutory provision, wrote 'It would be wrong for the courts to follow the will of Parliament, because this would breach the separation of powers.' However erudite, all arguments against the courts using Explanatory Notes as an aid to construction make me think of this comment.

[82] Criminal Justice Act 2003 (Commencement No 6 and Transitional Provisions) Order 2004, SI 2004/3033.

[83] *Makanjuola* [1995] 1 WLR 1348.

[84] And also 'Newton hearings.'

Home Office imagined they would only operate in respect of prosecutions that were instituted after it. The new provisions, it said, 'will apply to all cases in which charges are laid on or after 15 December.'

1.70 In January 2005, the Court of Appeal was called upon to decide the point in *Bradley*,[85] where it resolved the issue by deciding that the provisions operate in *trials* that begin after the commencement date, irrespective of when the charge was laid. In a judgment delivered by the Vice President, Rose LJ, they went out of their way to criticise the poor drafting of the Act, the absence from the Commencement Order of any transitional provisions, and the fact that (as explained in the Preface to this book) the government brought the bad character provisions into force ahead of the programme of judicial training.

1.71 For these purposes, a 'trial' includes a retrial. So, if a defendant was originally tried before 15 December 2004, and his retrial takes place after it, any issue relating to bad character evidence now falls to be decided under the new provisions. This was held by the Court of Appeal in *Benguit*,[86] in which they said that, in a retrial that took place in January 2005, it was a mistake for prosecuting counsel and the court, out of a desire to be fair to the defendant, to resolve the admissibility of bad character evidence by applying the earlier law, now that this had been repealed.

What is the Practical Impact of the New Provisions?

1.72 The result that was widely predicted to follow from the new provisions was an increase in convictions. This, indeed, was both the reason why the legislation was promoted (on the assumption that those convicted would be guilty) and the reason why it was opposed (by those who believed that the convicted persons would be innocent). At the time of writing, there is no statistical evidence yet to show us whether the conviction rate has increased since the new law on bad character evidence came into force; and as the new provisions came into force about the same time as a raft of other changes, it will be difficult to prove a causal link between the new law on bad character evidence and an increase in the conviction rate, even if the statistics, when available, show us that in this period an increase in the conviction rate has taken place. In the hope of obtaining some meaningful information on what the effect of the new provisions is, the Home Office has commissioned Morgan Harris Burrows, a firm of management consultants, to evaluate the operation and impact of the new law; but no results are expected

---

[85] [2005] EWCA Crim 20, [2005] 1 CrAppR 24 (397).
[86] [2005] EWCA Crim 1953.

before the end of 2006. Meanwhile, there is anecdotal evidence from various sources that the changes have brought about at least a slight increase in guilty pleas—particularly in sex cases, where the direct evidence of the commission of the offence is the uncorroborated word of the complainant.[87] There is some, but less, anecdotal evidence about fought cases where bad character evidence appears to have played an important part in securing a conviction: and most judges to whom the author has spoken report that, where bad character evidence is introduced in a fought case, the jury—very properly—appear to be much more interested in the evidence that implicates the defendant directly in the offence, than in the evidence of bad character. A side-effect of the new provisions which was widely predicted was that they would slow the course of justice down, by reason of the courts having to devote extra time to hearing argument about whether particular items of bad character evidence should be admitted. Anecdotal evidence does suggest that the courts are spending considerable amounts of time on this—and, in particular, on applications to admit the evidence of bad character of witnesses. However, it has not yet been suggested that this new area of work has overwhelmed them.

---

[87] A high-profile case of this type was that of the serial rapist, Petros Antia; see *Metropolitan Police Bulletin*, 15 June 2005.

2

DEFINITION OF 'BAD CHARACTER'

2.1 'Bad character' is defined by Criminal Justice Act 2003 **section 98**, which is as follows:

> References in this Chapter to evidence of a person's 'bad character' are to evidence of, or of a disposition towards, misconduct on his part, other than evidence which—
>
> (a) has to do with the alleged facts of the offence with which the defendant is charged, or
>
> (b) is evidence of misconduct in connection with the investigation or prosecution of that offence.

The term 'misconduct' is defined in section 112(1), which provides that:

> 'misconduct' means the commission of an offence or other reprehensible behaviour.

2.2 This definition of 'bad character' is based on the definition proposed by the Law Commission, but differs from it in two respects.

2.3 The first is that the Act defines 'misconduct' as 'the commission of an offence *or other reprehensible behaviour*,' whereas the equivalent in the Law Commission's scheme was the commission of an offence, or *'behaviour that, in the opinion of the court, might be viewed with disapproval by a reasonable person.'* The Law Commission's formula was used in the Bill, but the shorter 'other reprehensible behaviour' formula was substituted in Parliament. This was done to meet an objection that the Law Commission's formula was too wide—and could result in too much evidence being admissible, to the detriment of the defendant. This objection was based on muddled thinking, because the wider the definition of 'bad character,' the more forms of evidence which are *excluded* unless they pass through one of the 'gateways' listed in section 101, and hence the better the defendant is protected: whereas if evidence falls outside the definition of 'bad character' it is in principle admissible whenever the court considers it to be relevant. However, the two formulae seem virtually identical, and it is difficult to think of evidence that would pass one of the tests but be excluded by the other.

2.4 The second difference is that section 98 narrows the definition of 'bad character' in the Act so that it does not cover evidence of misbehaviour which is directly connected with the offence with which the defendant is charged, nor any mis-behaviour during the course of the investigation or prosecution.[1] Under the Law Commission's scheme, evidence of this type would have counted as evidence of 'bad character,' but a clause of their Draft Bill would have made it automatically admissible, without the need for leave. The government, as part of its policy of 'bending' the proposals in the direction of wider admissibility, produced a new formulation which excluded this type of evidence from the definition of 'bad character evidence' altogether.

2.5 The thought process behind this seems to have been that if this type of mis-behaviour fell outside the definition of 'bad character evidence,' it would therefore fall outside the scope of any ban on the use of such evidence that might be con-tained in the subsequent sections—and so be freely admissible. But unfortunately, things are not so simple. If such evidence falls outside the definition of 'bad char-acter' in the Act, it also falls outside the scope of the provision of the Act that repeals the common law rules on the admissibility of evidence of 'bad character'; which in turn means that the defendant can argue that such evidence is inadmis-sible at common law. As the common law rules would almost invariably have let such evidence in, such an argument is not likely to advance the defendant's case. However, there can be no doubt that evidence of this sort is potentially within the scope of the court's general discretionary powers to exclude—and some desperate defendants may request the court to exercise it in their favour.

2.6 So in practical terms, what sort of evidence will fall within the statutory definition of 'bad character' set out in section 98?

2.7 In the first place, there is evidence of 'the commission of an offence.' This evidence may take the form of a previous conviction,[2] or it may be evidence of pre-vious offences for which the defendant has not previously been tried, as where a defendant is prosecuted for a collection of similar offences, all of which he denies. Less obviously, it may also take the form of evidence that he has committed an offence of which he has been acquitted. In law, an acquittal is conclusive evidence of innocence to the extent that the defendant is no longer liable to prosecution or punishment for that offence. But it does not preclude the prosecution (or indeed the defence) from producing in other proceedings evidence to show that the accused was really guilty.[3]

---

[1] The scope of this exclusion is examined in §§2.22–2.27 below.
[2] By PACE 1984, s74, the fact that the defendant has a previous conviction gives rise to a rebuttable presumption against him that he was guilty of the offence; as against a non-defendant, it is generally conclusive proof. For what does and does not count in law as a conviction, see §4.48 below.
[3] *Z* [2000] 2 AC 483; *Terry* [2004] EWCA Crim 3252, [2005] QB 996.

2.8 In *Renda*,[4] the defendant, who was accused of robbery, had been prosecuted on an earlier occasion for assault occasioning actual bodily harm. At the earlier trial, the jury had found that he had approached someone from behind and struck him on the head with a large wooden table leg, but had found him unfit to plead, and the court had given him an absolute discharge. At the robbery trial, he had claimed to be a person of good character, and the judge allowed the prosecution to put the table leg incident in as evidence of bad character, admissible via 'gateway (f)' in order 'to correct a false impression given by the defendant' that he had a good one. On appeal, it was argued that a violent incident resulting in a finding of unfit to plead did not show 'bad character,' being neither a criminal conviction nor 'reprehensible behaviour.' The Court of Appeal did not accept this:

> We agree that the appellant was not 'convicted' of a criminal offence. We also accept that as a matter of ordinary language, the word 'reprehensible' carries with it some element of culpability or blameworthiness. What however we are unable to accept is the mere fact that the appellant was found unfit to plead some 18 months after an apparent incident of gratuitous violence has occurred, of itself, connotes that at the time of the offence his mental acuity was so altered as to extinguish any element of culpability when the table leg was used in such a violent fashion.

2.9 Following the proposal of the Law Commission, the CJA 2003 takes the position that evidence of the commission of an offence counts as evidence of bad character, whatever the nature of the offence. It leaves no room for the argument that because of the nature of the offence—a minor motoring offence, for example—it does not constitute evidence of bad character, and is therefore admissible without the need to put it through one of the 'gateways' created by the Act.

2.10 Secondly, 'evidence of bad character' includes evidence of 'other reprehensible behaviour.'

2.11 In abstract terms, behaviour is 'reprehensible' if it invites 'censure, rebuke or reprimand.'[5] It therefore includes a large part of the range of behaviour which it is considered defamatory to accuse other people of committing. However, 'reprehensible behaviour' is narrower. A statement is defamatory if it exposes a person to 'hatred, ridicule or contempt.' Behaviour that engenders hatred or contempt is clearly reprehensible, but not behaviour that provokes nothing worse than ridicule.

2.12 In concrete terms, examples of 'other reprehensible behaviour' would presumably include telling lies, drinking to excess, failing to pay one's debts, and

---

[4] [2005] EWCA Crim 2826, p 193 below.
[5] *Oxford English Dictionary* definition.

disobedience, absenteeism and other forms of serious misbehaviour when at work. It presumably also includes sexual misbehaviour, at any rate where this is of a kind of which most people disapprove, at least officially: prostitution, resort to prostitutes, promiscuity and cheating on a spouse or partner.

2.13 A delicate problem arises about forms of sexual behaviour on which public opinion is divided: in particular, homosexuality. Homosexual behaviour between consenting adults has been legal for nearly 40 years, and many people—and not just homosexuals—would emphatically reject the idea that it could still be classed as 'reprehensible behaviour.' On the other hand, there are still people who strongly disapprove of it, and tabloid newspapers usually regard allegations of this sort about prominent persons as very newsworthy. So many witnesses would consider evidence that they were homosexuals upsetting and embarrassing, and some defendants might fear that it would expose them to prejudice.

2.14 In the original version of this commentary, I suggested that, in order to resolve this problem, if a witness or defendant is likely to object to evidence of this sort about him (or her) being given, the court should be prepared to treat it as falling within the restrictions on evidence of 'bad character' for the purpose of restricting its admissibility.[6] However, having discussed the point with various people,[7] I no longer think that this is right. Instead, I now think the proper solution to this problem is to be found outside these provisions altogether, and in the Human Rights Act 1998 and the European Convention on Human Rights.

2.15 Under Article 8 of the Convention, everyone has 'a right to respect for his private and family life' and 'there shall be no interference by a public authority with the exercise of this right except such as is in accordance with the law and is necessary in a democratic society in the interests of national security, public safety or the economic well-being of the country, for the prevention of disorder or crime, for the protection of health or morals, or for the protection of the rights and freedom of others.' Under section 6 of the Human Rights Act 1998, public authorities are forbidden to act in ways that are incompatible with the rights guaranteed by the Convention, and the term 'public authority' includes a court. It follows that, when deciding whether or not to admit evidence that bears upon a person's sex-life, the court should remember the person's rights under Article 8, and only allow such evidence to be admitted if it is strictly necessary—where appropriate, carrying out a balancing exercise between the person's right to privacy under

---

[6] For a discussion of the point under the previous law see *Bishop* [1975] QB 274; and see §§4.93–4.95 below.

[7] In particular, Mr Justice Tugendhat, who wrote me a helpful letter suggesting the alternative solution which I am proposing now.

Article 8 and the defendant's right to a fair trial under Article 6.[8] In the case of an opposing witness whose sex-life the prosecution or defence wish to expose, this would provide, in practical terms, much the same protection as would otherwise be provided by section 100 of the CJA 2003 (see §3.8 *et seq* below).

2.16 Thirdly, evidence of 'bad character' includes not only evidence that the person in question has actually committed criminal offences or other reprehensible acts, but also evidence of his 'disposition towards' doing this. So, for example, it would include not only evidence that a person had planted bombs or committed burglaries by blowing open safes, but also that he had been collecting information about how to do so. In sex cases, it would also include evidence that the defendant had a particular sexual tendency: for example, where a person is accused of paedophile offences, evidence of his admission that he is sexually attracted to little children. As it counts as evidence of 'bad character', evidence of this sort would only be admissible against a defendant if it passed through one of the 'gateways' in section 101.

2.17 It is likely that evidence of disposition based on matters other than previous convictions will sometimes be disputed by the defence. In the sort of case described in the previous paragraph, the defendant might deny admitting that he is sexually attracted to children, or deny that the child pornography found on his office computer was downloaded by him. In principle, of course, evidence does not cease to be admissible because the defendant disputes it: and where he does, its truth or falsity is a matter for the jury to decide. However, if the disputed evidence is flimsy, the judge might properly decide to exclude it in his discretion—both in fairness to the defendant, and in order to avoid a prolonged investigation of 'satellite issues' which are of secondary importance. (The issue of discretionary exclusion is discussed further in §§1.21–1.28 above.)

2.18 In a learned article in the *Criminal Law Review*, Dr Munday expresses concern that the definition of 'bad character' in section 98 is dangerously vague. In his view, the phrase 'or other reprehensible behaviour' leaves the meaning of 'bad character' wide open, with potentially dire consequences: 'no matter how hard the courts endeavour to steady the ship, the Criminal Justice Act 2003 will prove a nightmare of interpretation.'[9]

---

[8] On this, see *Z v Finland* (1997) 25 EHRR 371, where the European Court of Human Rights considered whether a wife's rights under Article 8 were infringed by the disclosure and use in evidence of information about her HIV status. On the facts, the infringement of her right to privacy was held to be in principle justified by the prosecutor's need to use it as evidence against her husband, who was accused of a criminal offence, a key fact in which was the point in time at which he had become infected; but there was no justification for the part of the decision of the Finnish court that had the effect of allowing her medical details to become available to the public.

[9] Roderick Munday, 'What Constitutes 'Other Reprehensible Behaviour' under the Bad Character Provisions of the Criminal Justice Act 2003?' [2005] *Crim LR* 24.

2.19 The first case in which the Court of Appeal has had to confront this issue suggests that this problem is unlikely to cause too much difficulty in practice. In *Manister*,[10] the defendant was accused of serious sexual offences against a girl, A, allegedly committed when she was 13 and he was 39. The prosecution sought to support its case by demonstrating that Manister was sexually attracted to girls of this age-group, by adducing evidence that when 34 he had had a sexual relationship with B, a girl of 16, and that shortly before the alleged offence had said things to C, a 15-year-old girl, which made his sexual interest in her evident. None of his activity with B or C amounted to a criminal offence. The trial judge, however, ruled that it was 'other reprehensible behaviour,' hence evidence of 'bad character,' and hence admissible against the defendant via 'gateway (d).' The Court of Appeal thought that this behaviour could not properly be described as 'reprehensible,' and hence did not constitute 'evidence of bad character' for the purpose of section 98 and the rest of the Act. However:

> once it is decided that [this evidence] did not amount to 'evidence of bad character,' the abolition of the common law rules governing the admissibility of 'evidence of bad character' by section 99(1) did not apply. We have no doubt that the evidence . . . was admissible at common law, in the particular circumstances of this case, because it was relevant to the issue of whether the appellant had a sexual interest in A. It was capable of demonstrating a sexual interest in early or mid-teenage girls, much younger than the appellant, and therefore bore on the truth of his case of a purely supportive, asexual interest in A. It was not in our judgement unfair to admit the evidence (see section 78 of the Police and Criminal Evidence Act 1978).

2.20 So, evidence of dubious behaviour which is bad enough to be described as 'reprehensible' will constitute evidence of 'bad character' and, if sufficiently relevant to the issues in the case, will be admissible under sections 100 and 101 of the Act; and evidence of dubious behaviour which is not bad enough to earn this title will, if relevant, be admissible at common law, subject to the court's various discretionary powers to exclude.

2.21 In *Gleadall v Huddersfield Magistrates' Court*,[11] the defence sought to argue that, as an indirect result of the CJA 2003, the prosecution were now obliged to furnish them with further details about the character and antecedents of the prosecution witnesses than it had previously been the usual practice to provide. A step in this argument was (in effect) that section 98 had enlarged the definition of 'evidence of bad character' beyond the general notion of bad character which had existed in the common law before. This notion the Divisional Court rejected:

---

[10] Decided together with *Weir* [2005] EWCA Crim 2866, [2006] 1 CrAppR 19 (303), **p 206 below**.
[11] [2005] EWHC 2283 (Admin) (DC, Smith LJ and Simon J).

First, does the Criminal Justice Act extend the scope of evidence of bad character beyond the scope at common law? The District Judge held that it did not and that it merely provided a statutory definition which sought to encapsulate the meaning of bad character as it had been understood at common law. Mr Elvidge, who appeared before this court for the claimant, conceded the point. In my view he was right to do so.[12]

2.22 As we have seen, section 98 expressly excludes from the definition of 'bad character evidence' (and hence the statutory limits on its admission) any evidence of conduct or disposition, no matter how criminal or reprehensible, which 'has to do with the alleged facts of the offence with which the defendant is charged' or which 'is evidence of misconduct in connection with the investigation or prosecution of that offence.'

2.23 Conduct which 'has to do with the alleged facts of the offence with which the defendant is charged' undoubtedly includes other criminal acts which the defendant commits at the same time and place as the main offence: for example, when the burglar breaks the window in order to get into the house, or the when the robber hits his victim in the course of stealing the handbag.[13] It presumably also covers other criminal acts which were committed by way of preparation: for example, in a murder case, the theft or illegal purchase of the weapon. At one further remove, it would presumably also cover an earlier criminal act which was the reason why the later crime took place: for example, where a defendant beat his wife, a neighbour reported him to the police, and the defendant later assaulted the neighbour out of revenge. In this situation, there is a potential overlap between evidence that 'has to do with the alleged facts of the offence'—and hence is admissible because it falls outside the definition of bad character evidence—and evidence that falls inside the ban, but is admissible as 'important explanatory evidence' under section 101(1)(c). In practice, nothing of any legal significance depends on which of these two routes it is by which the evidence comes in.

2.24 That evidence of the defendant's misconduct is admissible where it 'has to do with the alleged facts of the offence with which the defendant is charged' is nothing new. In principle, such evidence was equally admissible under the rules relating to evidence of previous misconduct at common law, although there may have been occasions when it was suppressed through ignorance of the law or excessive caution.

---

[12] At §26.

[13] Or that, when the defendant's house was searched after he was arrested on suspicion of drug-dealing offences, the police discovered illegal weapons or ammunition: see *Edwards and Rowlands* [2005] EWCA Crim 3244, **p 230 below**, at §23.

2.25 Similarly, evidence of the defendant's misconduct 'in connection with the investigation or prosecution of that offence' was readily admissible before the Act. Thus, courts would routinely hear, for example, that the defendant had resisted arrest, or tried to suborn witnesses, or lied in response to questioning by the police. Indeed, the question of the weight that should be given to the defendant's lies under questioning is something which has produced a goodly crop of case law, none of which is directly affected by the Act.

2.26 It is important to note that evidence of 'misconduct in connection with the investigation or prosecution of that offence' falls outside the definition of 'bad character evidence' whether the author of the misconduct is the defendant, or anyone else.[14] This has a significant consequence as regards evidence of misconduct by the police—for example, mistreating the suspect or inventing a confession. Because this conduct falls outside the definition of 'bad character evidence' contained in section 98, evidence of it is admissible without reference to section 100, and hence without judicial leave.

2.27 However, it is important also to remember that the defendant who leads such evidence would have 'made an attack on another person's character'—which exposes him to the risk of having his own bad character examined by virtue of section 100(1)(g). Under the Law Commission's proposal, 'gateway (g)' would not have been opened by any attack on another person's character which involved accusations of misconduct that had to do with the alleged facts of the offence with which the defendant is charged, or accusations of misconduct in connection with the investigation or prosecution of that offence. However, this limitation did not appeal to the government and, contrary to the Law Commission's recommendations, it does not appear in the Act. On this important point, see §4.91 below.

---

[14] As where, for example, a defendant accused of robbery produces an explanation that includes an allegation that the complainant was 'high' on drugs: *Machado* (2006) 170 JPN 182.

3

THE BAD CHARACTER OF NON-DEFENDANTS

3.1 Section 100 of the CJA 2003 is as follows:

(1) In criminal proceedings evidence of the bad character of a person other than the defendant is admissible if and only if—

    (a) it is important explanatory evidence,

    (b) it has substantial probative value in relation to a matter which—

        (i) is a matter in issue in the proceedings, and

        (ii) is of substantial importance in the context of the case as a whole,

or

    (c) all parties to the proceedings agree to the evidence being admissible.

(2) For the purposes of subsection (1)(a) evidence is important explanatory evidence if—

    (a) without it, the court or jury would find it impossible or difficult properly to understand other evidence in the case, and

    (b) its value for understanding the case as a whole is substantial.

(3) In assessing the probative value of evidence for the purposes of subsection (1)(b) the court must have regard to the following factors (and to any others it considers relevant)—

    (a) the nature and number of the events, or other things, to which the evidence relates;

    (b) when those events or things are alleged to have happened or existed;

    (c) where—

        (i) the evidence is evidence of a person's misconduct, and

        (ii) it is suggested that the evidence has probative value by reason of similarity between that misconduct and other alleged misconduct,

the nature and extent of the similarities and the dissimilarities between each of the alleged instances of misconduct;

    (d) where—

        (i) the evidence is evidence of a person's misconduct,

> (ii)   it is suggested that that person is also responsible for the misconduct charged, and
>
> (iii) the identity of the person responsible for the misconduct charged is disputed,
>
> the extent to which the evidence shows or tends to show that the same person was responsible each time.
>
> (4)   Except where subsection (1)(c) applies, evidence of the bad character of a person other than the defendant must not be given without leave of the court.

3.2 At first sight, this provision looks as if it is primarily concerned with what Scots lawyers call 'the defence of incrimination': where the defence case is that the person who committed the offence was really someone else. And the section also looks as if it might concern 'background evidence' that implicates third parties— for example, where D is accused of a sexual offence against P, a minor, and the prosecution case is that it took place in a brothel run by a third party, X. But although it potentially applies in these 'third party' situations, this is not in fact its primary purpose. Its main aim is to restrict what can be put to witnesses in the course of cross-examination.

3.3 This is not immediately obvious, because unlike provisions in other legislation designed to restrict cross-examination,[1] section 100 does not explicitly say that 'no evidence may be adduced *and no question may be asked.*' Instead, it talks generally about when evidence of bad character is 'admissible.' So, on a casual reading, it is possible to assume that section 100 is simply about when a party can *adduce evidence,* rather than what can be done in cross-examination. But the wider purpose of the section is plain from its legislative history. Section 100 derives from parts of the Law Commission's Draft Bill which were drafted with a view to protecting witnesses from needlessly offensive cross-examinations. That section 100 controls the introduction of evidence via cross-examination is also underlined by the statutory context: the subsequent sections, dealing with evidence of the bad character of the defendant, are clearly meant to limit cross-examination—and use the same 'evidence is admissible' formula.

3.4 The type of cross-examination against which the Law Commission wished to see witnesses protected was, of course, primarily cross-examination as to credit: the extraction from the witness of discreditable incidents from his past, with a view to persuading the court that his evidence is not to be believed. The wording derives from the Law Commission's Report and Draft Bill, from which it appears that the draftsman meant the phrase in section 1(1)(b) referring to '[evidence that] has substantial probative value in relation to a matter which is a matter in issue in the

---

[1]   For example, Youth Justice and Criminal Evidence Act 1999 s41.

proceedings' to cover *both* evidence that is directly relevant to an issue in the proceedings *and* evidence bearing on the credibility of the witness who testifies about it. Unsurprisingly, therefore, the Court of Appeal in *Yaxley-Lennon* resoundingly rejected the argument of the appellant that section 100(1) is concerned with evidence of bad character relating to an issue, but not to credibility:[2]

> in our view, section 100(1) does cover matters of credibility. To find otherwise would mean that there was a significant lacuna in the legislation with the potential for unfairness. In any event, it is clear from paragraph 362 of the Explanatory Notes that the issue of credibility falls within the section.

Evidence Implicating Non-Defendants in the Offence

3.5 Although section 100 seems to have been primarily devised with a view to controlling the adduction of evidence relating to credit, there is no doubt that it also covers the adduction of evidence (whether in-chief or by cross-examination) that is relevant to issue. So it therefore potentially applies in cases where either the prosecution or the defence case involves heaping blame on someone other than— or in addition to—the defendant. Its potential application in this type of case is limited, however, by the restricted definition of 'bad character evidence' set out in section 98. As we have seen, section 98 excludes from the definition (and hence from the restrictions contained in sections 100 and 101) evidence of misbehaviour 'that has to do with the alleged facts of the offence' or 'is evidence of misconduct in connection with the investigation or prosecution of that offence.' To go back to the hypothetical case described above where the prosecution accuse D of having under-age sex with P in X's brothel, the fact that X runs a brothel clearly 'has to do with the alleged facts of the offence' and so would not count as 'bad character evidence,' and would be admissible without any reference to section 100. The same would no doubt be true where the prosecution accuse D of wounding P and D admits the injury but claims self defence. The evidence that P had attacked D qualifies the facts that the prosecution allege and so clearly 'has to do with the alleged facts of the offence.'[3]

3.6 But what about the case where D denies the wounding and runs a defence that the person who really did it was X? Is this also admissible without reference to section 100? Taking a commonsense view, evidence of this sort falls clearly within the spirit of section 98(a), which seeks to remove from the scope of 'bad character evidence' (and hence the restrictions on adducing it) all evidence directly related

---

[2] Reported together with *Weir* [2005] EWCA Crim 2866, [2006] 1 CrAppR 19 (303), **p 206 below**, at §73.
[3] See §2.26 above, and *Machado* (2006) 170 JPN 182.

to the commission—or non-commission—of the offence. However, if section 98(a) is read narrowly, it might be said to fall outside the scope of the phrase '[evidence which] has to do with the alleged facts of the offence with which the defendant is charged' because it does not 'have to do with' the 'alleged facts' meaning the facts *that are alleged by the prosecution.* In practical terms, this narrow reading has nothing to commend it and it surely ought to be rejected.

3.7 However, if the defence not only alleges that X did it, but seeks to support its theory by calling evidence of what X has done before, section 100 would undoubtedly apply. This is clear inter alia from section 100(3)(b), which requires the court, when deciding whether to admit evidence of a third party's misconduct, to weigh up various factors, one of which is declared to be:

  (d) where—

    (i)　the evidence is evidence of a person's misconduct,

    (ii)　it is suggested that that person is also responsible for the misconduct charged, and

    (iii)　the identity of the person responsible for the misconduct charged is disputed,

  the extent to which the evidence shows or tends to show that the same person was responsible each time.

3.8 *Section 100 and cross-examination of witnesses as to character.* According to section 100(1), evidence of a non-defendant's bad character is admissible:

  if and only if—

  (a)　it is important explanatory evidence,

  (b)　it has substantial probative value in relation to a matter which-

    (i)　is a matter in issue in the proceedings, and

    (ii)　is of substantial importance in the context of the case as a whole,

  or

  (c)　all parties to the proceedings agree to the evidence being admissible.

3.9 As previously mentioned (see §§3.3–3.4 above), there is nothing in this list that refers explicitly to evidence of a non-defendant's bad character being admissible where he is a witness and it is relevant to his credibility, but there is no doubt that the provision covers this. In the light of this, questions to a witness suggesting he is not credible because he is of bad character are clearly admissible—but they now have to pass the filter created by section 100(1), as elaborated by the subsections that follow it. The effect of these is to impose a test of what might be called 'enhanced relevance.' It is not enough that the evidence is merely 'relevant': if it is advanced as 'explanatory evidence' under subsection 101(1)(a) it must be '*important* explanatory evidence'; and if it is to be adduced as relevant to 'a matter in issue' in the proceedings, it must have '*substantial* probative value' in relation to that issue, and the issue must be one that is 'of *substantial* importance in the context of the case as a whole.' In addition to that, by virtue of section 100(4), such questions now require judicial leave.

3.10 How does this affect the previous law, which gave cross-examiners great freedom to question witnesses about discreditable incidents or tendencies, in order to undermine their credibility?

3.11 The first (and very obvious) point to make is that the general effect of section 100 is to restrict what could be done before, rather than to extend it. Section 100 clearly imposes restrictions that did not exist before. In *Gleadall v Huddersfield Magistrates' Court*,[4] as we have seen (§2.21 above), the Divisional Court rejected the notion that section 98, which defines 'bad character evidence' for the purpose of sections 100 and 101, widens the range of matters which count as 'bad character' beyond the scope of the concept as it was known before—hence indirectly opening the door for the cross-examination of witnesses about a wider range of discreditable matters.

Can a Witness be Asked whether he has a Criminal Conviction?

3.12 Hitherto, this has been covered by section 6 of the Criminal Procedure Act (CPA) 1865. This used to say:

> A witness may be questioned as to whether he has been convicted of any felony or misdemeanour, and upon being so questioned, if he either denies or does not admit the fact, or refuses to answer, it shall be lawful for the cross-examining party to prove such conviction.

The CJA 2003[5] amends this provision slightly so that in future it will read:

> *If upon a witness being lawfully* questioned as to whether he has been convicted of any felony or misdemeanour [. . .] he either denies or does not admit the fact, or refuses to answer, it shall be lawful for the cross-examining party to prove such conviction.

3.13 So, in future, the answer is that a witness may be asked in cross-examination whether he has a criminal conviction, but only where CJA 2003 section 100 applies; and this will normally mean satisfying section 100(1)(b), which (in effect)

---

[4] [2005] EWHC 2283 (Admin) (DC, Smith LJ and Simon J).
[5] CJA 2003 Sch 36, Part 5, para 79.

makes evidence of the witness's bad character admissible where the witness is giving evidence as to an *important* issue and the bad character makes a *major* dent in the witness's credibility. Both of these elements are important. Not only must the conviction make a major dent in the witness's credibility: the evidence that he or she has given must relate to a matter which 'is of substantial importance in the context of the case as a whole.'

3.14 Some convictions bear on the credibility of the witness directly, because they provide a reason for doubting the truth of the particular evidence the witness has given in this particular case. If the alleged victim of an assault claims that the defendant was the aggressor, we are less inclined to believe him when we discover that he has (say) five previous convictions for acts of violence himself. But other convictions bear on credibility only indirectly, by inviting us to reason 'a person who would do something like that is not a person whose word can be trusted.' Under the new law, there will be little difficulty about the admissibility of a witness's convictions in the first type of case, where they bear on his credibility directly. However, difficulties will arise in cases where, if at all, the witness's criminal record only undermines his credit indirectly.

3.15 As to how far convictions damage the credibility of a witness in this sense, the previous law contained two schools of thought. One was that any criminal conviction, however old or trivial, affected the credibility of a witness by definition—and could therefore be explored in cross-examination. The alternative view was that convictions must pass a certain threshold of gravity and freshness before a witness could properly be asked about them. This was the view of Lawton J in *Sweet-Escott*,[6] where he ruled that convictions for drunken driving and for petty theft 'including one for which a prison sentence had been imposed' were not material to the credit of a middle-aged witness, given that they were 20 years old and dated from his youth. The test, he said, was whether a fair-minded tribunal would think that these matters affected the standing of the witness. Under section 100, it seems to be the *Sweet-Escott* approach that now prevails.

3.16 Issues of freshness and gravity aside, must the previous offence, or the defendant's behaviour in trying to avoid a conviction for it, demonstrate a particular tendency to lie? Or does the law take the hard-nosed view that, as a general proposition, all convictions (other than trivial or ancient ones) undermine the credibility of those who have them?

3.17 Under the previous law, it was the second of these assumptions on which the courts operated. Thus, in *Paraskeva*,[7] for example, a conviction for assault was

---

[6] (1971) 55 CrAppR 316.
[7] (1982) 76 CrAppR 162.

quashed when, after the trial, it emerged that the alleged victim had a previous conviction for theft, about which the defence were unable to cross-examine him because they did not know about it. It was on this basis that it has always been the practice of the prosecution to inform the defence of any of their witnesses who have a criminal record. However, it is arguable that the position is now different.

3.18 As we shall see, under the new rules governing evidence of the bad character of the defendant, the defendant's previous convictions (and general bad character) may now be given where these suggest, inter alia, that 'the defendant has a propensity to be untruthful.'[8] In this new context, the Court of Appeal in *Hanson* made it plain that convictions should only be admitted as showing a propensity to be untruthful when they actually suggested that the defendant had earlier told a lie, either in committing the offence, or afterwards, by falsely denying that he had committed it to the police, or in court when giving evidence; and in the light of this, they said, his previous convictions—even for offences of 'dishonesty' such as theft—could not be adduced, without more, as showing his 'propensity to be untruthful.'

3.19 Logically, this line of reasoning could also be applied to the previous convictions of witnesses.[9] However, it would produce a major change, and one I suspect the courts would not wish to make. To take an extreme example, if the star prosecution witness at a trial had convictions for murder, rape, grievous bodily harm and arson, it would seem very odd if his criminal record now had to be withheld from the jury, because—thanks to his having invariably made full use of the right to silence—neither the crimes themselves nor his subsequent convictions show that he has ever lied. The narrow view the Court of Appeal took on when the defendant's previous convictions are admissible as suggesting a 'propensity to be untruthful' in *Hanson* is understandable within that context. If given too wide a scope, the provision allowing the court to hear about a defendant's criminal record where it shows he 'has a propensity to be untruthful' would circumvent the restrictions that the CJA 2003 attempts to impose on admitting the defendant's criminal record in order to show he has a propensity to commit crimes. But these considerations do not apply to witnesses. The defendant, unlike a witness, is on trial and runs the risk of being convicted and punished at the end.

3.20 In principle, witnesses can be asked in cross-examination not only about their criminal convictions, but more generally about their criminal activities,

---

[8] CJA 2003 s103(1)(b); see §§4.54–4.57 below.

[9] This issue also arises in situations where two defendants run 'cut-throat defences' and one wishes to undermine his co-defendant's case by bringing in his criminal record; see §4.71 below. And see generally Roderick Munday, 'Cut-throat Defences and the "Propensity to be Untruthful" under s.104 of the Criminal Justice Act 2003' [2005] *Crim LR* 624.

including criminal offences committed by them for which they have never been convicted. However, for reasons that are obvious, the courts are more reluctant to admit evidence of this type.

3.21 In *Yaxley-Lennon*,[10] the question before the Court of Appeal was whether the prosecution should have been permitted to ask the key defence witness to an offence of assault occasioning actual bodily harm about a caution she had received for possessing cocaine. The Court of Appeal thought not, agreeing with the trial judge's assessment that the caution 'has got as much to do with this case as the price of tomatoes.' In *Osbourne*,[11] the defendant was accused of robbing the licensee of a public house, who was the chief prosecution witness. The trial judge allowed the defence to ask the licensee about various malpractices in the course of running the pub as a result of which his books were often in the red, but refused to allow questions about his alleged practice of permitting drug-dealing on the premises. Of both these rulings the Court of Appeal approved. The malpractices that resulted in till shortages and inability to balance the books were relevant as providing a possible motive for the licensee's making a false claim that the defendant had robbed him, but the allegation that he permitted drug-dealing did not satisfy the conditions laid down by section 100.

3.22 In *Bovell*,[12] the defendant was accused of attacking a shopkeeper. The prosecution case was that the attack was unprovoked, the defence that the defendant was acting in self defence. The defendant appealed on the ground that he should have been permitted to ask the shop keeper about an incident in 2001 in which it was alleged that the shopkeeper had wounded someone with intent—a matter dropped by the authorities when the victim decided not to pursue it—and a conviction in 1993 for armed robbery. The Court of Appeal thought that it was right that the allegation in 2001 was not put to him; first, because the court doubted whether 'the making of a mere allegation is capable of being evidence within section 100(1)' and, secondly, because the facts relating to it were disputed, and examining it would therefore have led the court into a time-wasting and distracting examination of 'satellite matters.' The conviction in 1993, by contrast, could properly have been put to him, but if the defence had done so the defendant would have opened 'gateway (g),' as a result of which Bovell's own unsavoury criminal record would have been revealed to the jury; in the light of this, and the fact that the shopkeeper's evidence was corroborated by two other witnesses, Bovell's conviction was safe and was affirmed.

[10] Reported with *Weir* [2005] EWCA Crim 2866 [2006] 1 CrAppR 19 (303), **p 206 below.**
[11] Reported with *Renda* [2005] EWCA Crim 2826, **p 193 below.**
[12] [2005] EWCA Crim 1091, [2005] 2 CrAppR 27 (401), **p 163 below.**

3.23 Finally, it must be remembered that whether a given witness's criminal behaviour in the past satisfies the test of 'enhanced relevance' set out in section 100(1) will often depend on the facts of the case and the nature of his involvement in it, as well as the nature of his past behaviour. If D is on trial for assault and W, an independent witness who was undoubtedly present and who has no obvious motive to lie, asserts that D was the aggressor, it is of little relevance that W has a conviction for obtaining by deception. The main issue on these assumed facts is not W's honesty but his ability to observe. On the other hand, if W was a friend of the victim, or if W had come forward in response to the offer of a reward, then his honesty is a live issue and his track-record as a proven liar is obviously relevant.[13]

3.24 Plainly the judge has a degree of discretion here and his or her exercise of it will not usually be open to appeal. As the Court of Appeal said in *Renda and others*:[14]

> Several of the decisions or rulings questioned in these appeals represent either judgements by the trial judge in the specific factual context of the individual case, or the exercise of judicial discretion. The circumstances in which this Court would interfere with the exercise of a judicial discretion are limited. The principles need no repetition. However we emphasise that the same general approach will be adopted when the Court is being invited to interfere with what in reality is a fact specific judgement. As we explain in one of these decisions,[15] the trial judge's 'feel' for the case is usually the critical ingredient of the decision at first instance which this Court lacks. Context therefore is vital. The creation and subsequent citation from a vast body of so-called 'authority,' in reality representing no more than observations on a fact specific decision of the judge in the Crown Court, is unnecessary and may well be counterproductive. This legislation has now been in force for nearly a year. The principles have been considered by this Court on a number of occasions. The responsibility for their application is not for this Court but for trial judges.

Can a Witness Still be Asked, or Evidence Led to Suggest, that a Witness has Said Something Different to his Courtroom Testimony on an Earlier Occasion?

3.25 In principle, plainly yes. There is no difficulty, of course, where the overtone is that the witness has made a mistake, rather than told a lie. If there is no suggestion of lying, then the question will not relate to the 'bad character' of the witness. If the question (or evidence) does suggest that the witness has told a lie, then

---

[13] Those who attended the Judicial Studies Board training sessions will remember the hypothetical problem involving the witness appropriately named 'Seymour Cash.'
[14] [2005] EWCA Crim 2826, **p 193 below.**
[15] *Osbourne*, at §57; see also *Hanson* [2005] EWCA Crim 824, [2005] 1 WLR 3169, **p 153 below,** at §15.

section 100 is potentially applicable. However, in most cases the lie (if there was one) will have been told in the course of the investigation. As previously explained (§§2.22–2.27 above), the 'bad character' provisions of the CJA 2003 do not apply to bad character that takes the form of 'misconduct in connection with the investigation or prosecution of [the] offence.' So, if the suggestion is that the witness lied to the police, or told the truth to the police but subsequently lied in court, questions can clearly be asked about this without recourse to section 100. (But, as is explained elsewhere, a defendant who asks such a question risks the admission of evidence of his own bad character via 'gateway (g)': see §4.91 below.)

What is the Status Now of *R v Rowton*?

3.26 In *Rowton*,[16] it was held to be permissible for a party to attack the credit of his opponent's witness by calling another witness, asking if he knows the opponent's witness, and then asking—in the expectation of a negative answer—whether from what he knows of him he would believe his word on oath.[17] The implication of such evidence is that the first witness is in the habit of telling lies, which would fall within the definition of 'bad character' in section 98 and hence bring the issue within the framework of section 100. But such evidence would presumably pass the test laid down in section 100 (1)(b), because it would bear centrally upon the witness's credibility. So it would be admissible unless—as is unlikely—the evidence of the witness is not 'of substantial importance in the context of the case as a whole.'

What is the Status Now of *Toohey v Metropolitan Police Commissioner*?

3.27 In that case,[18] the House of Lords ruled that it is permissible to lead evidence suggesting that your opponent's witness is not to be believed because he is or was mentally disturbed. Section 100 does not affect this. Section 100 concerns evidence of 'bad character,' and although allegations of mental illness count as defamatory for the purpose of libel and slander, mental illness or disturbance clearly does not fall within the definition of 'bad character' laid down in section 98.

---

[16] (1865) 10 Cox 25.
[17] Cf *Richardson* [1969] 1 QB 299. It is not permissible to take the questioning further and ask the second witness why he would not believe the first.
[18] [1965] AC 595.

3.28 However, section 100 could enter the picture if the illness is one that manifested itself in reprehensible behaviour (eg mental problems which have led to violence). In many cases, the behaviour will be closely connected with the offence with which the defendant is charged, and hence the 'bad character' provisions of the CJA 2003 will not apply (see §2.22–2.27 above). Where this is not so, it would be open to the courts to decide that the 'bad character' aspect of the matter was purely incidental, the questions (or evidence) being primarily concerned with illness and hence outside the framework of Part 11 of the Act.

How does Section 100 relate to Section 41 of the YJCEA 1999 (Restricting Questions about the Sex-life of a Complainant in a Sex Case)?

3.29 In principle, these provisions operate in different areas. However, these areas overlap to a certain extent. To the extent that they overlap, the conditions set out in both provisions must be complied with.[19]

3.30 The first point to bear in mind is that the scope of section 41 of the Youth Justice and Criminal Evidence Act (YJCEA) 1999 is limited. It only applies where the defendant is on trial for a sexual offence, and the witness whose sex-life it is sought to examine is the complainant. Outside this context it has no application. So, for example, it does not come into the picture where the defendant is on trial for robbery and seeks to run what is usually called 'the guardsman's defence.'[20]

3.31 Where the situation is one to which section 41 of the YJCEA 1999 does apply, questions (or other evidence) about the complainant's sex-life may not involve a suggestion of bad character. They may, for example, relate to some neutral matter, such as whether or not the complainant had an ongoing sexual relationship with the defendant. If this is so, section 100 does not enter the picture. But the questions will often involve a suggestion of bad character: for example, where it is suggested that the complainant makes a habit of picking up men, getting them into compromising situations, and then demanding money. In such a case, the evidence would in theory have to pass the tests set out in *both* section 41 of the YJCEA 1999 *and* section 100 before it would be admissible. However, the tests set out in section 41 of the YJCEA are stricter than those set out in section 100, and as the Law Commission pointed out, 'evidence of sexual experience which is ruled admissible

---

[19] See CJA 2003 s112(3): 'Nothing in this Chapter affects the exclusion of evidence—. . . (b) under section 41 of the Youth Justice and Criminal Evidence Act 1999'.

[20] ie that the victim solicited the defendant for immoral purposes and when the defendant reacted angrily, the victim gave him the money to persuade him to keep quiet.

under section 41 will have substantial probative value, with the result that it would be ruled admissible under [what is now section 100] too'.[21]

3.32 If D is charged with something other than a sexual offence, and section 41 of the YJCEA 1999 does not apply, could a witness at his trial be asked embarrassing questions about his or her sex-life?

3.33 First, irrespective of whether the sexual behaviour in question would count as 'bad character,' questions about a person's sex-life would not be admissible unless they were either directly relevant to an issue or affected his or her credibility as a witness—neither of which will normally be the case. The fact that a person has a sex-life, or even what is euphemistically called an 'active' one, does not make him or her less likely to tell the truth on oath.

3.34 Secondly, if (unusually) a question about a witness's sex-life does bear upon credit or issue, then the question would be admissible without reference to section 100 if the sexual behaviour in question did not qualify as 'bad character' within the definition contained in section 98. This would be so, for example, if the question or evidence merely sought to show that the witness was the defendant's girlfriend or boyfriend, and hence likely to be biased.[22]

3.35 Thirdly, a question about the sex-life of a witness that does impugn his character will often be one that 'has to do with the alleged facts of the offence with which the defendant is charged' and hence fall outside the limited definition of 'bad character evidence' in section 98—and therefore outside the scope of section 100. This would be so, for example, in the case of the robber who runs the 'guardsman's defence.'

3.36 However, in the comparatively rare case where the witness's sexual behaviour (i) is relevant, (ii) reprehensible and (iii) not directly related to the facts of the case, then evidence about it would be admissible, but only where it passes the tests laid down by section 100. This could happen if the sexual behaviour was both disgraceful and showed the witness to be a person whose word is not to be trusted; for example, where a university employee is prosecuted for fraud in relation to travel expenses, the chief prosecution witness is the Head of Department, and the defence wish to discredit him by showing that he is in the habit of obtaining the sexual favours of his pupils by offering to falsify their exam records in their favour. The question would clearly relate to 'bad character' within section 98, and

---

[21] Law Commission, Evidence of Bad Character in Criminal Proceedings (Law Com no 273, Cm 5257, October 2001) §9.45.
[22] Unnecessary questions relating to the private life of a witness may infringe his or her rights under Article 8 of the European Convention on Human Rights; see §§2.14–2.15 above.

so would have to pass the requirements of section 100 in order to be admissible—which it would, presumably, because section 100(1)(d) would apply.

Does Section 100 Apply to 'Non-defendants' who are Dead?

3.37 This is an important loose end that section 100 leaves untied.

3.38 In practice, this issue will arise only rarely because of the limited definition of 'bad character evidence' set out in section 98. A recurrent situation where the defence heap blame on a deceased person is a murder prosecution in which the defendant admits the killing but runs a defence of provocation. This would undoubtedly be evidence that 'has to do with the alleged facts of the offence with which the defendant is charged' and hence would fall outside the definition of 'bad character evidence' and the restrictions on its use set out in section 100. Similarly, if a defendant claims that a police officer, now dead, fabricated his confession, this would fall outside the definition of 'bad character evidence' and the restrictions on its use in section 100, because it would be 'evidence of misconduct in connection with the investigation or prosecution of that offence.' However, there are some situations in which the issue will undoubtedly arise: for example, where the prosecution evidence includes a statement from a deceased witness,[23] whose credit the defence wishes to undermine by invoking his criminal record.

3.39 There is no hint as to whether section 100 was intended to apply to deceased non-defendants in either the Law Commission Report, or public discussions when the Criminal Justice Bill was being enacted. It seems, however, that section 100 was enacted with two aims in mind. The first was to protect people's reputations and feelings by preventing their trivial misdeeds being publicly paraded in legal proceedings to which they are barely relevant, and the second was to protect the court from being diverted from examining the central issues by 'red herrings.' The 'red herring' argument is valid, whether the person whose character is in issue is alive or dead. And although if a person is dead he presumably has no feelings and no longer cares for his good name, his friends and family may still greatly care on his behalf.[24] So, adopting a purposive approach, it looks as if 'non-defendants' are covered by section 100, whether they are alive or dead.

---

[23] Now clearly admissible under CJA 2003 s116(2)(a).

[24] It was partly considerations of this sort that led Parliament to amend the Criminal Evidence Act 1898 s1(f)(ii) (as it then was) in order to include deceased victims in the list of persons whose character the defendant could only attack at the risk of having his own bad character exposed. Earl Ferrers, supporting the amendment, said that in homicide cases it 'would spare the victim's family further suffering': Hansard, HL, vol 556 col 1248 (5 July 1994).

Does Section 100 Apply to 'Non-defendants' who are Not Identified?

3.40 In practice, it is not uncommon for defendants to claim that the offence for which they are on trial was in fact committed by some other person whose identity is unknown. A man is prosecuted for burglary on evidence that he was caught in the garden of the burgled house with a sack containing stolen goods, for example, and claims that he had entered the garden to relieve himself when an unidentified person climbed out of the window carrying the sack, and on seeing the defendant there he promptly dropped the sack and fled.

3.41 Where this situation arises, the evidence relating to the unknown person will usually be evidence which 'has to do with the alleged facts of the offence with which the defendant is charged' and, if this is so, it will fall outside the definition of 'bad character' in section 98 and hence outside the scope of section 100.[25]

3.42 In theory, situations could arise in which the bad character of an unknown person is an issue and the misbehaviour alleged against him does not relate to the alleged facts of the case.[26] If such a case did indeed arise, I believe that it would be sensible to interpret section 100 as inapplicable, on principle, to 'non-defendants' who cannot be identified. Unlike the 'non-defendant' who was once alive but now is dead, the unidentified person has no reputation to be destroyed, or friends or relatives who can suffer pain or outrage because his name is dragged through the mud. In the light of this, there seems to be no compelling reason for judicial leave to be obtained before the evidence is given.

The Requirement of Leave

3.43 Section 100(4) imposes a requirement of leave to admit evidence of a non-defendant's bad character, except where all the parties agree. Commentators have criticised this provision for several different reasons.

---

[25] Unless, that is, the 'narrow reading' of s98(a) is correct: see §3.6 above.

[26] For example, the defendant is accused of a theft allegedly committed when he was an inmate in a bail hostel, and in his defence points out that all the other inmates had the same opportunity to commit the offence as he did and most of them have criminal records: one of the hypothetical problems invented for the Judicial Studies Board seminars. This hypothetical case bears a close resemblance to *Lee* (1976) 62 CrAppR 33, where the Court of Appeal held that the defence ought to have been permitted to call evidence of this type—except that in Lee the other inmates were identified.

3.44 One commentator remarks that section 100(4) 'gives no guidance as to the factors the court may properly take into account when granting leave.'[27] This raises the question: what is the basis on which the court grants leave? Does section 100(4) give the judge a general discretion, or is his duty limited to deciding whether the tests laid down by section 100 are satisfied or not? As the basic test set out in section 100(1) is elaborated in detail by subsections (2) and (3), it seems probable that Parliament simply meant the judge to check that the conditions set out in section 100 are met—in which case the section is not open to criticism for offering insufficient guidance.

3.45 A further criticism is the apparent imbalance between the prosecution and the defence. Under the Law Commission's scheme, leave would have been required to adduce evidence of the bad character of *either* a witness *or* a defendant. The CJA 2003 scheme, however, imposes a leave requirement as regards witnesses, but not defendants. Although this has been criticised as inherently unfair,[28] it is probably not so, because the defendant—unlike a witness—can object to the evidence (see §1.44 above).

3.46 There seems little doubt, however, that the leave requirement will have the disadvantage of making certain trials more cumbersome.

---

[27] Rudi Fortson, who wrote the commentary in *Criminal Justice Act 2003—a Current Law Statute Guide*, annotated by DA Thomas and Rudi F Fortson (London, Sweet & Maxwell, 2004).
[28] See Colin Tapper, 'The Criminal Justice Act 2003: Evidence of Bad Character' [2004] *Crim LR* 533.

4

EVIDENCE OF THE DEFENDANT'S BAD CHARACTER

4.1 As previously mentioned, the Criminal Justice Act 2003 provides that evidence of the defendant's bad character is admissible if it passes through one of seven 'gateways'. To recapitulate, these are listed in **section 101** of the CJA 2003, which is as follows:

(1) In criminal proceedings evidence of the defendant's bad character is admissible if, but only if—

    (a) all parties to the proceedings agree to the evidence being admissible,

    (b) the evidence is adduced by the defendant himself or is given in answer to a question asked by him in cross-examination and intended to elicit it,

    (c) it is important explanatory evidence,

    (d) it is relevant to an important matter in issue between the defendant and the prosecution,

    (e) it has substantial probative value in relation to an important matter in issue between the defendant and a co-defendant,

    (f) it is evidence to correct a false impression given by the defendant, or

    (g) the defendant has made an attack on another person's character.

(2) Sections 102 to 106 contain provisions supplementing subsection (1).

(3) The court must not admit evidence under subsection (1)(d) or (g) if, on an application by the defendant to exclude it, it appears to the court that the admission of the evidence would have such an adverse effect on the fairness of the proceedings that the court ought not to admit it.

(4) On an application to exclude evidence under subsection (3) the court must have regard, in particular, to the length of time between the matters to which that evidence relates and the matters which form the subject of the offence charged.

4.2 This provision, of course, only applies to 'bad character' evidence that falls within the limited definition set out in section 98. So, where the evidence of the defendant's misbehaviour 'has to do with the alleged facts of the offence' or 'is evidence of misconduct in connection with the investigation or prosecution of that offence,' it is in principle admissible whether or not it passes through any of the 'gateways' listed in section 101. (See Chapter 2.)

The 'Gateways' are Not Mutually Exclusive

4.3 It should be obvious, I believe, that a particular item of bad character evidence could be admissible via more than one of these seven 'gateways' at once.[1] Where, for example, D1 and D2 are prosecuted for an armed robbery, evidence that they had jointly been involved in what the tabloid newspapers would call a 'crime spree' together could be admissible via 'gateway (c)' as important explanatory evidence,[2] and also—depending on the nature of the previous crimes—via 'gateway (d)' as showing propensity. Similarly, where a sadistic murder was committed in circumstances which make it clear that it must have been the work either of D1 or D2 on his own, or both of them together, the fact that D1 has a track-record for acts of sadistic violence could be admissible either via 'gateway (d)' as showing propensity, or—where each one blames the other—via 'gateway (e)' as relevant to 'an important matter in issue between the defendant and a co-defendant.' In *Somonathan*,[3] where a Hindu priest had been convicted for sexual offences against a member of his congregation, evidence of his inappropriate behaviour towards female worshippers at his previous temple was held to be admissible both via 'gateway (d)'—because it showed disposition—and 'gateway (f)'—because it corrected the false impression he had given that he was a respected priest whose standing in the Hindu community was high. Further, as is explained below, the particular 'gateway' through which a given piece of evidence is admitted does not limit the use which the tribunal of fact may later make of it.[4]

Gateways (a) and (b); Consent of all Parties; Evidence from the Defence.

4.4 Of the gateways listed in section 101, those described in subsections (1)(a) and (b) require little comment or explanation. By section 101(1)(a), evidence of the defendant's bad character is admissible when 'all parties to the proceedings agree,' and by section 101(1)(b) it is admissible in the rather more likely event that the evidence comes from the defence; as it might, for example, where the defendant produces an alibi that he was in prison at the time, or committing a less serious offence somewhere else—or, as in one famous case, that he failed to tell the police

---

[1] For a contrary view, however, see Roderick Munday, 'The Purposes of Gateway (g): Yet Another Problematic of the Criminal Justice Act 2003' [2006] *Crim LR* 300.

[2] *Pettman*, Court of Appeal, 5 May 1985, CA no 5048/C/82; see §4.9 below.

[3] Reported with *Weir* [2005] EWCA Crim 2866 [2006] 1 CrAppR 19 (303), **p 206 below**; see further §4.84 below.

[4] See further §4.105 below. Furthermore, where at trial bad character evidence is wrongly admitted through a 'gateway' that is not open, the Court of Appeal is likely to dismiss the appeal if the evidence in question could have been admitted through a different one: see *Lambrou, Constantinou and Gun* [2005] EWCA Crim 3595.

when he found his girlfriend dead because, in the light of his criminal record, he thought they were bound to accuse him of killing her.[5]

4.5 Where evidence of the defendant's bad character is admitted by the defence, they will do so with a specific aim in mind; but in *Enright and Gray*,[6] the Court of Appeal made it plain that, where this is so, they have no power to limit the use the tribunal of fact makes of it to that particular purpose. Enright was arrested by the police in the course of a drugs raid, and on arrest they handcuffed him. The defence, fearing that the jury would infer from the handcuffing that he was a major criminal, put his criminal record in evidence, which consisted of a long catalogue of middle-range offences, including drink-related violence, criminal damage, assault on the police and one conviction for possessing drugs. In his direction to the jury, the judge indicated that they could take account of these convictions in deciding whether he had committed the offence with which he was now charged, and also in deciding whether his evidence was truthful. The Court of Appeal rejected the defence argument that convictions put in voluntarily by the defence could not be made use of for these purposes (although they also thought that, on the facts of this case, the previous convictions were of little if any relevance to either credibility or issue).

Gateway (c): Important Explanatory Evidence

4.6 By section 101(1)(c), bad character is admissible where it is 'important explanatory evidence.' The scope of this 'gateway' is explained in **section 102**, which makes it plain that to be admissible under this gateway the evidence must be *both* important *and* explanatory. It is as follows:

> For the purposes of section 101(1)(c) evidence is important explanatory evidence if—
>
> (a) without it, the court or jury would find it impossible or difficult properly to understand other evidence in the case, and
> (b) its value for understanding the case as a whole is substantial.

4.7 This 'gateway' closely reflects the pre-existing common law.[7] In *Pettman*,[8] Purchas LJ said that bad character evidence is admissible:

---

[5] The case of Tony Mancini, accused of the 'Brighton Trunk Murder' in 1934.

[6] Reported with *Edwards and Rowlands* [2005] EWCA Crim 3244, **p 230 below.**

[7] For further details of this, see Roderick Munday, *Evidence* (3rd edn, Oxford, OUP, 2005) §§7.27–7.31; *Archbold* (2006) §§13-30–13-46; Peter Murphy and Eric Stockdale *Blackstone's Criminal Practice* (2006) §F12-7.

[8] Court of Appeal, 5 May 1985, CA no 5048/C/82.

where it is necessary to place before the jury evidence of part of a continual background of history relevant to the offence charged in the indictment and without the totality of which the account placed before the jury would be incomplete or incomprehensible, then the fact that the whole account involves including evidence establishing the commission of an offence with which the accused is not charged is not of itself a ground for excluding the evidence.

This statement of principle has been quoted and applied in many later cases.

4.8 The 'important explanatory evidence' gateway featured in the Law Commission's scheme, but it would have been restricted by a requirement of judicial leave, to be given (inter alia) only where the court was satisfied that 'the evidence carries no risk of prejudice to the defendant,'[9] or where, despite the risk of prejudice, 'the interests of justice nevertheless require the evidence to be admissible.' These restrictions would probably have reduced the amount of bad character evidence which was admissible under the 'important explanatory evidence' principle at common law and, unsurprisingly, they are not included in the Act. There is no requirement of judicial leave and, although section 101(3) gives the court an explicit power to exclude evidence of the defendant's bad character that is in principle admissible via some of the 'gateways' listed in section 101, this power does not extend to evidence admissible under gateway (c)—'important explanatory evidence.' (On the question whether the court could exclude such evidence under its general discretionary powers, see §1.21–1.28 above.)

4.9 Cases in which the principle now encapsulated in 'gateway (c)' was applied under the earlier law include the following: a conspiracy to commit a robbery in Acton, to prove which evidence was admissible of a burglary committed jointly by the defendants in Brighton some weeks earlier, because it showed they were involved in criminal projects together;[10] a sex case, where the defendant's previous offences against the alleged victim and other members of the family were admissible to explain how the one with which he was charged came to be committed, and why the victim did not complain about it;[11] a murder, in which evidence was admitted of the defendant's previous acts of violence towards the victim;[12] and a prosecution for possessing explosives for an unlawful purpose, where the defendant claimed to be an ordinary law-abiding citizen and disclaimed all knowledge of the explosives, and the prosecution was permitted to produce in evidence a video of the defendant training with a terrorist group in Pakistan.[13] A further example,

---

[9] A condition which, if literally applied to evidence admissible for the prosecution, could never be complied with; see §1.55 above.

[10] *Pettman*, n 8 above.

[11] *TM* [2000] 2 CrAppR 266.

[12] *Fulcher* [1995] 2 CrAppR 251.

[13] *Sidhu* (1994) 98 CrAppR 59.

given as a hypothetical case by the Law Commission, would be a prosecution for a fraud offence, in which evidence could be given of other fraudulent incidents in order to show the fraudulent nature of the business in the running of which the offence in question was committed.[14]

4.10 The 'important explanatory evidence' principle has now been considered by the Court of Appeal in several reported cases since the bad character evidence provisions of the Criminal Justice Act 2003 came into force. In *Chohan*,[15] the defendant was accused of a robbery. A key prosecution witness was one Donna Marsh, who claimed to have seen the defendant running away from the scene of the crime. She recognised him, she said, because he was the 'dealer' from whom she regularly bought heroin. The trial judge admitted this part of her evidence because, in his view, it constituted 'important explanatory evidence'—explanatory, because it explained why she was able to recognise him—and hence admissible via 'gateway (c)': a ruling which the Court of Appeal said was correct.[16] In *Van Nguyen*,[17] the defendant was accused of growing cannabis, a flourishing crop of which the police had found growing at the house which he shared with various people, including his brother, who had pleaded guilty to the same offence, in the light of evidence that his fingerprints were found on the plants and the equipment. At trial, the main issue was whether or not the defendant Van Nguyen had played any part in the cultivation. The trial judge admitted prosecution evidence that Van Nguyen was someone who took heroin and used methadone, evidence the judge held to be admissible by virtue of 'gateway (d),' believing that it was relevant to the issue of whether Van Nguyen did in fact help his brother cultivate the plants. The Court of Appeal quashed the conviction, because in their view his habit of using heroin and methadone shed no light on this particular issue whatsoever. In their view, the evidence might have been admissible as 'background to the offence charged'—presumably because it explained why he and the other *dramatis personae* were all living together under the same roof. But as such, it did not deserve to become, as it did, 'the centre of focus of the trial.' In *Smith*,[18] the prosecution, at the trial of the defendant for indecent offences against young girls, sought to adduce evidence of other indecent acts with other girls, committed in the same area around the same time. The trial judge refused to admit this evidence via 'gateway (c)' as 'background evidence' and the Court of Appeal said this was correct.

---

[14] Law Commission, *Evidence of Bad Character in Criminal Proceedings* (Law Com no 273, Cm 5257, October 2001) 132.

[15] Decided together with *Edwards* [2005] EWCA Crim 1813, [2006] 1 CrAppR 3 (31), **p 169 below**.

[16] I think this evidence might also have been admissible via 'gateway (d),' as 'relevant to an important matter in issue between the defendant and the prosecution': namely, whether the person Donna Marsh saw running away from the scene of the robbery was in fact the defendant.

[17] Decided together with *Highton* [2005] EWCA Crim 1985, [2005] 1 WLR 3472, **p 153 below**.

[18] Reported together with *Edwards and Rowlands* [2005] EWCA Crim 3244, **p 230 below**.

(The trial judge had, however, admitted the evidence via 'gateway (d)' because it showed propensity—a ruling of which the Court of Appeal also approved.)

Gateway (d): Evidence Relevant to 'an Important Matter between the Defendant and the Prosecution'; Evidence of Propensity

4.11 By section 101(1)(d), evidence of the defendant's bad character is admissible where 'it is relevant to an important matter in issue between the defendant and the prosecution.' By section 112(1), an 'important matter' is defined as 'a matter of substantial importance in the context of the case as a whole.'

4.12 This 'gateway,' like the others, originates with the proposals of the Law Commission—although, as will be explained below, it has been widened far beyond what the Law Commission had in mind. Under the earlier law, evidence incidentally revealing the defendant's bad character was always admissible where it shed light on a 'matter in issue' in the sense of a specific factual question on which prosecution and defence was in dispute: for example, where the defendant was prosecuted for obtaining money by deception by passing off fake jewellery as genuine, his defence was that he had acted in good faith, and the prosecution were allowed to prove his previous convictions for similar offences in order to suggest he knew fake jewellery when he saw it and he therefore acted with dishonest intent.[19] The Law Commission approved of this and proposed a 'gateway' relating to 'evidence going to a matter in issue' with this principle in mind.

4.13 The primary effect of section 101(1)(d) is to do what the Law Commission intended, that is, to codify the principle that evidence which incidentally reveals the defendant's bad character is admissible if it is directly relevant to a particular disputed issue in the case. So, in any case where the evidence would have been admissible under the old law because it was relevant to a 'matter in issue' in this sense, it will undoubtedly be admissible under the new law as well. So, to this limited extent, it is true that the old rules on 'similar fact evidence' still apply.

4.14 That this is so is clear from the post-Act case of *Benguit*.[20] The defendant was accused of murdering a young woman who had been killed as she walked home from a nightclub by an assailant who inflicted three stab wounds to her back. One

---

[19] *Francis* (1874) LR 2 CCR 128.
[20] [2005] EWCA Crim 1953 (23 July 2005).

of the issues at the trial[21] was whether, on the night the murder was committed, the defendant was carrying a knife, which he denied, asserting that although people involved in the drug scene (as he was) often carried knives, he never did so. The prosecution claimed that he carried one habitually, and called two witnesses who gave evidence that, on other occasions, they had seen him in possession of a large knife. At trial, which took place just after the bad character evidence provisions of the CJA 2003 came into force, it was wrongly assumed that the earlier rules still applied and, applying those rules, the judge held this evidence to be admissible. The Court of Appeal said that the question should have been decided with reference to the CJA 2003, but held that this evidence was admissible under the new law, as showing that he was in fact in the habit of carrying a knife.[22]

4.15 Under the Law Commission's proposals, evidence of bad character would have been admissible via the 'matter in issue' gateway only where it satisfied a test of 'enhanced relevance': to make it admissible, it would not have been enough that the bad character evidence had some degree of relevance to the disputed issue—it would have been necessary to persuade the court that, in relation to it, it had 'substantial probative value.' This restrictive form of words did not appeal to the government, and under section 101(1)(d) such evidence is in principle admissible provided it is '*relevant* to an important matter in issue between the defendant and the prosecution.' In *Somonathan*,[23] the Court of Appeal laid stress upon this point, rejecting as it did so an obiter dictum from Lord Phillips in the civil case of *O'Brien v Chief Constable of South Wales Police*,[24] in which he had suggested that, in criminal proceedings, the test of admissibility under CJA 2003 was now 'enhanced probative value.'

4.16 As previously mentioned (§1.11 above), the Law Commission also proposed a further limitation in that evidence of the defendant's bad character should be admissible only where the court gave leave. This limitation did not appeal to the government either and has not found its way into the Act. However, section 101(3) gives the court an explicit power to exclude evidence otherwise admissible

---

[21] In fact, it was the defendant's third trial—second retrial after two previous juries had disagreed. The first ground of appeal was that a trial in these circumstances necessarily amounted to an abuse of process, an argument the Court of Appeal rejected.

[22] In his judgment, which was delivered unreserved, Latham LJ said that 'the gateway was passed' without explicitly mentioning 'gateway (d)'; but from the context, it is clear that it was gateway (d) that he had in mind.

[23] Reported together with *Weir* [2005] EWCA Crim 2866, [2006] 1 CrAppR 19 (303), **p 206 below**, at §§35–36.

[24] [2005] UKHL 26, [2005] 2 AC 534, at §33. In *Edwards*, a differently-constituted Court of Appeal had earlier cited this passage, without disapproval: [2005] EWCA Crim 1813, [2006] 1 CrAppR 3 (31), **p 169 below** at §54.

via gateway (d) or (g) if 'on an application by the defendant to exclude it, it appears to the court that the admission of the evidence would have such an adverse effect on the fairness of the proceedings that the court ought not to admit it.'

4.17 If the primary effect of section 101(1)(d) is to ensure that evidence revealing the defendant's bad character is admissible if it sheds light on a specific issue in dispute, it has a far wider reach than this, because its meaning is extended by **section 103**, which is as follows:

(1) For the purposes of section 101(1)(d) the matters in issue between the defendant and the prosecution include—

  (a) the question whether the defendant has a propensity to commit offences of the kind with which he is charged, except where his having such a propensity makes it no more likely that he is guilty of the offence;

  (b) the question whether the defendant has a propensity to be untruthful, except where it is not suggested that the defendant's case is untruthful in any respect.

(2) Where subsection (1)(a) applies, a defendant's propensity to commit offences of the kind with which he is charged may (without prejudice to any other way of doing so) be established by evidence that he has been convicted of—

  (a) an offence of the same description as the one with which he is charged, or

  (b) an offence of the same category as the one with which he is charged.

(3) Subsection (2) does not apply in the case of a particular defendant if the court is satisfied, by reason of the length of time since the conviction or for any other reason, that it would be unjust for it to apply in his case.

(4) For the purposes of subsection (2)—

  (a) two offences are of the same description as each other if the statement of the offence in a written charge or indictment would, in each case, be in the same terms;

  (b) two offences are of the same category as each other if they belong to the same category of offences prescribed for the purposes of this section by an order made by the Secretary of State.

(5) A category prescribed by an order under subsection (4)(b) must consist of offences of the same type.

(6) Only prosecution evidence is admissible under section 101(1)(d).

4.18 The history of this inelegant provision is that it is a last-minute amalgamation of two separate clauses that appeared in the original Bill. In the original Bill, what is now section 101(1) appeared as clause 87:

(1) For the purposes of section 101(1)(d) the matters in issue between the defendant and the prosecution include—

  (a) the question whether the defendant has a propensity to commit offences of the kind with which he is charged, except where his having such a propensity makes it no more likely that he is guilty of the offence;

(b) the question whether the defendant has a propensity to be untruthful, except where it is not suggested that the defendant's case is untruthful in any respect.

4.19 And in addition there was a further clause 86, in which the government proposed a separate gateway, designed to make the defendant's previous convictions admissible on the simple basis that they were convictions for the same or a similar offence. The 'similar offences' gateway provoked strong opposition in Parliament, and clause 86 was eventually removed; but in the removal, some of the key parts of it were inserted into clause 87 dealing with 'matters in issue.' This rearrangement was a concession by the government, which had eventually accepted the argument that evidence of the defendant's previous convictions for offences listed in clause 86 should only be admissible in cases where his propensity to commit offences of a particular type is a live issue at the trial.[25] The result is a big, rather clumsy provision that expands section 101(1)(d) by grafting onto it some further grounds of admissibility, none of which bear much relation to what the Law Commission (and lawyers generally) would regard as a 'matter in issue.'

4.20 The general drift of what is meant in section 103 is not difficult to grasp. In essence, it seems to tell us that 'gateway (d)' must be read in such a way that:

(1) That evidence of the defendant's bad character is admissible if it shows he has a propensity to commit 'offences of the kind with which he is charged' (section 103(1)(a)).

(2) One possible way in which this may be done is by showing he has previously committed an offence 'of the same description' as this offence or 'of the same category' (section 103(2)–(5)).

(3) Evidence of the defendant's bad character is also admissible if it 'shows he has a propensity to be untruthful' (section 103(1)(b)).

If this is what section 103 really provides, then it obviously extends 'gateway (d)' far beyond the sort of situation the Law Commission had in mind—and the bad character of the defendant has become admissible in a far wider range of situations than it was at common law.

4.21 As is explained below, however, the drafting is not well done and it is possible to read section 103 in various narrower senses, the result of which would be (in effect) 'business as before,' with evidence of the defendant's bad character continuing to be admissible only in the limited situations in which it was admissible at common law. As we shall see, the Court of Appeal has so far shown no inclination to accept these arguments, but section 103 has yet to be considered by the House of Lords and for this reason it is worth examining them.

[25] See the explanation by Baroness Scotland, Hansard, HL, vol 654 col 2080 (20 November 2003).

Bad Character Admissible to Show Propensity: Scope of Section 103(1)(a)

4.22 As we have seen, section 103(1)(a) provides that:

(1) For the purposes of section 101(1)(d) the matters in issue between the defendant and the prosecution include—

(a) the question whether the defendant has a propensity to commit offences of the kind with which he is charged, except where his having such a propensity makes it no more likely that he is guilty of the offence.

The general idea behind the provision appears from the Explanatory Notes, according to which:

> Section 103(1)(a) makes it clear that evidence which shows that a defendant has a propensity to commit offences of the kind with which he is charged can be admitted under this head. For example, if the defendant is on trial for grievous bodily harm, a history of violent behaviour could be admissible to show the defendant's propensity to use violence.[26]

4.23 In other words, the purpose of the provision is to ensure that, in future, evidence of the defendant's bad character is not only admissible where it sheds light on some specific disputed issue, but also—to the extent that it shows he has a propensity to commit offences of this sort—where it sheds light on the *general* issue of whether he committed the offence or not.

4.24 However, the drafting is confusing. The purpose of section 103(1)(a) is to elaborate section 101(1)(d), which says that evidence of the defendant's bad character is admissible when 'it is relevant to an important issue between the defendant and the prosecution.' But in doing so, it interprets the phrase 'a matter in issue' in a different sense. A 'matter in issue' normally means 'a specific question of fact on which the prosecution and defence disagree,' and this clearly is the sense in which the phrase is used in section 101(1)(d). But in section 103(1)(a), the phrase is used in a different and looser sense. In section 103(1)(a), it does not seem to mean a specific factual matter which the prosecution has alleged and which the defence has decided to deny. Instead, it seems to mean 'one of those matters which the court ought to take into account when reaching its decision.' And it was put there in this form, it seems, with the aim of making the court, when deciding the general question of the defendant's guilt or innocence, consider whether or not he has a propensity to commit the sort of offence for which he is on trial. This shift of

---

[26] At §371. On the current status of Explanatory Notes as an aid to construction, see §§1.65–1.66 above.

meaning gives rise to various arguments which, if accepted, would limit the effect of the provision.

4.25 The first turns on the phrase 'in issue.' For most legal purposes, a matter is 'in issue' when the parties are in dispute about it, and not where they are agreed. In the light of this, it looks as if it might be open to a defendant with a string of previous convictions for similar offences in the past to *admit* that he has a propensity to commit offences of the type with which he is now charged—and from this to argue that, as his propensity to commit such offences is not 'in issue,' the prosecution are not entitled to put even the existence of these convictions before the court (let alone the details). In answer to this, however, it could be said that a propensity is a matter of degree, and where the defendant admits a propensity, this still leaves room for argument about how strong it is—and that the evidence of the defendant's previous convictions can still be used to shed light on that.[27]

4.26 The second argument turns on the meaning of the word 'important,' which qualifies the phrase 'matter in issue' where it originally appears in section 101(1)(d). Where 'a matter in issue' means 'a matter in dispute,' then the word 'important' clearly adds something. But where that phrase is used to mean 'a matter that the court should take into account,' it is not clear what intelligible meaning the word 'important' can bear. However, it could be used to found an argument to the effect that section 103(1)(a) only allows in evidence of bad character where this is 'important'—and to be 'important' it must go beyond showing a mere tendency to commit this type of offence and illuminate some specific factual issue.[28] The objection to this argument, of course, is that it would recreate the previous law, which is expressly abolished by section 99(1),[29] and which we know it was the general intention of Parliament—or at any rate, the desire of those who introduced this legislation—to replace with something wider.

4.27 The third argument is based on the second sentence of section 103(2)(a). This says that one of the issues in a case on which bad character evidence is to be admissible is 'whether the defendant has a propensity to commit offences of the kind with which he is charged, *except where his having such a propensity makes it no more likely that he is guilty of the offence.*'[30] What is the meaning of this final sentence? On the face of it, it looks like another peg upon which the defence can hang

---

[27] For this argument, and the answer to it, I am indebted to judges participating at the Judicial Studies Board seminars.

[28] See n 27 above.

[29] 'The common law rules governing the admissibility of evidence of bad character in criminal proceedings are abolished.' See §1.20 above.

[30] Emphasis added.

an argument that evidence of the defendant's previous misconduct is not admissible merely because it shows he has a general tendency to commit this sort of offence, and that it is only admissible where (as under the earlier law) it is directly relevant to some specific issue.

4.28 From the Explanatory Notes it is clear that the phrase 'where his having such a propensity makes it no more likely that he is guilty of the offence' was meant to serve a different and more restricted purpose. It was simply meant to prevent bad character evidence being admitted 'where there is no dispute about the facts of the case and the question is whether those facts constitute the offence (for example, in a homicide case, whether the defendant's actions caused death).'[31] An Explanatory Note in these terms was before Parliament at the time this provision was enacted,[32] so it was clear from the outset what the draftsman had mind; and I believe it would be proper, and sensible, for the courts to assume that the draftsman's intention was also the intention of Parliament when the section was enacted.[33]

4.29 To the disappointment of anyone who may have been hoping that the new provisions would in the end mean 'business as before,' though conducted in different words, the Court of Appeal has so far made it very plain that the new law really does mean a new start, and important pieces of bad character evidence will indeed be admissible via 'gateway (d)' which would have been excluded under the earlier law.

4.30 In *Hanson and others*,[34] the Court of Appeal said that, under the new law, it is no longer true that 'what used to be referred to as striking similarity must be shown before convictions become admissible,' and that evidence of bad character is now admissible on the basis that it shows a tendency to commit offences of this general type. Similarly, in *Somonathan*,[35] the Court of Appeal pointed out that section 99 abolishes the common law rules on the admissibility of evidence of bad character and said 'The 2003 Act completely reverses the pre-existing general rule. Evidence of bad character is now admissible if it satisfies certain criteria (see section 101(1)) and the approach is no longer one of inadmissibility subject to exceptions.' 'If evidence of a defendant's bad character is relevant to an important issue between the prosecution and the defence,' they added, 'then, unless there is an application to exclude the evidence, it is admissible.' The test, they also pointed

---

[31] At §371.
[32] See §305 of the Explanatory Notes that accompanied the Bill.
[33] *Pace* Dr Roderick Munday; see in particular his article in [2005] *Crim LR* 337, referred to at §1.65 above.
[34] *Hanson* [2005] EWCA Crim 824, [2005] 1 WLR 3169; **p 153 below.**
[35] Decided together with *Weir* [2005] EWCA Crim 2866, [2006] 1 CrAppR 19 (303), **p 206 below.**

out, was now simple relevance: it was not necessary to show that the evidence had any kind of 'enhanced probative value' or 'enhanced relevance.'[36]

4.31 In the individual cases heard and decided by the Court of Appeal, this new approach is evident.

4.32 Thus, in *Hanson*, the Court of Appeal upheld a conviction for stealing a carrier bag containing £600 from a bedroom to which the defendant had access, the defendant having pled guilty when the judge ruled that he would permit the prosecution to prove his previous convictions for dishonesty. In *Gilmore*,[37] they upheld a theft conviction against a man caught in suspicious circumstances with a bag of stolen goods which he claimed to have found abandoned in an alleyway—the jury hearing evidence of his three previous convictions for shoplifting.

4.33 Similarly, three cases clearly indicate that where the defendant is prosecuted for a sexual offence, bad character evidence is now generally admissible where it shows his sexual tastes. So in *P*,[38] the Court of Appeal upheld a conviction for rape and indecent assault committed on a girl of 10, the jury having heard evidence of the defendant's conviction for a similar offence against a girl of 11. In *Weir*, a man's conviction for sexually assaulting a girl of 13 was upheld, the Court of Appeal holding that evidence had been rightly admitted via 'gateway (d)' of his previously being cautioned for taking an indecent photograph of a child. In *Manister*,[39] in which a 39-year-old man was convicted of indecent assault upon a girl of 13, the Court of Appeal held that evidence had been rightly admitted of his recent involvement with two other girls in their mid-teens.[40]

4.34 The case law also suggests that where the defendant is charged with an offence of violence, and his defence is that the alleged victim started it by making an attack on him, the defendant's previous acts of personal violence are admissible to bolster the prosecution case that it was he who was the aggressor. So, in *Duggan*,[41] the Court of Appeal upheld a conviction for wounding with intent, holding that evidence had been rightly admitted via 'gateway (d)' of the defendant's having previously been convicted of assault.

---

[36] Rejecting a suggestion earlier made in *Duggan*; see *Edwards and others* [2005] EWCA Crim 1813, p 169 below, at §54.

[37] Decided together with *Hanson*, n 34 above.

[38] Decided together with *Hanson*, n 34 above.

[39] Decided together with *Weir*, n 35 above.

[40] With neither of these two other girls did D's behaviour amount to criminal offences and the Court of Appeal thought that it could not properly be classed as 'evidence of bad character' within the definition set out in CJA 2003 s98. This being so, they said, it was not admissible (or inadmissible) by virtue of s101. However, they indicated that it was admissible at common law, as tending to show that the defendant was sexually attracted to the 13-year-old complainant. See §2.19 above.

[41] Decided together with *Edwards* [2005] EWCA Crim 1813, [2006] 1 CrAppR 3 (31), p 169 below.

4.35 In a further group of cases, the Court of Appeal has upheld convictions where, at trial, evidence of the defendant's record of similar offences was admitted where the issue was identification. In *Brima*,[42] a murder case, the victim was stabbed in the stomach and killed during a mêlée. Various pieces of evidence pointed to Brima as the assailant, including the testimony of X, who claimed that he had helped Brima to dispose of some bloodstained clothes. The defence case was mistaken identity, and that the real murderer was X. The Court of Appeal held that the trial judge had been right to admit evidence of Brima's two previous convictions: one for stabbing, and one for a robbery, in the course of which he had held a knife to his victim's throat. Similar in principle are *Smith*[43] and *Blake*,[44] although the offences in question were burglary rather than homicide.

4.36 Under the previous law, there would have been no question of the prosecution putting in evidence the defendant's previous convictions for offences of dishonesty as part of their case that he is guilty of a theft. Nor would it usually have been possible for the prosecution to produce evidence of the defendant's sexual preferences to back up their case that he is guilty of a sexual offence. In *Wright*, for example, a headmaster's convictions for buggery with his young male pupils was quashed because the trial court had admitted evidence of his possession of homosexual pornography and a guide to homosexual brothels in Paris.[45] Similarly, evidence of the defendant's disposition to acts of violence would not normally have been admissible against him when he was accused of an offence of violence. In *Dolan*, for example, the defendant's conviction for the murder of his baby son was quashed because evidence had been admitted at his trial of his tendency to fly into a rage when things went wrong: a tendency which had shown itself on several previous occasions when he had smashed up the furniture.[46] This evidence, said the Court of Appeal, was inadmissible, inter alia 'because it went to propensity.' Nor, in the absence of 'stricking similarity', would evidence of previous convictions have been admitted to support a disputed identification. The new cases clearly show that the bad character evidence provisions of the CJA 2003 have brought about a major change.

---

[42] [2006] EWCA Crim 408.
[43] (2006) 170 JPN 142.
[44] (2006) 170 JPN 144.
[45] (1990) 90 CrAppR 325; and see *B (RA)* (1997) 2 CrAppR 88.
[46] [2003] EWCA Crim 1859, [2003] Crim LR 41, [2003] 1 CrAppR 18 (281).

Showing Propensity by Reference to Convictions for Similar Offences: Section 103(2)–(5)

4.37 Section 103(1)(a), which expands the scope of 'gateway (d)' as described in section 100(1)(d), is itself expanded by the next three subsections of section 100,[3] which are as follows:

(2) Where subsection (1)(a) applies, a defendant's propensity to commit offences of the kind with which he is charged may (without prejudice to any other way of doing so) be established by evidence that he has been convicted of—

(a) an offence of the same description as the one with which he is charged, or
(b) an offence of the same category as the one with which he is charged.

(3) Subsection (2) does not apply in the case of a particular defendant if the court is satisfied, by reason of the length of time since the conviction or for any other reason, that it would be unjust for it to apply in his case.
(4) For the purposes of subsection (2)—

(a) two offences are of the same description as each other if the statement of the offence in a written charge or indictment would, in each case, be in the same terms;
(b) two offences are of the same category as each other if they belong to the same category of offences prescribed for the purposes of this section by an order made by the Secretary of State.

(5) A category prescribed by an order under subsection (4)(b) must consist of offences of the same type.

4.38 At the time of writing, one Order has so far been made under subsection (4)(b). This Order[47] establishes two groups. The first consists of theft, robbery, burglary, aggravated burglary, taking vehicles without consent, handling, going equipped for stealing, making off without payment, plus attempts to commit these offences (and committing them as an accessory). The second comprises 36 offences involving sex with minors. It has been rumoured that a further Order is being considered, which will create a further category of offences of personal violence, but so far no text has yet been published.

The Relationship between Section 103(2) and 103(1)(a)

4.39 What exactly is the relationship between section 103(2) and section 103(1)(a)? Does section 103(2) add something to section 103(1)(a) or subtract something from it? When the prosecution seeks to establish propensity by reference to previous convictions, are those convictions admissible *only* if the conditions set out in section

[47] Criminal Justice Act 2003 (Categories of Offences) Order 2004, SI 2004/3346.

103(2) are satisfied? Or can the prosecution use evidence of previous convictions, even if they fall outside the requirements of section 103(2)? For example, take a case where D is charged with manslaughter of the child of the woman with whom he was then living, and the defence case is that the person who struck the child the fatal blow was not him, but her. He has previous convictions for assault occasioning actual bodily harm, all committed against previous cohabitees or their children. These offences do not fall within section 102(2)(a) and are not bracketed with manslaughter in any Order that has yet been made under section 103(2)(b). Are these previous convictions nevertheless admissible to establish the defendant's propensity to commit offences 'of the kind with which he is now charged'?

4.40 The most obvious construction of the provisions is that section 103(2)–(5) add to the range of possibilities already created by section 103(1)(a), rather than restrict them: from which it would follow that the prosecution *can* use previous convictions to establish propensity under section 103(1)(a), even though they do not fall within section 103(2). This is clear from the phrase in brackets in the first paragraph of section 103(2): 'Where subsection (1)(a) applies, a defendant's propensity to commit offences of the kind with which he is charged *may (without prejudice to any other way of doing so)*[48] be established by evidence that he has been convicted of [offences of the types listed in the rest of this subsection].' The word 'may' indicates a route that is available to the prosecution if it wishes to take advantage of it, not one down which it is obliged to go. And the phrase 'without prejudice to any other way of doing so' clearly suggests that section 103(2) is meant to add something to the scope of section 103(1)(a), not to restrict it. In order to read section 103(2) as limiting section 103(1)(a) rather than expanding it, it would be necessary to give that phrase a strained interpretation.

4.41 Another argument in favour of what might be called the 'expansive' construction of subsections section 103(2)–(5) is that the 'restrictive' interpretation would produce extremely odd results. If D was prosecuted for murdering child X, it would not be possible to use 103(2)(a) to prove that he has been convicted of grievous bodily harm against his other children, Y and Z, by beating them to within an inch of their lives, because these convictions would not be covered by section 103(2); but if he was prosecuted for shoplifting it would be possible to prove his previous conviction for taking a conveyance without the owner's consent, because—bizarrely—this previous offence would be: because both theft and taking a conveyance without the owner's consent appear together in one of the lists contained in the Order which has been made under section 103(4)(b).

---

[48] Emphasis added.

4.42 In *Hanson*,[49] the Court of Appeal came down firmly in favour of the expansive view: 'In referring to offences of the same description or category, section 103(2) is not exhaustive of the type of conviction which might be relied upon to show evidence of propensity to commit offences of the kind charged.' And the same view was expressed again, in the clearest terms, in *Weir*, where the Court expressly adopted the arguments put forward in favour of this view in the original version of this commentary, as written for the Judicial Studies Board.[50]

Scope of Section 103(2): the Need for the Previous Conviction to Show Propensity

4.43 However, when dealing with this question, the Court of Appeal in *Hanson* also stressed that just because a defendant has a criminal record that falls within the categories set out in section 103(2), it does not follow that it is automatically admissible. In the Court's clear view, before it is admitted the defendant's record must be one which can fairly be said to show a propensity to do the sort of thing of which the defendant is currently accused—even though, as previously mentioned, there need not be a 'striking similarity' between the previous offence or offences and the one currently alleged. To show a 'propensity,' it seems, the record must show one or other of two things: either that the defendant has a taste for, or at least a willingness to engage in, conduct that most people would have no desire to do at all, or would emphatically wish to avoid; or else, where the behaviour in question is not particularly unusual, that the defendant, unlike most people, makes a habit of it. The Court said:

> §7. Where propensity to commit the offence is relied upon there are thus essentially three questions to be considered. 1. Does the history of the conviction(s) establish a propensity to commit offences of the kind charged? 2. Does that propensity make it more likely that the defendant committed the offence charged? 3. Is it unjust to rely on the convictions(s) of the same description or category; and, in any event, will the proceedings be unfair if they are admitted?
>
> §8. In referring to the offences of the same description or category, section 103(2) is not exhaustive of the types of conviction which might be relied upon to show evidence of propensity to commit offences of the kind charged. Nor, however, is it necessarily sufficient, in order to show such a propensity, that a conviction should be of the same description or category as that charged.
>
> §9. There is no minimum number of events necessary to demonstrate such a propensity. The fewer the number of convictions the weaker is likely to be the evidence of propensity. A single previous conviction for an offence of the same description or category will often not show propensity. But it may do so where, for example, it shows a

---

[49] [2005] EWCA Crim 824, [2005] 1 WLR 3169; **p 153 below.**
[50] At §7.

tendency to unusual behaviour or where its circumstances demonstrate probative force in relation to the offence charged: compare *Director of Public Prosecutions v P* [1991] 2 AC 447, 460–461. Child sexual abuse or fire setting are comparatively clear examples of such unusual behaviour but we attempt no exhaustive list. Circumstances demonstrating probative force are not confined to those sharing striking similarity. So, a single conviction for shoplifting will not, without more, be admissible to show propensity to steal. But if the modus operandi has significant features shared by the offence charged it may show propensity.[51]

Need to Provide Details of the Offence in Addition to the Bare Fact of the Conviction

4.44 From this it will be clear that, at least in certain cases, the admissibility or otherwise of a defendant's previous convictions will depend on how similar they were to the offence of which he is currently accused: and this means that in practice there may be factual disputes about the details of the offences of which he was convicted (or indeed about whether he committed them at all). As to this, the Court of Appeal in *Hanson* had the following to say:

> It will often be necessary, before determining admissibility, and even when considering offences of the same description or category, to examine each individual conviction rather than merely to look at the nature of the offence or at the defendant's record as a whole. The sentence passed will not normally be probative or admissible at the behest of the Crown. Where past events are disputed, the judge must take care not to permit the trial unreasonably to be diverted into an investigation of matters not charged in the indictment.[52]

In the same case, they also said:

> We would expect the relevant circumstances generally to be capable of agreement, and that, subject to the trial judge's ruling as to admissibility, they will be put before the jury by way of admission. Even where the circumstances are genuinely in dispute, we would expect the minimum indisputable facts to be thus admitted. It will be very rare indeed for it to be necessary for the judge to hear evidence before ruling on admissibility under this Act.[53]

4.45 In *Bovell*, the Court of Appeal made the following additional point:

> it is necessary for all parties to have the appropriate information in relation to convictions and other evidence of bad character, whether in relation to the defendant or some other person, in good time. This can only be achieved if the rules in relation to the

---

[51] On this point see also *Tully and others*, (2006) 170 JPN 243.
[52] At §12. See further, §§5.15–5.20 below.
[53] At §17.

giving of notice are complied with. It is worth mentioning that the basis of a plea in relation to an earlier conviction may be relevant where it demonstrates differences from the way in which the prosecution initially put the case. In other words, a mere reference to the statement of a complainant in an earlier case may not provide the later court with the material needed to make a decision as to the admissibility of the earlier conviction.[54]

Power of the Court to Exclude Evidence Otherwise Admissible under Section 103(2) by Virtue of Section 103(3)

4.46 By section 103(3):

> Subsection (2) does not apply in the case of a particular defendant if the court is satisfied, by reason of the length of time since the conviction or for any other reason, that it would be unjust for it to apply in his case.

This provision is in addition to the duty imposed on the court by section 101(3), which (as we have already seen) provides that:

> The court must not admit evidence under subsection (1)(d) or (g) if, on an application by the defendant to exclude it, it appears to the court that the admission of the evidence would have such an adverse effect on the fairness of the proceedings that the court ought not to admit it.

In respect of bad character evidence which the prosecution seeks to admit via section 102(2), these two provisions clearly overlap, to the point where it is permissible to wonder why, given the existence of section 101(3), it was thought necessary to include section 103(3) at all. However, there is one important respect in which section 103(3) goes further than section 101(3): for section 101(3) to operate it is necessary for the defence to make an application, whereas it is open to the judge to apply section 103(3) on his own initiative.

4.47 In practice, it seems likely that section 103(3) will be the main vehicle by which the courts exclude evidence of past convictions which the prosecution seek to introduce via section 102(2) and which the court feels do not really establish 'a propensity'; and section 101(3) will be the vehicle through which the court excludes evidence of bad character otherwise admissible via 'gateway (d)' on more general grounds—in particular, because the court considers that it would cause the court to waste excessive time on 'satellite issues' or because it is being adduced to support a case that is otherwise extremely weak.[55]

---

[54] [2005] EWCA Crim 1091, [2004] 2 CrAppR 27 (401), **p 163 below**, at §2.
[55] See §§1.29–1.32 above.

What is Meant by 'a Conviction' for the Purposes of Section 103(2)?

4.48 Section 103(2) provides that the defendant's propensity to commit the sort of offence with which he is now charged may 'be established by evidence that he has been convicted' of criminal offences of the various types specified in section 103(2)(a) and (b). In law, a defendant is 'convicted' either when he pleads guilty to the offence with which he is charged or when, following a not guilty plea, the court finds him guilty of it.[56] It does not constitute 'a conviction' in the eye of the law where a person submits to a formal caution or when, on being sentenced for an offence of which he stands convicted, he asks for another offence to be 'taken into consideration' for the basis of sentencing.[57] It therefore follows, as the Court of Appeal pointed out in *Weir*,[58] that section 103(2) may not be used as the vehicle for putting before the court as evidence of propensity the fact that the defendant has previously been cautioned for a similar offence, or asked for one to be taken into consideration. In so holding, the Court of Appeal made it clear that in such a case it is still open to the prosecution to make evidential use of the incident that gave rise to the caution by relying on the general words of section 103(1)(a); and on that basis, they upheld the defendant's conviction for indecent assault on a 13-year-old girl, the trial court having heard evidence that, some four years previously, the defendant had been cautioned for taking an indecent photograph of a child, contrary to section 1 of the Protection of Children Act 1978.

'Gateway (d)' and 'Cross-admissibility' where the Defendant Faces a Single Trial on an Indictment Charging two or More Similar Offences[59]

4.49 So far, the discussion about 'gateway (d)' has proceeded on the assumption that D is being prosecuted for offence X, and the point at issue is the admissibility or otherwise of his previous convictions in respect of offences Y and Z. But what is the position where D was never charged with offences Y and Z, and is now being prosecuted on a single indictment charging all three of these offences together? Under the new law, to what extent (if any) can the court take account of the evidence in relation to offences Y and Z in deciding whether or not D has committed offence X?

---

[56] *Shergill and others* [1999] 2 CrAppR(S) 341; *Webster* [2004] 2 CrAppR(S) 25.
[57] *Nicholson* [1947] 2 All ER 535.
[58] [2005] EWCA Crim 2866, [2006] 1 CrAppR 19 (303), **p 206 below**, at §5.
[59] Or in a magistrates' court, one trial in respect of two or more informations charging similar offences.

4.50 Under the previous law, the evidence in respect of counts Y and Z would have been admissible on count X if it went beyond showing a mere propensity to commit the sort of offence in question and had 'positive probative value' in relation to some specific issue in dispute. Where this would have been the case before, I believe it is equally the case under the new provisions. As we have seen (see §§4.11–4.14 above), evidence revealing that the defendant is of bad character is admissible through 'gateway (d)' where it is relevant to 'an important matter in issue between the defendant and the prosecution'—which it would be in this case.

4.51 A more difficult question arises where, under the previous law, the three counts would have been properly joined but the evidence would not have been 'cross-admissible.' In such a case, section 112(2) requires us, for the purpose of deciding whether the evidence on one count is admissible on the other, to treat each count as if it were 'charged in separate proceedings.' So, in respect of count X, the evidence on counts Y and Z would in principle be evidence of 'bad character' and would not be let in by virtue of section 98(a), which ordinarily removes from the definition of evidence of 'bad character' any evidence which 'has to do with the alleged facts of the offence with which the defendant is charged.' This would mean that, to be admissible on count X, the evidence in respect of counts Y and Z would need to pass through one of the 'gateways' set out in section 101. This it would do, I believe, if, though the evidence would not have been 'cross-admissible' at common law, it nevertheless suggests that the defendant 'has a propensity to commit offences of the kind with which he is charged.'

4.52 In practical terms, the result will be that where counts for different offences are properly joined, it will happen more frequently than in the past that the evidence on one count is admissible on the other.

Gateway (d) and Evidence of Propensity: is Expert Evidence Admissible?

4.53 A final question in relation to section 103(1)(a) is the basis on which the defendant's previous convictions are to be admissible as evidence of propensity. Is this to be done by rule of thumb and common sense? Where a defendant is charged with burglary, for example, can the courts simply take it as a given that a long string of convictions for burglary clearly shows that he has a propensity to commit burglaries, one isolated conviction for burglary many years ago fails to show this clearly, and previous convictions for reckless driving do not show it at all? Or is this a matter on which scientific evidence is relevant and admissible: so that, for example, the defence could produce a statistical expert to argue that, contrary to what one might imagine, persons with this particular defendant's pattern of previous burglaries do not have a particular propensity to commit burglaries? Or with the even more extreme consequence that the prosecution must produce evidence of this sort before they are allowed to put the defendant's previous convictions in? In broad terms, it seems appropriate to look at statistics of this sort when considering whether the policy behind the character evidence provisions is a fair one, but admitting detailed statistical evidence in particular cases would, by contrast, be a source of great confusion. Judicial common sense seems preferable.

Evidence of Propensity to be Untruthful: Section 103(1)(b)

4.54 According to section 103(1)(b), matters in issue between the defendant and the prosecution include:

> the question whether the defendant has a propensity to be untruthful, except where it is not suggested that the defendant's case is untruthful in any respect.

In principle, this provision clearly makes admissible evidence that shows that the defendant is a compulsive liar, but such evidence is unlikely to be available. The important practical question is whether, and if so when, it enables evidence to be given of the defendant's previous criminal offences.

4.55 When dealing with witnesses, the common law has traditionally taken the position that criminal convictions of all types undermine the speaker's credibility. This is the spirit that lay behind section 6 of the Criminal Procedure Act 1865, which in its original form permitted a witness to be cross-examined about any criminal convictions. The previous law also adopted a similar attitude towards the credibility of defendants, to the limited extent that the law admitted evidence of their bad character to bear upon their credibility. Where a defendant in his evidence had cast 'imputations on the character' of the prosecutor or various other persons, section 1(3)(ii)—originally 1(f)(ii)—of the Criminal Evidence Act (CEA) 1898 allowed him to be cross-examined on his character in order to undermine his credibility. The case law on this provision proceeded on the assumption that questions could be asked about any offences, because all convictions are relevant to credibility.[60] In effect, the law acted on the basis that 'character is indivisible.'

4.56 Surprisingly, perhaps, 'indivisibility of character' was not the idea that lay behind section 103(1)(b). According to the Explanatory Notes, 'This is intended to enable the admission of a limited range of evidence such as convictions for

---

[60] Although a minority line of cases suggested that cross-examination should be principally directed to offences of dishonesty: *Watts* (1983) 77 CrAppR 126; *Owen* (1983) 83 CrAppR 100.

perjury or other offences involving deception (for example, obtaining property by deception), as opposed to the wider range of evidence that will be admissible where the defendant puts his character in issue by, for example, attacking the character of another person.'[61] In other words, some convictions suggest that the defendant is an untruthful person, and others do not.

4.57 If this logic is followed through, and evidence of convictions is admissible to the extent that lying or dishonesty was involved, it ought to follow that evidence could also be given of any conviction that followed a contested trial in which the defendant had given evidence on oath to protest his innocence. This line was taken by the Court of Appeal in *Hanson*,[62] in which it said:

> As to propensity to untruthfulness, this, as it seems to us, is not the same as propensity to dishonesty. It is to be assumed, bearing in mind the frequency with which the words honest and dishonest appear in the criminal law, that Parliament deliberately chose the word 'untruthful' to convey a different meaning, reflecting a defendant's account of his behaviour, or lies told when committing an offence. Previous convictions, whether for offences of dishonesty or otherwise, are therefore only likely to be capable of showing a propensity to be untruthful where, in the present case, truthfulness is an issue and, in the earlier case, either there was a plea of not guilty and the defendant gave an account, on arrest, in interview, or in evidence, which the jury must have disbelieved, or the way in which the offence was committed shows a propensity for untruthfulness, for example by the making of false representations.

(How far, if at all, this logic applies when the issue of the defendant's truthfulness arises in the context of 'gateway (e)' or 'gateway (g)' is discussed later: see §4.70 and §4.110 below.)

Evidence of Propensity and the Powers and Duties of the Court to Exclude

4.58 As previously mentioned, section 101(3) requires the court to exclude evidence otherwise admissible under the 'matter in issue' gateway if it appears to the court that its admission would make the trial unfair. It is probable that defence applications under this subsection will be common, and that the basis of the argument will often be that admitting the evidence would result in 'moral prejudice'[63]—in other words, it would inflame the jury against the defendant and predispose them to convict him in order to punish him for what he did before, even though they are not convinced that he is guilty of the offence of which he is currently accused.

---

[61] At §374.
[62] *Hanson* [2005] EWCA Crim 824, [2005] 1 WLR 3169, **p 153 below**, at §13.
[63] The term adopted by the Law Commission in their Working Paper, LC Consultation Paper no 141 §7.2; IH Dennis, *The Law of Evidence* (2nd edn, London, Sweet & Maxwell, 2002) 622.

4.59 In my view, this is not a sensible basis on which the courts should exclude 'bad character' evidence which is adduced to show propensity. It should do so, in my view, where the evidence consists of incidents which are trivial. It should be prepared to do so if the evidence is old and stale (§§4.111–4.116 below). But if the evidence is relevant, in that it would make a tribunal of reasonable people more inclined to convict, it should in principle be admitted. As suggested earlier (§§1.29–1.32 above), the real dangers with bad character evidence are its use to bolster up a weak case in which there is little or no other evidence, and the risk that it will divert the attention of the court into time-wasting 'satellite issues.' If this is so, the discretion to exclude should be exercised with an eye to these matters, rather than to the allegedly inflammatory nature of the evidence it is sought to exclude. In principle, it cannot be right to exclude evidence that is clearly relevant for fear that it might make the fact-finders shocked or angry with the accused. Were this so, it would make it impossible for the criminal justice system to deal with the most serious cases or offenders.[64]

4.60 As previously mentioned (§1.37 above), an appeal court will be reluctant to criticise the way in which the trial court has exercised (or refused to exercise) its powers to exclude bad character evidence, provided that it considered and evaluated the relevant factors in the course of making its decision.

The Admissibility of Old Convictions

4.61 On this, see §§4.111–4.116 below.

Gateway (e): Relevant to an Issue Between Co-defendants

4.62 By section 101(1)(e), evidence of the defendant's bad character is admissible where 'it has substantial probative value in relation to an important matter in issue between the defendant and a co-defendant.' By section 112(1), an 'important matter' is defined as 'a matter of substantial importance in the context of the case as a whole.'

4.63 Insofar as 'gateway (e)' might be used by one defendant to undermine his co-defendant's credibility, its meaning is elaborated by **section 104**, which is as follows:

---

[64] Compare the remarks of the Court of Appeal in the 'House of Horrors' case, when rejecting the defence argument that the horrific nature of the case had attracted extensive press coverage so adverse to the accused that the court could no longer give her a fair trial: 'In our view it could. To hold otherwise would mean that if allegations of murder are sufficiently horrendous as inevitably to shock the nation, the accused cannot be tried. That would be absurd.' *West* [1996] 2 CrAppR 374, at 386.

(1) Evidence which is relevant to the question whether the defendant has a propensity to be untruthful is admissible on that basis under section 101(1)(e) only if the nature or conduct of his defence is such as to undermine the co-defendant's defence.

(2) Only evidence—

  (a) which is to be (or has been) adduced by the co-defendant, or
  (b) which a witness is to be invited to give (or has given) in cross-examination by the co-defendant,

is admissible under section 101(1)(e).

'Gateway (e),' it seems, largely preserves the position under the pre-existing common law.[65]

4.64 The common law was initially reluctant to allow D1 to adduce evidence of D2's bad character. However, it would do so, rather grudgingly, where the evidence that D1 wished to call revealed D2 to be a person of bad character if this supported some specific aspect of D1's defence. Thus, in *Thompson and others*,[66] D1 had given his version of events to the police in a statement, in the course of which he had mentioned that D2 had told him that D2 and D3 'always torch our jobs when we finished them, it covers up the evidence.' In the light of this, the Court of Appeal held that that D1 was entitled to call evidence at trial to show that D2 and D3 did indeed 'torch their jobs' when they had committed burglaries, because this evidence suggested that D1 was telling the truth when he made his statement to the police. Then in 2004, the House of Lords in *Randall*[67] held—less technically and rather more intelligibly—that where an issue arises at trial as to which of two joint defendants committed the offence, D1 can use evidence of D2's propensity to do this sort of thing in an attempt to persuade the court that it was D1 who really did it. So, in that case, where the prosecution alleged that a man had been beaten to death by both of them, and each one blamed the other, D1—who had a relatively clean record—should have been allowed to use D2's history of domestic burglaries (including one in which the occupier was threatened with a hammer) in order to support his case that the murder was the work of D2 alone.[68] In addition, where D2 gave evidence against D1, the earlier law gave D1 a statutory right[69] to cross-examine him on his bad character, with a view to undermining his credibility as a witness.

---

[65] On which see *Archbold* (2005 edn) §8-214; *Blackstone's Criminal Practice* (2006) F12-35.

[66] [1995] 2 CrAppR 589.

[67] [2004] 1 WLR 56; and see *Price* [2004] EWCA Crim 1359, [2005] CrimLR 304.

[68] This principle only applies, of course, where there is an issue as to which of two defendants committed the offence. In other words, D1 is only permitted to make use of D2's propensity to commit this sort of offence where it tends not only to suggest that D2 committed it, but that D1 did not. See *B(C)* [2004] EWCA Crim 1254, [2004] 2 CrAppR 34 (570).

[69] Under s1(3)(iii) (formerly 1(f)(iii)) of the CEA 1898.

4.65 The Law Commission's Draft Bill aimed to confirm the earlier law, but would have added a requirement of judicial leave. The scheme in the CJA 2003 broadly follows the Law Commission's proposals, but omits the leave requirement (and in respect of this 'gateway,' section 101(3) confers no judicial discretion to exclude).

4.66 Section 101(1)(e) provides that evidence of the defendant's bad character is admissible if 'it has substantial probative value in relation to an important matter in issue between the defendant and a co-defendant.' In using the words 'substantial probative value,' the phraseology is slightly more restrictive than is used in section 101(1)(d), where bad character is admissible if 'it is relevant to an important matter in issue between the defendant and the prosecution.' Although the difference between these forms of words is slight, it does have a possible significance, which is explained in §4.70 below. It is safe to assume that this 'gateway' enables D1 to adduce evidence of D2's bad character in an attempt to show that D2 committed the offence, in the same way as he was entitled to do at common law.

4.67 The CJA 2003 has repealed section 1(3)(iii) of the CEA 1898[70] and D1's right to adduce evidence to undermine the credibility of D2 who has testified against him is now a matter that falls within the 'gateway' in section 101(1)(e). In this respect it is qualified by **section 104(1)**:

> Evidence which is relevant to the question whether the defendant has a propensity to be untruthful is admissible on that basis under section 101(1)(e) only if the nature or conduct of his defence is such as to undermine the co-defendant's defence.

The result is much the same as under section 1(3)(iii) of the CEA 1898. This provision enabled D1 to cross-examine as to character D2 who had 'given evidence against' him: a phrase that the case law interpreted as 'giving evidence in such a way as to undermine his defence.'[71]

4.68 However, there is one possible respect in which D1's right to adduce evidence of D2's bad character in order to undermine D2's credibility may be wider under the new law than it was under the old. Under the old law, D1 could only adduce evidence of D2's bad character to this end by cross-examining under section 1(3)(iii) of the 1898 Act; and, obviously, he could not cross-examine D2 unless D2 gave evidence. And where D2 put forward a defence that heaped the blame on D1 without actually going into the witness-box, the case law suggested that D1 was unable to call D2's truthfulness into question by calling evidence of his bad character.[72] Section 104, unlike section 1(3)(iii) of the CEA 1898, is not

---

[70] CJA 2003 Sch 37, Part 5.
[71] *Murdoch and Taylor* [1965] AC 574; *Crawford* [1998] 1 CrAppR 338; *Rigot* [2000] 7 Archbold News 2.
[72] *Knutton* (1993) 97 CrAppR 115.

phrased in such a way as to make D2's presence in the witness-box a precondition for D1's being able to adduce evidence of his bad character in order to dent his credibility, in a situation where 'the nature or conduct of [D2's] defence is such as to undermine the co-defendant's defence.'

4.69 Where one co-defendant seeks to adduce evidence of the other's bad character with a view to undermining his credibility, is there any general limit to the sort of evidence that he may produce? Is he limited to evidence that clearly demonstrates that his co-defendant has told lies: for example, evidence that he has convictions for obtaining property by deception, or evidence that in previous trials he has given evidence that was disbelieved? Or does this corner of the law operate on the simpler basis that the rogues are less worthy of belief than law-abiding citizens, with the result that he can call any evidence that shows his co-defendant is a rogue?

4.70 The previous law operated on the second basis: where D1 had given evidence against D2, D2 was permitted to cross-examine D1 on his convictions for (in effect) anything and everything, including offences with no particular connection with telling lies.[73] As we have seen, 'gateway (d)' as extended by section 103(1)(b) now permits the prosecution to call evidence of bad character which shows that the defendant has a propensity to lie: and in that context, the Court of Appeal in *Hanson*[74] said that, when exploiting this new possibility, the prosecution may only adduce evidence that specifically shows his tendency to lie. It has been suggested that, to be consistent, the courts might now be expected to take the same line with 'gateway (e).'[75] I do not think this suggestion is correct. The prosecution's new power to adduce evidence of the defendant's bad character in order to show his propensity to lie is something which the courts were right to construe narrowly, because if construed broadly to allow the adduction of any evidence which shows the defendant is a rogue, it would short-circuit the scheme under which the prosecution has been given only a limited right to adduce evidence of bad character which shows the defendant has a propensity to commit the type of offence with which he is now charged. But that is not a reason for adopting the same approach where 'gateway (e)' is involved, and the issue is how much one defendant may reveal about the character of a co-defendant who has sought to put the blame for the offence on him.

4.71 If the conditions set out in sections 101(1)(e) and 104 are met, the court is obliged to admit the evidence that D1 wishes to use against D2. Section 101(3),

---

[73] For one example out of many, see *Hoggins* [1967] 1 WLR 1223 (a criminal record for offences of violence).

[74] [2005] EWCA Crim 824, [2005] 1 WLR 3169, **p 153 below**; see above, §§4.54–4.57.

[75] See Roderick Munday, 'Cut-throat Defences and the "Propensity to be Untruthful" under s104 of the Criminal Justice Act 2003' [2005] Crim LR 624.

which requires the court to exclude bad character evidence if 'it appears to the court that the admission of the evidence would have such an adverse effect on the fairness of the proceedings that the court ought not to admit it' applies only to bad character evidence admissible via 'gateways (d) and (g),' and hence does not apply to evidence admissible to which 'gateway (e)' applies. Although in general terms the courts appear to have a discretion to exclude otherwise admissible evidence of bad character by virtue of section 78 of PACE 1984,[76] this provision is expressly limited to 'evidence on which the prosecution proposes to rely.' However, a court confronted by a defendant who wishes to adduce against his co-defendant some highly prejudicial piece of bad character evidence, the relevance of which is only marginal, is not left completely powerless. In order to open 'gateway (e),' section 101(1)(e) requires the evidence to have 'substantial probative value' in relation to 'an important' matter in issue between the defendant and a co-defendant. If the bad character evidence is only marginally probative, or it is probative only in relation to some minor matter, then the judge should rule that it does not satisfy the conditions for admissibility under section 101(1)(e).[77]

4.72 Where D1 is allowed to call evidence of D2's bad character via 'gateway (e)' in an attempt to persuade the court that he (D1) is innocent, is the tribunal of fact permitted to take this evidence into account as part of the case against D2—or is it supposed to consider it only in relation to the question of whether D1 might be innocent? In *Randall*, Lord Steyn said, at the end of his speech (and obiter), the following:

> [§35] For the avoidance of doubt I would further add that in my view where evidence of propensity of a co-accused is relevant to a fact in issue between the Crown and the other accused it is not necessary for a trial judge to direct the jury to ignore that evidence in considering the case against the co-accused. Justice does not require that such a direction be given. Moreover, such a direction would needlessly perplex juries.

On the implications of this, two views are possible. One is that, in such a case, the prosecution have a windfall: the 'bad character' evidence that the co-accused (B) has adduced may be used to strengthen the prosecution case against the other defendant (A). The other is that it should not be so used, unless it could have been adduced by the prosecution against A via one of the other 'gateways': but that, to avoid confusing juries, judges need not direct juries to take notice of it when considering whether B may be innocent, whilst simultaneously ignoring it in deciding whether A is guilty.[78] In *Robinson*, the latest of a series of Court of Appeal decisions on this point, the court inclined towards the second view: but in so doing, the

---

[76] §§1.21–1.28 above.

[77] For a practical example, see *Edwards and Rowlands* [2005] EWCA Crim 3244, **p 230 below**.

[78] [2004] EWCA Crim 1254; [2004] 2 CrAppR 34 (570); *Price* [2004] EWCA Crim 1359; *Mertens* [2004] EWCA Crim 2252, [2005] Crim LR 301; *Murrell* [2005] EWCA Crim 382, [2005] Crim LR 869.

court said that, where the 'bad character' evidence could not have been adduced by the prosecution through one of the other 'gateways', prosecuting counsel should avoid making use of it in his or her closing speech.[79] Although the facts of *Robinson* arose before the new law on bad character evidence came into force, the Court of Appeal referred to it—with the suggestion that, in principle, the position is still the same.[80] (The broader question of how bad character evidence, once admitted, may be used is discussed below (see §§4.105–4.110 and §5.46).

4.73 Section 104(2) makes it plain that, where the *adduction* (as against the use) of bad character evidence is concerned, 'gateway (e)' is open to the defence, but not the prosecution. It is as follows:

> (2) Only evidence—
>> (a) which is to be (or has been) adduced by the co-defendant, or
>> (b) which a witness is to be invited to give (or has given) in cross-examination by the co-defendant,
>
> is admissible under section 101(1)(e).

However, as is explained below (§4.85 *et seq* below), a defendant who conducts his defence in such a way as to attack the character of his co-defendant will thereby open 'gateway (g),' as a result of which the prosecution will certainly be able to adduce evidence of his bad character.[81]

4.74 A final point to note in connection with 'gateway (e)' is that, of course, a court may properly decide to admit bad character evidence via that gateway which it earlier refused to admit through 'gateway (d).' Even though 'gateway (e)' sets a higher standard in some ways than is set by 'gateway (d),' the conditions that each sets are different; and furthermore, the court has what is (in effect) a discretion to exclude evidence otherwise admissible via 'gateway (d)' which it does not have in respect of 'gateway (e).'

'Gateway' (f): Evidence to Correct a False Impression

4.75 Under the previous law, evidence of a defendant's bad character was admissible, within limits, if he had made the running by leading evidence that he had a good one.

---

[79] *Robinson* [2005] EWCA Crim 3233 (at §83).
[80] The Court of Appeal certified a point of public importance, but refused leave to appeal.
[81] As in *Dowds* (reported together with *Bovell* [2005] EWCA Crim 1091, [2005] 2 CrAppR 27 (401)), p 163 below.

4.76 The justice of enabling the defendant's bad character to be displayed in order to correct a false impression was universally accepted, but the details of the previous law were widely thought to be unsatisfactory. Its problems were examined by the Law Commission, which identified three deficiencies.

4.77 First, it seemed that the existing law made no provision to correct a false impression which was conveyed not expressly, but by implication: by dress, for example, or by conduct, as where a defendant with a criminal record makes much of the fact that other possible culprits have criminal records for offences similar to that charged—so conveying the false impression that he has not.

4.78 Secondly, the power to correct the false impression only arose where the false impression had been given by witness evidence, either from the defendant,[82] or from the mouth of a defence witness.[83] There was no power to correct the false impression if it was conveyed in a speech by the defendant's lawyer, for example, or in a statement that he made to the police and which was later read to the court.

4.79 Thirdly, the existing rules were thought to have an element of 'overkill' in them, in that if the defendant claimed quite truthfully that he had a good character in one respect, the prosecution could prove that he had a bad one in another. In the leading case of *Winfield*, a defendant prosecuted for indecent assault led evidence of his previous good conduct towards women—and it was held that the prosecution were entitled to cross-examine him about a previous conviction for dishonesty.[84] Although the 'indivisibility of character' rule was defended by some,[85] the Law Commission thought it was unduly harsh. Disagreeing with Humphrys J in *Winfield*,[86] the Law Commission thought that that on principle the defendant ought (in effect) to be able to 'put half of his character in issue.'

4.80 Here, the government accepted the Law Commission's analysis of the problem, and adopted most of Law Commission's proposed solution. The provisions of the CJA 2003 that deal with this matter are based on the Law Commission's Draft Bill but some of its refinements have been removed: in particular, the requirement for judicial leave, and the Law Commission's clauses providing that bad character evidence otherwise admissible through this 'gateway' must be excluded if it would be unduly prejudicial. Section 101(3), under which the court is required to exclude bad character evidence which is admissible via certain of the

---

[82] In which case he exposed himself to cross-examination as to credit under CEA 1898 s1(3)(ii).
[83] When the witness could be cross-examined and evidence called in rebuttal: as in *Redd* [1923] 1 KB 104.
[84] (1939) 27 CrAppR 139.
[85] Roderick Munday, *Evidence* (2nd edn, London, Butterworths, 2003) §8.18.
[86] (1939) 27 CrAppR 139.

statutory 'gateways' if it appears to the court that its admission would make the trial unfair, does not apply where the evidence is admitted to correct a false impression (although it does seem that, in this situation, the court could exclude the evidence under section 78 of the Police and Criminal Evidence Act 1984).[87]

4.81 Section 101(1)(f) of the Act provides that evidence of bad character is admissible 'if it is evidence to correct a false impression given by the defendant' and this 'gateway' is further explained in **section 105**:

    (1) For the purposes of section 101(1)(f)—

        (a) the defendant gives a false impression if he is responsible for the making of an express or implied assertion which is apt[88] to give the court or jury a false or misleading impression about the defendant;

        (b) evidence to correct such an impression is evidence which has probative value in correcting it.

    (2) A defendant is treated as being responsible for the making of an assertion if—

        (a) the assertion is made by the defendant in the proceedings (whether or not in evidence given by him),

        (b) the assertion was made by the defendant—

            (i) on being questioned under caution, before charge, about the offence with which he is charged, or

            (ii) on being charged with the offence or officially informed that he might be prosecuted for it,

and evidence of the assertion is given in the proceedings,

        (c) the assertion is made by a witness called by the defendant,

        (d) the assertion is made by any witness in cross-examination in response to a question asked by the defendant that is intended to elicit it, or is likely to do so, or

        (e) the assertion was made by any person out of court, and the defendant adduces evidence of it in the proceedings.

    (3) A defendant who would otherwise be treated as responsible for the making of an assertion shall not be so treated if, or to the extent that, he withdraws it or disassociates himself from it.

    (4) Where it appears to the court that a defendant, by means of his conduct (other than the giving of evidence) in the proceedings, is seeking to give the court or jury an impression about himself that is false or misleading, the court may if it appears just to do so treat the defendant as being responsible for the making of an assertion which is apt to give that impression.

    (5) In subsection (4) 'conduct' includes appearance or dress.

---

[87] See §§1.21–1.28 above.

[88] Roderick Munday in *Evidence* (3rd edn, Oxford, OUP, 2005) §7.59 comments that the phrase 'apt to' is unusual in a statute. This may be so, but if it is, I do think that it is problematic: it simply means 'likely to' or 'liable to.' The phrase originated in the Law Commission's Draft Bill, attached to *Evidence of Bad Character in Criminal Proceedings* (Law Com no 273, Cm 5258, October 2001).

(6) Evidence is admissible under section 101(1)(f) only if it goes no further than is necessary to correct the false impression.

(7) Only prosecution evidence is admissible under section 101(1)(f).

4.82 This provision appears to meet all three of the defects that the Law Commission identified in the previous law. Between them, subsections 105(1), (4) and (5) take care of the problem about misleading impressions given by conduct, or by implication. Section 105(2) deals with the problem about false impressions that are conveyed other than by the defendant or one of his witnesses when testifying. Although section 105(2)(a) does not expressly say that an assertion is made 'by the defendant' when it is made by his lawyer on his behalf, it is clear that this was what Parliament intended.[89] By providing that 'evidence is admissible under section 101(1)(f) only if it goes no further than is necessary to correct the false impression,' section 105(6) reverses the decision in *Winfield* that for these purposes 'character is indivisible'.

4.83 In the 12 months since these provisions came into force, the Court of Appeal has considered 'gateway (f)' in a number of cases. In *Dowds*,[90] one of two joint defendants at a burglary pointed out, in the course of his evidence, that his co-defendant had committed another burglary the day before. The Court of Appeal held (unsurprisingly)[91] that he had 'made an attack on another person's character' and so had opened 'gateway (g)'; but they added for good measure that, by making pointed reference to his co-defendant's track-record for burglary without mentioning his own worse one, he had 'created a false impression'—and had thereby opened 'gateway (f)' as well. In *Renda*, the Court of Appeal also considered the ambit of section 105(3), which provides that a defendant is not treated as responsible for making an assertion where he 'withdraws it or dissociates himself from it'; this, they said, does not apply where—as in that case—the defendant, far from withdrawing the assertion voluntarily, had been forced under cross-examination to admit that it was false.[92] In *Renda*,[93] the Court of Appeal made the point that sections 101(1)(f) and 105 mark a new start; it is therefore not particularly helpful for counsel to ply the court with cases decided under the old law on whether (in the words of the CEA 1898) the defendant had 'put his character in issue.'

---

[89] See the Explanatory Notes to clause 10 of the Law Commission's Draft Bill, Report, n 80 above, at 219; and see para 309 of the Explanatory Notes. 'Section 105(2) sets out the circumstances in which a defendant is to be treated as being responsible for an assertion. These include the defendant making the assertion himself, either in his evidence *or in his representative's presentation of his case.*' (emphasis added).

[90] Decided with *Bovell* [2005] EWCA Crim 1091, [2005] 2 CrAppR 27, **p 163 below**, at §32.

[91] *Pace* Roderick Munday, *Evidence* 3rd edn, (Oxford, OUP, 2005) §7.70. The point is further discussed in n 226 below.

[92] At §21.

[93] [2005] EWCA Crim 2826, **p 193 below**, at §19.

4.84 In *Somonathan*, the Court of Appeal considered the meaning of section 105(6), which provides that 'Evidence is admissible under section 101(1)(f) only if it goes no further than is necessary to correct the false impression.' The defendant was a Hindu priest, who appealed from his conviction for twice raping a woman member of the congregation at his current temple. In his defence he 'put himself forward as a man who not only had no previous convictions but also enjoyed a good reputation as a priest, particularly at Tooting, where he had previously been employed [in another temple].' In fact this was not true, as he had left his previous employment under a cloud. In order to correct the false impression he had given, the prosecution were allowed to call the chairman of the Board of Trustees of the Tooting temple, who gave evidence that the priest's contract had not been renewed because of complaints of his indiscreet behaviour towards women, and because he was untruthful. On appeal, the defendant argued that, by reason of section 105(6), the prosecution should have been required to limit this part of their evidence to a bare statement that the priest's contract had not been renewed because there had been unspecified complaints. Affirming the conviction, the Court of Appeal said: 'The gateway having been opened the prosecution was entitled to adduce a full account of what, according to their witness, brought the Tooting contract to an end.'[94]

Gateway (g): 'the Defendant has Made an Attack on Another Person's Character'

4.85 Under the previous law, where the nature or conduct of the defence was 'such as to involve imputations on the character of the prosecutor or the witnesses for the prosecution, or the deceased victim of the alleged crime,' CEA 1898 section 1(3)(ii) permitted the prosecution to cross-examine the defendant on his character.

4.86 This law was potentially harsh, for two reasons. First, it made no difference whether the defendant's 'imputation' was a gratuitous attack on the general character of a prosecution witness, or something that had to be said because it was an integral part of the defence (for example, that the defendant's alleged confession had been fabricated by the police). Secondly, the law was said to be unduly harsh because, although in theory the purpose of revealing the defendant's bad character was to blunt the effect of his 'imputation' by showing that his word was less than credible, there was an obvious possibility that the magistrates or jury would treat his bad character in a cruder way as something that simply made it more likely that he had committed the offence; this was particularly so in cases where the

---

[94] [2005] EWCA Crim 2866, [2006] 1 CrAppR 19 (303), **p 206 below**, at §43.

evidence of bad character consisted of convictions for similar offences in the past. It was in an attempt to palliate this harshness that the courts decided that a cross-examination as to character under section 1(3)(ii) of the CEA 1898 could only take place where the judge granted leave.

4.87 Conversely, in another way the old law was also thought to be unduly lenient, because the only way in which it permitted the defendant's bad character to be revealed was by cross-examining him when he gave evidence.[95] So, if the defendant kept out of the witness-box he could cast imputations on all and sundry, with no fear that his own bad character would be revealed.

4.88 The Law Commission was much exercised about these problems. In the hope of dealing with them, it produced a long, complicated provision in clause 9 of its Draft Bill. Where a defendant made 'an attack on another person's character,' the prosecution would have been entitled to adduce evidence of the defendant's bad character—by cross-examining him if he gave evidence, or if not, by other means. But, unlike section 1(3)(ii) of the CEA 1898, the new provision would not be triggered by any 'attack' that was an integral part of the defence case. The only evidence the prosecution would be entitled to call would have been evidence bearing on the defendant's credibility. Such evidence would only be admissible on leave. And the clause contained cautious phrases intended to ensure that leave would only be given when the bad character evidence would not be unfairly prejudicial.

4.89 The solution adopted by the CJA 2003 is simpler and more brutal. Section 101(1)(g) provides that evidence of the defendant's bad character is admissible if 'the defendant has made an attack on another person's character,' and **section 106** elaborates this phrase as follows:

(1) For the purposes of section 101(1)(g) a defendant makes an attack on another person's character if—

    (a) he adduces evidence attacking the other person's character,

    (b) he (or any legal representative appointed under section 38(4) of the Youth Justice and Criminal Evidence Act 1999 (c. 23) to cross-examine a witness in his interests) asks questions in cross-examination that are intended to elicit such evidence, or are likely to do so, or

    (c) evidence is given of an imputation about the other person made by the defendant—

        (i) on being questioned under caution, before charge, about the offence with which he is charged, or

        (ii) on being charged with the offence or officially informed that he might be prosecuted for it.

---

[95] *Butterwasser* [1948] 1 KB 4.

(2) In subsection (1) 'evidence attacking the other person's character' means evidence to the effect that the other person—

    (a) has committed an offence (whether a different offence from the one with which the defendant is charged or the same one), or

    (b) has behaved, or is disposed to behave, in a reprehensible way;

and 'imputation about the other person' means an assertion to that effect.

(3) Only prosecution evidence is admissible under section 101(1)(g).

4.90 Like the Law Commission's proposal, this allows the prosecution to adduce evidence of the defendant's bad character by any means, so enabling them to do so by evidence in-chief where he launches his attack on the character of others not from the witness-box but from the safety of the dock. But it drops the aspects of the Law Commission's draft clause that were designed to blunt the harshness of the previous law.

4.91 Under the Law Commission's proposal, this gateway to the revelation of the defendant's character would not have been opened by any attack on another person by means of 'evidence that has to do with the alleged facts of the offence with which the defendant is charged, or evidence of misconduct in connection with the investigation or prosecution of that offence.'[96] So, for example, the defendant would not have risked his record being exposed if he accused the police of inventing his confession. But section 106 of the Act contains no such limit. Indeed, section 106(2) expressly states that an attack on another person's character 'means evidence to the effect that the other person (a) has committed an offence (whether a different offence from the one with which the defendant is charged or the same one), or (b) has behaved, or is disposed to behave, in a reprehensible way.' So, in *Hanson*, the Court of Appeal said that the pre-Act authorities 'will continue to apply when assessing whether an attack has been made on another person's character, to the extent that they are compatible with s106.'[97]

4.92 Like the previous law, the new provision potentially applies not only where the defendant accuses someone else of having committed a criminal offence,

---

[96] Draft Bill, clause 9(2)(a), Report, n 88 above, at 216.

[97] *Hanson* [2005] EWCA Crim 824, [2005] 1 WLR 3169, **p 153 below**, at §14. In a recent article, David Wolchover suggests that—contrary to the view expressed in this paragraph–'gateway (g) is *not* opened by an attack that forms an integral part of the defence: see 'Gateway (g): Casting imputations and putting in the defendant's form', [2006] *Archbold News*, issue 2, 6–9. This view is based on a dictum un *Ball* (reported with *Renda* [2005] EWCA Crim 2826), a rape case where the trial judge refused to allow the prosecution to call evidence of the defendant's bad character by reason of the simple fact that the defence case was that the allegation of rape was fabricated, and the Court of Appeal described his ruling as 'impeccable'. This dictum looks to me like an endorsement of the judge's exercise of a discretion to exclude evidence otherwise admissible, rather than a limitative interpretation of the provision. *Ball* is further discussed in §4.100 below.

but also where he accuses him of misbehaviour that falls outside the scope of the criminal law. This is expressly provided for by section 106(2)(b), which defines 'evidence attacking the other person's character' as including evidence that the other person 'has behaved, or is disposed to behave, in a reprehensible way.'

4.93 As in the context of section 98 and the definition of 'bad character,' so here too the scope of 'reprehensible behaviour' raises a delicate problem where a defendant attributes homosexual behaviour to a person who is not homosexual (or who does not wish to be publicly identified as one). Thirty years ago, the Court of Appeal in *Bishop*[98] dealt with the issue robustly by saying that, even if homosexual practices were now legal, to call somebody a practising homosexual was still to cast an 'imputation' on his character, and the defendant who did so thereby exposed himself to cross-examination on his criminal record.

4.94 Earlier in this commentary, when discussing the scope of 'reprehensible behaviour' as an element in the definition of 'bad character,' and hence what sort of evidence about a person fell within the restraints set by sections 100 and 101, it was suggested that nowadays homosexual practices should not be seen as falling within the scope of 'reprehensible behaviour': but in that context it was also suggested that calling evidence of this sort about another person could potentially infringe a person's right to privacy under Article 8 of the European Convention on Human Rights, and in principle the court could therefore restrain unnecessary evidence about such matters in order to comply with its duties under the Human Rights Act 1998 to respect Convention rights.[99]

4.95 If the view expressed in the previous paragraph is correct, then a defendant who imputes homosexual behaviour to another person does not thereby 'attack his character' for the purpose of opening 'gateway (g).' And here, the Human Rights Act 1998 does not enable us to solve the problem: if a court could properly invoke its duty to protect 'Convention rights' in order to stop such evidence being given, it could hardly use this as the basis for inventing a new rule, external to the bad character evidence provisions of the CJA 2003, allowing the prosecution to expose the defendant's bad character as 'tit for tat' for his invading someone else's right to privacy. The conclusion must be that, under the new law, a defendant who calls another person a homosexual does not thereby expose his bad character to view by opening 'gateway (g).' However, where a defendant ascribes homosexuality to another person it will often be in circumstances that imply some other behaviour that is reprehensible behaviour beyond any shadow of a doubt. A defendant accused of robbery who runs the 'guardsman's defence,' for example,[100] will

---

[98] *Bishop* [1975] QB 274, (1975) 59 CrAppR 246.
[99] Above, §§2.13–2.15.
[100] See Chapter 3, n 18.

almost invariably accuse the complainant of committing a sexual offence; and in *Bishop*,' the alleged burglar's explanation for his fingerprints in the complainant's flat—that he and the complainant were homosexual lovers—also carried the implication that the complainant had lied in his evidence.

4.96 Another restriction proposed by the Law Commission, and not adopted by Parliament, was a requirement of judicial leave. However, where bad character evidence is potentially admissible under sections 101(1) and 106, section 101(3) does require the court to exclude it where it believes 'that the admission of the evidence would have such an adverse effect on the fairness of the proceedings that the court ought not to admit it.'

4.97 And 'gateway (g)' is wider than the previous law in that, under section 1(3)(ii) of the CEA 1898, the defendant exposed his bad character to public view only where he had attacked 'the character of the prosecutor or the witnesses for the prosecution, or the deceased victim of the alleged crime.' Under the new law, the defendant potentially triggers the exposure of his bad character if he makes an attack 'on any person.' This phrase is very wide.[101] One consequence is that 'gateway (g)' applies, inter alia, where in the course of his evidence one co-defendant attacks the character of another: as in *Dowds*,[102] where in the course of denying that he was responsible for a burglary, the defendant informed the court that his co-defendant had committed another burglary only the day before.

4.98 Surprisingly, the Act does not tell us whether section 101(1)(g) is brought into play by the defendant attacking the character of a person who is dead. When discussing section 100 of the Act, which regulates the admission of bad character evidence relating to non-defendants, the view was expressed that 'non-defendants' included persons who are now dead (see §§3.37–3.39 above). One of the reasons there given was that, although dead people do not feel hurt or humiliated when their characters are publicly attacked, their living relatives may well do so. This reasoning would suggest the section 101(1)(g) does apply where the person attacked is dead. A pointer in the same direction is the fact that, under the previous law, section 1(3)(ii) of the CEA 1898 allowed the defendant to be cross-examined on his bad character when he had cast imputations on a range of people—which was extended in 1994 to include 'the deceased victim of the alleged crime.'[103]

---

[101] As Roderick Munday points out, in principle a defendant could even find that he had opened 'gateway (g)' if he abuses the judge or prosecuting counsel! *Evidence* 3rd edn, (Oxford, OUP, 2005) §7.69.

[102] Reported with *Bovell* [2005] EWCA Crim 1091, [2005] 2 CrAppR 27 (401), **p 163 below**.

[103] For a contrary view, see Roderick Munday, *Evidence* (3rd edn, Oxford, OUP, 2005) §7.69. Dr Munday severely criticised the change in 1994: see 'A Sample of Law-making' (1995) 145 *New LJ* 855, at 895. However, in *Hanson* [2005] EWCA Crim 824, [2005] 1 WLR 3169, **p 153 below**, Rose LJ at §5 said that 'gateway (g)' applied '. . . where the defendant has made an attack on the character of another person who will often, though not always, be the victim of the alleged crime, *whether alive or dead.*'

4.99 As with 'gateway (f),' the scope and operation of 'gateway (g)' has been considered on several occasions by the Court of Appeal in the 12 months since the bad character evidence provisions of the CJA 2003 were brought into force.

4.100 The decision in *Ball*[104] illustrates the widened scope of what now may constitute making 'an attack on the character of another person.' Ball appealed against his conviction for raping a woman with whom he had spent the evening drinking in a public house. When interviewed by the police he admitted the sexual intercourse, but 'told the police that most of the men in the local public house had had sexual intercourse with the complainant. He criticised the complainant's sexual promiscuity in very disparaging terms. She was easy. "She's a bag really, you know what I mean, a slag."' His statement to the police, with this character sketch of the complainant included, was put in evidence by the prosecution as part of the prosecution case. The trial judge held that, by virtue of section 106(1)(c), these disparaging remarks made to the police constituted an 'attack on the character of another person,' which opened 'gateway (g)': and, rejecting a defence application under section 101(3), he allowed the prosecution to put the defendant's criminal record in evidence. The Court of Appeal upheld this decision.

4.101 Two further decisions deal with the application, in relation to 'gateway (g),' of the duty of the court under section 101(3) to exclude bad character evidence which the court believes 'would have such an adverse effect on the fairness of the proceedings that the court ought not to admit it.' In *Dowds*,[105] the Court of Appeal said that, even if (as seemed highly improbable on the facts) the defendant had not really intended by his evidence to attack the character of his co-defendant by what he said about him, it did not make the admission of evidence of his previous convictions unfair; what mattered was the actual impact of his evidence, and his mens rea or otherwise in giving it was irrelevant.

4.102 More significantly, in *Edwards*,[106] the Court of Appeal held that, where at the start of the proceedings the prosecution apply to admit evidence of the defendant's bad character via 'gateway (d),' and the judge excludes it by applying section

[104] Reported together with *Renda* [2005] EWCA Crim 2826, **p 193 below.**
[105] Reported with *Bovell* [2005] EWCA Crim 1091, [2005] 2 CrAppR 27 (401), **p 163 below**; under the Law Commission's original proposal, what is now 'gateway (g)' would also have been opened by the defendant's attack on any person, including in principle a co-defendant. However, the opening of 'gateway (g)' would not have been triggered by any attack on a person's character that 'has to do with the alleged facts of the offence with which the defendant is charged': which in practice would have reduced the scope of 'gateway (g)' in relation to cut-throat defences, although the result would have been the same in *Dowds*, presumably, where the defendant did not merely blame his co-defendant for the crime, but also informed the court about a different offence he had committed earlier. For an argument that the courts ought on principle to read the phrase 'other person' in s101(1)(g) as excluding co-defendants, see Roderick Munday, *Evidence* 3rd edn, (Oxford, OUP, 2005) §7.70.
[106] *Edwards* [2005] EWCA Crim 1813, [2006] 1 CrAppR 3 (31), **p 169 below.**

101(3), it is permissible for the prosecution to make a further application to admit it via 'gateway (g)' if the defendant in the course of his evidence then launches an attack on the character of the prosecution witnesses; and that when the second application is made, it is open to the judge to reconsider his initial ruling and admit the evidence, notwithstanding his initial ruling that to do so would make the trial unfair. To the argument that to admit a certain piece of evidence against the defendant either makes the proceedings unfair or it does not, the Court of Appeal responded thus:

> As it seems to us, the difficulty with that submission is that the fairness of the proceed-
> ings, and the impact on it of admitting the evidence, has to be gauged at the time at which
> the application is made and by reference to the gateway under which admissibility is
> sought. At the initial stage there had been no attack on the character of the prosecution
> witnesses. In this regard, when dealing with the matter at the time of the second applica-
> tion, the Recorder . . . said this: 'I have come to the conclusion that there is a difference
> now between the prosecution arguments, the difference being the sustained attack upon
> the character of the police, and it seems to me that, even though these convictions are of
> a serious nature and of some age, the jury are entitled to know about these convictions,
> that I think they would be misled seriously if they did not know of this matter.' In our
> judgment, that was a conclusion which was not only open to the Recorder, it is one which
> he was, in the circumstances as we have described them, right to reach.

4.103 Even more significantly, the Court of Appeal has now ruled on the purposes for which the evidence of the defendant's bad character admitted via 'gateway (g)' may be used once it has come in.

4.104 This point was a loose end which the wording of the Act had significantly failed to tie. Under the previous law, the theory was that any evidence of the defendant's bad character admitted under section 1(3)(ii) of the CEA 1898 because he had cast imputations on the character of others in the course of his defence, was evidence only insofar as it bore upon his credibility as a witness, and at trial the judge was supposed to direct the jury to this effect; though the theory was not particularly realistic, given that section 1(3)(ii) did not limit the type of bad character evidence that could be called, and in practice the evidence would often be that the defendant had committed previous offences similar to the one for which he was currently on trial.[107] Under the Law Commission's proposals, evi-dence admitted via what is now 'gateway (g)' would, like evidence admitted under section 1(3)(ii), have been admissible in relation to credit only. The CJA 2003, however, leaves the matter open. Section 106 contains nothing that expressly lim-its either the nature of the evidence that the prosecution may bring in via 'gateway (g)', or the purpose for which the court is entitled to use it—and on this point the Explanatory Notes are less than helpful. According to paragraph 382:

---

[107] See eg, *Powell* [1985] 1 WLR 1364.

Evidence admissible under section 101(1)(g)—as under section 101(1)(f)—will primarily go to the credit of the defendant. Currently a jury would be directed that evidence admitted in similar circumstances, under the 1898 Act, goes only to credibility and is not relevant to the issue of guilt. Such directions have been criticised and the new statutory scheme does not specify that this evidence is to be treated in such a way. However, it is expected that judges will explain the purpose for which the evidence is being put forward and direct the jury about the sort of weight that can be placed on it.

4.105 The approach now adopted by the Court of Appeal is, in essence, 'once it's in, it's in.' Even though the different 'gateways' listed in section 101(1) may have been created with distinct purposes in mind, once evidence of the defendant's bad character has passed through one of them, the use the court may make of it depends on the nature of the evidence, not the 'gateway' through which it was admitted. In *Highton*, the Court of Appeal, in a judgment delivered by Lord Woolf CJ, said this:

> . . . the 2003 Act does not expressly identify the purpose for which the bad character evidence can be used if it passes through one of those gateways and is therefore admissible. Two different interpretations are contended for by counsel appearing for the appellants and the Crown. The appellants contend that the purposes for which admissible evidence of bad character can be used are confined by the terms of the gateway through which the evidence is admitted. The Crown, on the other hand, contends that once the evidence becomes admissible by passing through any gateway, it can be used for any purpose for which bad character evidence is relevant in the particular case.[108]

Having examined the arguments, the court continued:

> We therefore conclude that a distinction must be drawn between the *admissibility* of evidence of bad character, which depends upon it getting through one of the gateways, and *use* to which it may be put once it is admitted. The use to which it may be put depends upon the matters to which it is relevant rather than upon the gateway through which it was admitted. It is true that the reasoning that leads to the admission of evidence under gateway (d) may also determine the matters to which the evidence is relevant or primarily relevant once admitted. That is not true, however, of all the gateways. In the case of gateway (g), for example, admissibility depends on the defendant having made an attack on another person's character, but once the evidence is admitted, it may, depending on the particular facts, be relevant not only to credibility but also to propensity to commit offences of the kind with which the defendant is charged.[109]

It is important, said the court, that in a jury trial the judge should give the jury a clear direction as to the issues in respect of which any given piece of bad character evidence is relevant: a point which is further explored in Chapter 5.

---

[108] [2005] EWCA Crim 1985, [2005] 1 WLR 3472, **p 183 below**, at §2.
[109] At §10.

4.106 The decision in *Highton* has been criticised.[110] First, it is said that under the previous law, where the prosecution were permitted to adduce evidence of the bad character of a defendant who had 'cast an imputation' in the course of his defence, the theoretical basis was that the evidence was called to dent his credibility, not to show his propensity to commit the offence—and juries had to be directed to take the evidence into account for this purpose only. So, to interpret the new provisions as allowing the tribunal of fact to treat such evidence as showing the defendant's propensity to commit the offence as well is to increase the ways in which bad character evidence may be used to the detriment of the defendant. Secondly, it is said that the proper 'gateway' for the admission of evidence of propensity to commit the offence is 'gateway (d),' as expanded by section 103: if evidence that the prosecution wants to use to show the defendant's propensity to commit the offence fails to pass the tests set out in that provision, it should not—it is said—be smuggled in through any of the other 'gateways.'

4.107 I find neither of these points convincing. To take the second first, evidence that is said to demonstrate the defendant's propensity to commit the offence does not get in through 'gateway (d)' merely because the evidence has this effect. In practice, two further conditions are necessary: (i) the prosecution must make the attempt to put it in through 'gateway (d)' and (ii) the court must allow this to be done. Evidence that undoubtedly shows the defendant's propensity to commit the offence may fail to gain admission either because the prosecution initially decides that it would be fairer not to use it, or because, when it seeks to do so, the judge in the early stages of the proceedings rules that fairness to the defendant requires him to exclude it using section 101(3) or section 103(3). Decisions taken on the basis of what seems fair to the defendant at the outset might deserve to be revisited if he turns the proceedings into a mud-slinging match once he gets into the witness-box.[111]

4.108 To return to the first point, evidence of the defendant's bad character is not in practice clearly divisible into two groups: group A that shows propensity and group B that shows that his word is less worthy of belief. In practice, there is a spectrum, and in practice much evidence of this sort shows both. The case of the defendant who is accused of shoplifting and who claims to have walked out of the shop having innocently forgotten to pay, and who has been convicted five times for similar offences in the past, on each occasion pleading not guilty and advancing an identical defence, is an obvious example. In such circumstances, to tell a

---

[110] Roderick Munday, 'The Purposes of Gateway (g): Yet Another Problematic of the Criminal Justice Act 2003' [2006] *CrimLR* 300; and see the commentary by AJR on *Murrell* [2005] Crim LR 869. For a slightly less critical comment, see D. Wolchover, 'Gateway (g): casting imputations and putting the defendant's form', [2006] *Archbold News*, issue 2, 6–9.
[111] See *Edwards* [2005] EWCA Crim 1813 [2006] 1 CrAppR 3 (31), **p 169 below**.

jury that his previous convictions are evidence of his untruthfulness when giving evidence but not of his tendency to steal from shops is counter-intuitive, and unsatisfactory for that reason.

4.109 Directions to juries that evidence which is logically relevant to issue A may only be considered in relation to issue B, to which it is less relevant than to issue A, are certain to be confusing and unlikely in practice to be followed. Thirty years ago, they were famously castigated by Sir Rupert Cross as 'gibberish':[112] and they have not become any more comprehensible in the interval. Furthermore, to believe that a direction of this sort is both necessary and desirable presupposes a mind-set about the qualities and abilities of juries that is schizophrenic. The notion that jurors should be kept as far as possible in ignorance of the defendant's bad character is based on the assumption that they are morons deaf to reason: once they discover the defendant has a criminal record, they will disregard the rest of the evidence (if any) and convict him on that fact alone. But expecting them to disregard the defendant's previous similar offences when deciding whether he committed the one with which he is now charged, whilst simultaneously remembering it when deciding if he is telling the truth when he says that he did not, assumes they have the mental agility of an Acquinas. In reality, the practical effect of requiring judges to deliver directions of this kind is to sow the seeds of unmeritorious appeals in cases where they understandably forget to give them, without advancing the overriding objective of criminal justice, which is the acquittal of the innocent and the conviction of the guilty. In my view, the decision in *Highton* marks a break with the past that is proper and desirable, and it is a good thing that such directions no longer have to be given on these confusing lines.

4.110 A rule requiring bad character evidence admitted via 'gateway (g)' to be used exclusively for deciding whether a defendant's evidence is credible would make sense, perhaps, if the only evidence that could be admitted via 'gateway (g)' were evidence which suggests that he has a tendency to lie, while suggesting nothing else. This was, in effect, the scheme that the Law Commission put forward in its Report and the Draft Bill attached to it. But Parliament rejected it, and enacted the scheme contained in section 106 instead. There is no suggestion in section 106 that the bad character evidence admissible via 'gateway (g)' is restricted in this way, and it would require a heroic effort of interpretation to read this restriction into it. If—as surely is the case—'gateway (g)' lets in evidence of the defendant's bad character in general, the ruling in *Highton* must be correct.

---

[112] 'The Evidence Report: Sense or Nonsense—A Very Wicked Animal Defends the 11th Report of the Criminal Law Revision Committee' [1973] Crim LR 329, 332–34.

Evidence of the Defendant's Bad Character—General; the Admissibility of 'Stale' Convictions

4.111 Common sense suggests that, broadly speaking, the older a piece of bad character evidence is, the less cogently it suggests that the defendant is guilty of the offence for which he is now on trial—and hence the more willing the court should be to exclude it. This will not invariably be so. Evidence which shows the defendant has the skill or knowledge to pick the lock of a particularly complex safe, or that he has a particularly unusual sexual tendency, would not necessarily lose its probative force with the passage of time. But evidence that merely shows that, years ago, the defendant was a burglar or a shoplifter sheds little or no light on whether he has committed a similar offence 25 years later. And if, in the interval, the defendant has apparently 'gone straight,' it would seem doubly unfair to admit it.[113]

4.112 Section 101(4) makes it plain that the court should be willing to take this into account in applying section 101(3) to exclude bad character evidence otherwise admissible through the 'matter in issue' gateway, or through the 'attack on the character of another' gateway: in respect of both of which the court must exclude if it believes the admission of the evidence would render the proceedings unfair. By **section 101(4):**

> On an application to exclude evidence under subsection (3) the court must have regard, in particular, to the length of time between the matters to which that evidence relates and the matters which form the subject of the offence charged.

4.113 In *Hanson*,[114] the Court of Appeal said that, in deciding whether a previous conviction was 'stale,' it regarded 'the date of commission as generally being of more significance than the date of conviction when assessing admissibility.' As previously explained,[115] section 101(3) is duplicated to some extent by section 103(3), which also requires the court to exclude evidence of stale convictions in certain circumstances. But here, surprisingly, the matter that the court is required to consider is 'the length of time since the conviction.'

---

[113] Compare the words of the Court of Appeal in *Hanson* [2005] EWCA Crim 824, [2005] 1 WLR 3169, **p 153 below**, at §11: 'Old convictions, with no special feature shared with the offence charged, are likely seriously to affect the fairness of the proceedings adversely, unless, despite their age, it can properly be said that they show a continuing tendency.'
[114] *Ibid.*
[115] See above, §§4.46–4.47.

4.114 Section 101(4) does not affect the position where the evidence is admissible through one of the 'gateways' other than (d) or (g), and the scope of section 103(3) is even narrower. However, in the relatively rare case that the bad character evidence takes the form of a conviction incurred when the defendant was under the age of 14, its admissibility is restricted by **section 108**. It may only be admitted where the conviction was for an offence triable only on indictment, and so is the offence for which the defendant is now on trial—and in addition, the court has a general discretion to exclude:

(1) Section 16(2) and (3) of the Children and Young Persons Act 1963 (c. 37) (offences committed by person under 14 disregarded for purposes of evidence relating to previous convictions) shall cease to have effect.
(2) In proceedings for an offence committed or alleged to have been committed by the defendant when aged 21 or over, evidence of his conviction for an offence when under the age of 14 is not admissible unless—

 (a) both of the offences are triable only on indictment, and
 (b) the court is satisfied that the interests of justice require the evidence to be admissible.

(3) Subsection (2) applies in addition to section 101.[116]

4.115 The duty where necessary to exclude under section 108(2) is wider than the duty created by section 101(3), because it applies across the board and is not limited to any particular 'gateway.'

4.116 As previously mentioned (§§1.21–1.28 above), it is now safe to assume that the general powers of the court to exclude evidence under section 78 of PACE 1984 or at common law extend to evidence of bad character otherwise admissible under the CJA 2003. If this is correct, then these powers could be used to exclude evidence of bad character which is very stale, even if the situation is not covered by sections 101(3), 103(3) or 108(2).

---

[116] In its original form, what is now s108 consisted of what is now subsection (1) only. Subsections (2) and (3) were a late addition by the House of Lords.

5

PRACTICAL ISSUES

Attitude of the Crown Prosecution Service

5.1 The Director of Public Prosecutions has publicly encouraged Crown Prosecutors to make use of the new tools that the bad character evidence provisions of the Criminal Justice Act 2003 have given them. For the use of Crown Prosecutors, the Crown Prosecution Service (CPS) has issued its own detailed guide to the new legislation, and how it should be used, which it has published on the CPS website.[1] This begins as follows:

> The effect of these provisions will mean that non-defendants will be better protected from attacks on their character than previously. In relation to a defendant's bad character, such evidence is likely to play a greater part in the investigation and prosecution of cases and may form an essential part of the evidence against a defendant. This means that police and prosecutors will need to know the details of the defendant's previous misconduct at the earliest opportunity in order to assess whether such evidence should be used as part of the prosecution case.

This official guidance is updated from time to time, to take account of Court of Appeal decisions.[2]

Information Relevant to Bad Character: Recording, Storage and Access

5.2 In the past, information tending to show that a person has committed an offence has been recorded and stored locally. Each court kept (and still keeps) its own records of the convictions and sentences that it imposes. In addition, each of the 43 police forces in England and Wales kept (and still keep) their own records of information in relation to offences, offenders, and suspects.

5.3 Obviously, the fact that this sort of material is stored locally rather than centrally is a serious problem to anyone who wishes to discover whether any

---

[1] www.cps.gov.uk/legal/section13/chapter_u.html
[2] I am grateful to the Director of Public Prosecutions for a long and helpful letter on these matters.

particular witness, suspect or defendant has a disreputable past. Where someone is a witness or a suspect in a case in Cambridge, how is a policeman, prosecutor or a defence lawyer to find that he has a conviction in Carlisle, a caution in Cardiff, or in Canterbury was the subject of a police investigation leading to a trial and an acquittal?

5.4 To some extent, this problem has been resolved by the Police National Computer (PNC), on which certain types of information about crimes and criminals are now stored centrally, in a form in which they can be readily accessed by any police force and the other official criminal justice agencies. This arrangement, however, has (or at any rate, had until recently) a number of serious shortcomings. One of these was that information relating to criminal behaviour that did not consist of convictions, cautions, reprimands and warnings was not logged on the PNC, and was usually to be found only in the files of the local police force, where other police forces and other criminal justice agencies would not find it easy to access. A further problem was inaccuracy. Details of convictions held on the PNC were placed there not by the courts, but by the police, and in consequence were sometimes inaccurate or incomplete. The existence of these problems was among the criticisms of the existing system made by the Bichard Report[3] into the Huntley case.[4] Practical steps are now being taken to address them. A computer link-up is being planned to enable one police force to access information when held only in the files of another, and there is also a move to transfer the responsibility for entering the details of convictions from the police to the courts. But, surprisingly, no general IT system as yet exists to enable all the individual courts to have computerised access to the records of the others.

5.5 When a defendant or a witness has been convicted of a criminal offence, the details of the offence may be more important as a piece of evidence than the mere fact of the conviction, as we have seen.[5] For these details, it may be necessary to look back into the police or CPS files relating to the case. At one time, the different police forces and agencies were left to follow their own practices as to how and for what period of time material relating to past cases was kept. More recently, minimum standards have been prescribed by the Home Secretary in a code[6] made

---

[3] A Public Inquiry Report on Child Protection Procedures in Humberside Police and Cambridgeshire Constabulary, particularly the Effectiveness of Relevant Intelligence-based Record Keeping, Vetting Practices since 1995 and Information Sharing with other Agencies, HC 653 (June 2004). Online at www.homeoffice.gov.uk/pdf/bichard_report.pdf

[4] The murder by Ian Huntley, a school caretaker at Soham, of Holly Wells and Jessica Chapman, which he committed in the summer of 2002, and of which he was convicted in December 2003.

[5] See §4.44 above.

[6] Criminal Procedure and Investigations Act 1996: Code of Practice under Part II.

under the Criminal Procedure and Investigations Act 1996. In *Bovell*,[7] the Court of Appeal drew attention to the fact that the current version of the code prescribes minimum periods for retaining material relating to investigations which are rather short: evidence must be retained at least until a convicted person is released from custody, or discharged from hospital, in cases where the court imposes a custodial sentence or a hospital order, or, in all other cases, six months from the date of conviction. If materials relating to past cases were routinely destroyed at this point, evidence that the CJA 2003 has now made admissible in later prosecutions for subsequent offences would often be unavailable when needed. It seems likely that, in the light of these comments, the code will be amended. Until recently, some police forces have tended to 'weed' information held on suspects and convicted persons fairly quickly for fear of contravening the data protection principles contained in the Data Protection Acts. A recent decision of the Information Tribunal has clarified the application of these principles to police records, giving the green light to the retention of such data for long periods.[8]

5.6 Although the police and the CPS are able to 'trawl' for evidence of bad character using the PNC and other facilities, these facilities are not available for defence lawyers. Unless they have the means to finance their own private enquiries, defendants in practice have to make do with such information on the bad character of the prosecution witnesses as they are given by the police and by the CPS. What are the duties of the police and prosecutors in this respect? Case law from before the bad character evidence provisions of the CJA 2003 came into force requires the prosecution to tell the defence about their witness's previous convictions, except for minor traffic offences—and in the case of police officers, disciplinary proceedings and Court of Appeal decisions quashing convictions because of their misconduct; if they fail to do so, the defendant is likely to have grounds for appeal.[9] As regards evidence of other reprehensible behaviour which undermines the credit of the prosecution's witnesses, they are required to share this with the defence if they happen to have it, but they are under no obligation to go looking for it.[10] In *Gleadall v Huddersfield Magistrates' Court*,[11] a defendant sought to argue that an incidental consequence of the new statutory provisions on bad character evidence was that the police were now under a duty to carry out further investigations into the character of their witnesses, at any rate where the defence request this. This argument was rejected by the Divisional Court; the court said that the rules

---

[7] [2005] EWCA Crim 1091, [2005] 2 CrAppR 27 (401), **p 163 below**, at §2.
[8] *Chief Constables of West Yorkshire, South Yorkshire and North Wales v Information Commissioner*, Information Tribunal, 12 October 2005; available online at www.informationtribunal.gov.uk/decisions/information_tribunal_judgement_new.pdf
[9] *Paraskeva* (1982) 76 CrAppR 162; *Guney* [1998] 2 CrAppR 242.
[10] *Guney*, n 9 above.
[11] [2005] EWHC 2283 (Admin).

in relation to the duties of the police and CPS to seek out and disclose information bearing on the credibility of their witnesses are the same as they were before the CJA 2003 came into force.

Proving a Conviction

5.7 The standard procedure for proving that a person has been convicted (or acquitted) of an offence within the United Kingdom is to obtain a formal certificate from the court concerned. This is done under section 73 of the Police and Criminal Evidence Act 1984, which is as follows:

(1) Where in any proceedings the fact that a person has in the United Kingdom been convicted or acquitted of an offence otherwise than by a Service court is admissible in evidence, it may be proved by producing a certificate of conviction or, as the case may be, of acquittal relating to that offence, and proving that the person named in the certificate as having been convicted or acquitted of the offence is the person whose conviction or acquittal of the offence is to be proved.

(2) For the purposes of this section a certificate of conviction or of acquittal—

   (a) shall, as regards a conviction or acquittal on indictment, consist of a certificate, signed by the proper officer of the court where the conviction or acquittal took place, giving the substance and effect (omitting the formal parts) of the indictment and of the conviction or acquittal; and

   (b) shall, as regards a conviction or acquittal on a summary trial, consist of a copy of the conviction or of the dismissal of the information, signed by the proper officer of the court where the conviction or acquittal took place or by the proper officer of the court, if any, to which a memorandum of the conviction or acquittal was sent;

   and a document purporting to be a duly signed certificate of conviction or acquittal under this section shall be taken to be such a certificate unless the contrary is proved.

(3) In subsection (2) above 'proper officer' means—

   (a) in relation to a magistrates' court in England and Wales, the designated officer for the court; and

   (b) in relation to any other court, the clerk of the court, his deputy or any other person having custody of the court record.

(4) The method of proving a conviction or acquittal authorised by this section shall be in addition to and not to the exclusion of any other authorised manner of proving a conviction or acquittal.

5.8 Section 73(4) makes it plain that, in principle, convictions and acquittals may be proved in other ways as well: for example, by the defendant's admission. If other forms of evidence are used, however, the information they produce may be unreliable, and the court may decide to reject such evidence for that reason. The point arose in *Duggan*,[12] where the prosecution, in order to establish the defendant's conviction, had used material derived from the PNC. Confusion followed, because this material suggested that his previous conviction was for assault occasioning actual bodily harm, whereas the defence claimed that it was for common assault only: as was indeed the case, as became clear when a certificate of conviction was eventually obtained. The Court of Appeal rejected the defendant's argument that the judge should have refused to admit the evidence as unreliable, because the judge had admitted it on condition that the prosecution accepted the defence version of what the offence in issue was, and so no harm was done to him. But clearly, if the judge had admitted the evidence without imposing this condition, the outcome on appeal might have been different.[13]

5.9 Section 73 of PACE 1984 only applies to convictions imposed by courts in the United Kingdom: in other words, those sitting in England, Scotland and Northern Ireland.[14] It does not apply to convictions imposed in the Isle of Man or the Channel Islands—nor, a fortiori, to those imposed by foreign courts. At common law, convictions recorded by such courts were formally proved by producing a copy of the record authenticated by the seal of the court, plus further evidence that the seal was what it purported to be. Section 7 of the Evidence Act 1851 relaxed these requirements slightly as regards convictions imposed by courts in 'any foreign state or in any British colony.' Where this provision applies, the conviction may now be formally proved by producing a copy of the record, duly sealed, without the need to produce further evidence establishing the authenticity of the seal. But as the Channel Islands and the Isle of Man are neither 'foreign states' nor 'British colonies' they fall outside the scope of the provision, and in consequence the formal method for proving convictions imposed by Manx and Channel Island courts still presupposes separate proof of the authenticity of the seal.[15] Presumably, foreign convictions, like convictions from UK courts, may also be proved by other and less formal types of evidence;[16] but unless the other evidence produced takes the form of an admission from the defendant, difficult issues of reliability are likely to arise.

---

[12] Reported with *Edwards* [2005] EWCA Crim 1813, [2006] 1 CrAppR 3 (31), **p 169 below.**

[13] As in *Ainscough* (2006) 170 JPN 223 (CA, 14 March).

[14] By the Interpretation Act 1978 Sch 1, the term 'United Kingdom' means 'Great Britain and Northern Ireland.'

[15] *Archbold* (2006) §9-97.

[16] This is stated in the headnote to *Mauricia* [2002] 2 CrAppR 377; but the judgment does not in fact support the proposition, because the case was concerned with the problem not of proving foreign convictions, but proving the foreign conviction was actually imposed upon the person who is now before the English court.

5.10 Proving that an earlier court (whether British or foreign) imposed a conviction on a person of a given name does not, of course, conclusively establish that it was actually imposed on the person who is now before the court today. If the person now before the court disputes this, it will be necessary to produce further evidence establishing that the two people are really one and the same. In the context of proving the offence of driving whilst disqualified, it was once suggested that this must be done by one or other of three methods: a formal admission from the defendant under section 10 of the Criminal Justice Act 1967, comparison of fingerprints pursuant to section 99 of the Criminal Evidence Act 1948, or evidence from a person who was in court at the time the original conviction was imposed.[17] However, subsequent case law establishes that this may be done by 'any admissible evidence in the ordinary way'.[18]

Legal Effect of Proving a Conviction

National Convictions

5.11 To what extent, in law, does the fact of a conviction establish that the convicted person committed the offence? As regards UK convictions proved by using section 73 of the PACE 1984, the answer is provided by section 74, which, as amended by the CJA 2003,[19] is as follows:

(1) In any proceedings the fact that a person other than the accused has been convicted of an offence by or before any court in the United Kingdom or by a Service court outside the United Kingdom shall be admissible in evidence for the purpose of proving that that person committed that offence, where evidence of his having done so is admissible, whether or not any other evidence of his having committed that offence is given.

(2) In any proceedings in which by virtue of this section a person other than the accused is proved to have been convicted of an offence by or before any court in the United

---

[17] *R v Derwentside Justices, ex parte Heaviside* [1996] RTR 384.
[18] *Mauricia*, n 15 above, at 385; *West Yorkshire Probation Board v Boulter* [2005] EWHC 2342 Admin, [2006] 1 WLR 232; *Pattison v DPP* [2005] EWHC Admin 2938, 170 JPN 22; *Burns* [2006] EWCA Crim 617, cf *Moran v Crown Prosecution Service* (2000) 164 JP 562.
[19] CJA 2003 Sch 36, para 85 amended PACE 1984 s74(1) by removing the words 'where to do so is relevant to any issue in those proceedings, that that person committed that offence' and replaced them with the words 'that that person committed that offence, where evidence of his having done so is admissible.' Schedule 37 Part I removed the following words from s74(2): 'insofar as that evidence is relevant to any matter in issue in the proceedings for a reason other than a tendency to show in the accused a disposition to commit the kind of offence with which he is charged.' Both changes were brought into force on 15 December 2004, by the Criminal Justice Act 2003 (Commencement No 6 and Transitional Provisions) Order 2004, SI 2004/3033, which also brought into force the main provisions of the Act concerning evidence of bad character.

Kingdom or by a Service court outside the United Kingdom, he shall be taken to
have committed that offence unless the contrary is proved.

(3) In any proceedings where evidence is admissible of the fact that the accused has
committed an offence, if the accused is proved to have been convicted of the offence

(a) by or before any court in the United Kingdom; or
(b) by a Service court outside the United Kingdom,

he shall be taken to have committed that offence unless the contrary is proved.

(4) Nothing in this section shall prejudice—

(a) the admissibility in evidence of any conviction which would be admissible apart
from this section; or
(b) the operation of any enactment whereby a conviction or a finding of fact in any
proceedings is for the purposes of any other proceedings made conclusive evidence of any fact.

The effect of this provision is to create a rebuttable presumption that the person
who was convicted of the offence actually committed it. It is open to him, or to
anyone else, to claim that despite the conviction he did not, but anyone who makes
this claim bears the burden of persuading the court that the convicted person was
innocent.

5.12 Supplementary provisions are contained in PACE 1984 section 75:

(1) Where evidence that a person has been convicted of an offence is admissible by
virtue of section 74 above, then without prejudice to the reception of any other
admissible evidence for the purpose of identifying the facts on which the conviction
was based—

(a) the contents of any document which is admissible as evidence of the conviction;
and
(b) the contents of the information, complaint, indictment or charge-sheet on
which the person in question was convicted,

shall be admissible in evidence for that purpose.

(2) Where in any proceedings the contents of any document are admissible in evidence
by virtue of subsection (1) above, a copy of that document, or of the material part
of it, purporting to be certified or otherwise authenticated by or on behalf of the
court or authority having custody of that document shall be admissible in evidence
and shall be taken to be a true copy of that document or part unless the contrary is
shown.

(3) Nothing in any of the following—

(a) section 14 of the Powers of Criminal Courts (Sentencing) Act 2000 (under
which a conviction leading to probation or discharge is to be disregarded except
as mentioned in that section);
(b) section 247 of the Criminal Procedure (Scotland) Act 1995 (which makes similar provision in respect of convictions on indictment in Scotland); and

(c) section 8 of the Probation Act (Northern Ireland) 1950 (which corresponds to section 13 of the Powers of Criminal Courts Act 1973) or any legislation which is in force in Northern Ireland for the time being and corresponds to that section,

shall affect the operation of section 74 above; and for the purposes of that section any order made by a court of summary jurisdiction in Scotland under section 228 or section 246(3) of the said Act of 1995 shall be treated as a conviction.

(4) Nothing in section 74 above shall be construed as rendering admissible in any proceedings evidence of any conviction other than a subsisting one.

5.13 As regards defendants who have previous convictions, section 103(2) of the CJA 2003 is phrased so as to suggest that the mere fact that a person has been convicted of an offence establishes as a matter of law that he has a disposition to commit offences of that sort, and it could indeed be read in just this sense. I do not think that it should be, however. In principle, a conviction surely shows a disposition towards a certain type of criminal behaviour only to the extent that it causes us to believe that the defendant actually committed the offence of which he has a conviction from an earlier court, and it should be open to the defendant whose previous convictions are admitted under this provision to argue that, contrary to what might appear, he was innocent.

Foreign Convictions

5.14 Section 73 of PACE 1984, which creates a rebuttable presumption that the person who was convicted of the offence actually committed it, was enacted to reverse a common law rule known as 'the rule in *Hollington v Hewthorn*,[20] according to which a criminal conviction, so far from creating a presumption in a later case that the convicted person was guilty of the earlier offence, was *not even admissible as evidence* to that effect. Unfortunately, however, the provision is expressly limited to convictions imposed by UK courts. The consequence of this appears to be that, as regards foreign convictions, the rule in *Hollington v Hewthorn* survives and if a prosecutor sought to establish the defendant's propensity to commit an offence by proving a foreign conviction, the defendant could require the court to exclude the fact of the conviction and prove that he committed the offence by other means. In these days of increased travel, particularly within Europe, this result would be extremely inconvenient, and might persuade the courts to decide that the rule in *Hollington v Hewthorn* is now defunct.[21]

---

[20] [1943] KB 587.

[21] Or alternatively, it might persuade Parliament to give this messy corner of the law the attention it rather urgently deserves. (I am grateful to Ms Recorder Cherie Booth QC for drawing these issues to my attention.)

Previous Convictions: the Need for Details

5.15   As we have seen, when judges are required to make decisions about the admissibility of previous convictions, they will sometimes need to know the details in order to make a proper decision. If the prosecution seek to argue that the defendant's convictions for theft undermine his credibility on oath, for example, one relevant matter will be whether he pleaded guilty or not guilty, and if he pleaded not guilty, whether or not he gave evidence.[22] In *Hanson*,[23] the Court of Appeal said that the prosecution, when giving notice or making an application, should state whether it intends to rely on the mere fact of the conviction, or also on the circumstances of it.

5.16   Where is such information to be found? The prosecution may find the necessary details are supplied in the certificate of conviction and the supplementary documents admissible under sections 73–75 of PACE 1984. If they are not, then in principle they will have to prove them by producing other forms of legally admissible evidence. In practice, this will usually be either direct oral evidence from the witnesses to the earlier offence, or, if the witness is unavailable, a previous statement made by the witness, admissible as an exception to the hearsay rule by virtue of sections 114 and 116 of the CJA 2003.

5.17   Is it possible to circumvent this requirement by proving the underlying facts by producing information about the details (or alleged details) of the earlier offence or offences that the police have logged in their records? According to the Court of Appeal in *Humphris*,[24] the answer to this question is 'no.' In this case, the trial judge had admitted such evidence, relying on section 117 of the CJA 2003, which makes exceptions to the hearsay rule in relation to 'business and other documents.' This, said the Court of Appeal, was wrong: one of the requirements of section 117 is that the person who 'supplied the information' in the document had 'personal knowledge of the matters dealt with.' In the case of police records, the person who 'supplied the information' is the police officer who entered the details in the records—who in this case did not have 'personal knowledge' of them.

5.18   The details of the earlier offences may be disputed by the defence, and such disputes raise among other things the spectre of judges being asked to hear oral evidence when making preliminary rulings on the admissibility of bad character evidence. In *Hanson*, the Court of Appeal was anxious to discourage this:

---

[22] See *Hanson* [2005] EWCA Crim 824, [2005] 1 WLR 3169, **p 153 below**, at §13; and see §§4.44–4.45 above.
[23] See n 21 above.
[24] [2005] EWCA Crim 2030, (2005) 169 JP 441.

. . . in a conviction case the Crown needs to decide, at the time of giving notice of the application, whether it proposes to rely simply upon the fact of conviction or also upon the circumstances of it. The former may be enough when the circumstances of the conviction are sufficiently apparent from its description, to justify a finding that it can establish propensity, either to commit an offence of the kind charged or to be untruthful and that the requirements of sections 103(3) and 101(3) can, subject to any particular matter raised on behalf of the defendant, be satisfied. For example, a succession of convictions for dwelling-house burglary, where the same is now charged, may well call for no further evidence than proof of the fact of the convictions. But where, as will often be the case, the Crown needs and proposes to rely on the circumstances of the previous convictions, those circumstances and the manner in which they are to be proved must be set out in the application. There is a similar obligation of frankness upon the defendant, which will be reinforced by the general obligation contained in the new Criminal Procedure Rules to give active assistance to the court in its case management (see rule 3.3). Routine applications by defendants for disclosure of the circumstances of previous convictions are likely to be met by a requirement that the request be justified by identification of the reason why it is said that those circumstances may show the convictions to be inadmissible. We would expect the relevant circumstances of previous convictions generally to be capable of agreement, and that, subject to the trial judge's ruling as to admissibility, they will be put before the jury by way of admission. Even where the circumstances are genuinely in dispute, we would expect the minimum indisputable facts to be thus admitted. It will be very rare indeed for it to be necessary for the judge to hear evidence before ruling on admissibility under this Act.[25]

5.19 The admissibility or otherwise of an item of bad character evidence will depend on its relevance to particular issues and its probative value. In determining this, in principle the court is required by section 109 to make the decision on the assumption that the evidence is true (see §5.31 below). On the face of it, this provision could perhaps be read as requiring the court, in a case where the details of a past offence are disputed, to assume when ruling on admissibility that the prosecution version of events is correct. However, even if it is theoretically possible for the judge to circumvent the disputed issue in this way, it would not necessarily be sensible to do this, because if the judge did admit the evidence on this assumption, the defence might still adduce its own evidence at the trial to show the prosecution version of events is wrong.[26]

5.20 Where bad character evidence is admitted and the underlying facts of the previous misbehaviour are difficult to prove and seriously disputed, this is likely to result in disputed evidence about the details of the earlier offence being called at trial. Where this happens, the trial is certain to take longer and there is an obvious risk that the attention of the tribunal of fact will be diverted away from the

---

[25] [2005] EWCA Crim 824, [2005] 1 WLR 3169, **p 153 below**, at §17.
[26] I am grateful to Judge John Phillips for this point.

central issues. As previously mentioned,[27] the need to prevent too much time being spent on 'satellite issues' is something judges should bear in mind when an application to call bad character evidence is decided. As the Court of Appeal said in *Hanson*, 'Where past events are disputed the judge must take care not to permit the trial unreasonably to be diverted into an investigation of matters not charged in the indictment.'[28]

May Bad Character be Established by Proving a Previous Allegation, as Against a Previous Conviction?

5.21 There is no doubt that a person's bad character may be established by proving he has committed offences of which he has not been convicted, where this can be done by producing witnesses to give direct oral evidence alleging he committed them. Indeed, the House of Lords in *Z* held that this can be done where the defendant has not merely avoided conviction for the earlier offence, but has actually been tried for it and acquitted.[29] More recently, the Court of Appeal in *Smith*[30] held (unsurprisingly) that the same could be done where a prosecution for the earlier offence had been launched and then stayed as an abuse of process.

5.22 But can the prosecution (or the defence, where they wish to attack a prosecution witness) attempt to show that a person has a tendency towards a certain type of misbehaviour by producing, not witness evidence as to what he did on an earlier occasion, but merely evidence that on a previous occasion someone who is not to be called as a witness has made a complaint against him? In principle, I believe that the answer to this question is 'yes, sometimes.' However, there are serious difficulties.

5.23 The first is that the evidence of the previous allegation constitutes hearsay, as now defined by section 114 of the CJA 2003, because it would be 'a statement not made in oral evidence in the proceedings' and would be called 'as evidence of [a] matter stated in it': ie, to suggest that the person concerned did the thing which the previous complainant said he did. Against the argument that section 114 applies, it might be said that the statement would be used, not as evidence that the person did the thing he was alleged to have done, but as evidence of his tendency to do such things: but this must be wrong, because it only shows his tendency to do such

---

[27] See §§1.33–1.37 above.
[28] At §12.
[29] *R v Z* [2000] 2 AC 483.
[30] Reported together with *Edwards and Rowlands* [2005] EWCA Crim 3244, **p 230 below**.

things because it shows that, on at least one occasion, he actually did it. In principle, therefore, it would be admissible only if one of the conditions set out in section 114(1)(a)–(d) are met.[31]

5.24 Assuming that one of these conditions can be met—for example, that the person who made the complaint is not available and cannot be produced to give oral evidence—there is a further problem, in that when admissible hearsay is used in an attempt to show bad character the court is being asked to admit evidence which is doubly problematic: first, because it is hearsay, which the law traditionally regards with suspicion because it may be unreliable and is difficult to check, and secondly, because it is evidence of bad character, which the law traditionally regards with suspicion for fear that it will be given excessive weight. Of course, it is possible to imagine some circumstances in which such evidence could be both convincing and highly relevant, for example, where over a period of time a series of allegations have been made, all by different people, none of whom had any apparent motive to fantasise or lie. But in other cases, evidence of this sort will be of little weight and the courts would be wise to exclude it, even where it is potentially admissible: as the Court of Appeal suggested in *Bovell*, where the evidence in question was that a prosecution witness had once been accused of a malicious wounding by a person who, having made the accusation, had then withdrawn it.[32]

Requirement to Give Notice of Bad Character Evidence: the Criminal Procedure Rules

5.25 **Section 111** of the CJA 2003 creates a power to make Rules so far as may be 'necessary or expedient for the purposes of this Act' and sketches out a list of matters they should cover, at the head of which is a requirement for those wishing to adduce evidence of bad character to give notice. Rules were duly made, which are now to be found in Part 35 and Part 68.21 of the consolidated Criminal Procedure Rules. For the details, readers should consult the Rules, which are set out in Appendix III.

---

[31] Section 114(1) is as follows:

'(1) In criminal proceedings a statement not made in oral evidence in the proceedings is admissible as evidence of any matter stated if, but only if—

(a) any provision of this Chapter or any other statutory provision makes it admissible,
(b) any rule of law preserved by section 118 makes it admissible,
(c) all parties to the proceedings agree to it being admissible, or
(d) the court is satisfied that it is in the interests of justice for it to be admissible.'

[32] [2005] EWCA Crim 1091, [2005] 2 CrAppR 27 (401), **p 163 below**. In *Edwards and Rowlands* [2005] EWCA Crim 3244 (**p 230 below**) the Court of Appeal expressly said, at §1 (vii), that an allegation could sometimes be evidence of bad character.

5.26 In broad terms, they require a party wishing to adduce evidence of bad character, whether of the defendant or a non-defendant, and whether by calling evidence or by cross-examination, to give notice to the court and all other parties to the proceedings within 14 days of various 'trigger' events, which differ according to whether the case is to be heard in the Crown Court or in the magistrates' court. A party who wishes to oppose a non-defendant's bad character being introduced must give notice of his intention within 14 days of receiving the application to admit it, and a defendant who wishes to oppose the introduction of evidence of his own bad character must also give notice within 14 days. The form in which these notices are to be given, and the information they must contain, are set out in a Practice Direction, which is also set out in Appendix III.

5.27 Compliance with the notice requirements set out in the Rules are not mandatory, and Rule 35.8 gives the court a wide power to dispense with them. It is as follows:

The court may—

(a) allow a notice or application required under this rule to be given in a different form, or orally; or

(b) shorten a time-limit under this rule or extend it even after it has expired.

5.28 It is obviously necessary for the court to have power to waive the requirement for advance notice of bad character evidence, because there will be many cases in which the 'gateway' through which it becomes admissible is only opened at the trial: for example, where, at trial, the defendant makes an unexpected attack upon the character of another person, thereby opening 'gateway (g).'[33] But the court may, of course, allow bad character evidence to be given even where the requirements of notice could have been complied with, if it thinks the interests of justice require this.

5.29 But the courts should not waive the need to comply with the notice requirements too lightly, because they exist to serve a purpose: to give the side against which the evidence is to be called a proper chance to challenge it if it is inaccurate, and so to make sure that the decision of the court is based so far as possible on the truth and not on falsehood. Where the prosecution, without good reason, seeks to adduce evidence of a defendant's bad character without due notice, and the defence seriously wish to contest it but are unable to do so effectively because it is too late, the court should refuse to waive compliance with the time limits. Where, on the other hand, the defence are not prejudiced by the delay, the court is free to admit bad character evidence if it thinks it might help the court to reach a

---

[33] As happened in *Dowds*—see *Bovell and Dowds* [2005] EWCA Crim 1091, [2005] 2 CrAppR 27 (401), **p 163 below.**

factually accurate result, even though the notice requirements have not been complied with. In *R (on the application of Robinson v Sutton Coldfield Magistrates' Court*[34], the Divisional Court rejected the defence argument that the court should waive compliance with the notice requirements only where it found 'exceptional circumstances'.

Deciding Applications to Admit Bad Character Evidence and Applications for Such Evidence to be Excluded

5.30 This subject has been covered in the previous chapters of this book. To recapitulate:

(1) Evidence, or questions, revealing a *non-defendant's* 'bad character,' as restrictively defined in section 98, are admissible only with leave (§3.43–3.46 above).

(2) Evidence, or questions, revealing the 'bad character' (as so defined) of *a defendant* are admissible if any of the 'gateways' listed in section 101(1)(a)–(g) are open.

(3) Section 101(3) of the Act imposes on the court a duty to exclude evidence of the defendant's bad character that would otherwise be admissible through the 'gateways' provided by section 100(1)(d) and (g) where it appears to the court that admitting it would make the trial unfair; section 103(3) imposes a duty on the court to exclude evidence of the defendant's bad character otherwise admissible under section 103(2) if the court is satisfied that to apply section 103(2) would be unjust; and section 108(2) and (3) confer a more general discretion to exclude such evidence if the evidence relates to criminal convictions imposed on the defendant when he was under 14.

(4) As far as evidence of the defendant's bad character is concerned, admissibility is almost certainly subject to the court's general discretion to exclude prosecution evidence under section 78 of PACE 1984, and—to the extent that it adds anything to section 78—the court's common law discretion to exclude evidence that is more prejudicial than probative; but where such evidence passes the tests for admissibility contained in the Act, its exclusion under these general powers should not usually be necessary (see §§1.21–1.28 above).

(5) Objections to the admission of evidence of the defendant's bad character based on the European Convention on Human Rights and the Human Rights Act 1978 will usually be ill-founded (§§1.38–1.48 above).

---

[34] [2006] EWHC 307 Admin, (2006) 170 JPN 83.

Assumption of Truth in Assessment of Relevance or Probative Value

5.31 In deciding whether to admit evidence of bad character, sections 100 to 106 of the Act require the court to make decisions about whether such evidence is 'relevant' and 'important.' In making such a decision, **section 109** requires the court to assume that the evidence is true, unless its falsehood is very obvious:

> (1) Subject to subsection (2), a reference in this Chapter to the relevance or probative value of evidence is a reference to its relevance or probative value on the assumption that it is true.
> (2) In assessing the relevance or probative value of an item of evidence for any purpose of this Chapter, a court need not assume that the evidence is true if it appears, on the basis of any material before the court (including any evidence it decides to hear on the matter), that no court or jury could reasonably find it to be true.[35]

Duty to Stop the Case because the Evidence is 'Contaminated'

5.32 The basic rule is that the weight (if any) to be given to any piece of evidence is a matter for the jury, not the judge. So, if the prosecution evidence, if believed, shows the defendant to be guilty, the judge should not stop the case merely because he finds it unconvincing. As the Court of Appeal held in *Galbraith*,[36] the judge who finds the prosecution evidence unconvincing should only stop the case where he or she 'comes to the conclusion that the prosecution evidence, taken at its highest, is such that a jury properly directed could not properly convict upon it.'

5.33 To this rule, there are a number of exceptions where the judge is required or permitted to stop the case because he considers the prosecution evidence to be of poor quality, notably where it consists of eye-witness identification.[37] To these exceptions, the CJA 2003 adds a new one relating to evidence of bad character.[38] Where the case against the defendant consists of a series of incidents, described by a series of witnesses, the court must stop the case if it comes to the conclusion that the witnesses have colluded, or that their evidence is the result of suggestion, to

---

[35] Section 109 confirms the position under the previous law: see *R v H* [1995] 2 AC 596.
[36] (1981) 73 CrAppR 124.
[37] *Turnbull* [1977] QB 224; and also where it consists of nothing but the extra-judicial confession of a person who is mentally handicapped: *Mackenzie* (1996) 93 CrAppR 98.
[38] And, by s125, a second new one in relation to unconvincing hearsay.

the point where a conviction on the evidence would be unsafe. **Section 107** is as follows:

(1) If on a defendant's trial before a judge and jury for an offence—

    (a) evidence of his bad character has been admitted under any of paragraphs (c) to (g) of section 101(1), and

    (b) the court is satisfied at any time after the close of the case for the prosecution that—

        (i) the evidence is contaminated, and

        (ii) the contamination is such that, considering the importance of the evidence to the case against the defendant, his conviction of the offence would be unsafe,

the court must either direct the jury to acquit the defendant of the offence or, if it considers that there ought to be a retrial, discharge the jury.

(2) Where—

    (a) a jury is directed under subsection (1) to acquit a defendant of an offence, and

    (b) the circumstances are such that, apart from this subsection, the defendant could if acquitted of that offence be found guilty of another offence,

the defendant may not be found guilty of that other offence if the court is satisfied as mentioned in subsection (1)(b) in respect of it.

(3) If—

    (a) a jury is required to determine under section 4A(2) of the Criminal Procedure (Insanity) Act 1964 (c. 84) whether a person charged on an indictment with an offence did the act or made the omission charged,

    (b) evidence of the person's bad character has been admitted under any of paragraphs (c) to (g) of section 101(1), and

    (c) the court is satisfied at any time after the close of the case for the prosecution that—

        (i) the evidence is contaminated, and

        (ii) the contamination is such that, considering the importance of the evidence to the case against the person, a finding that he did the act or made the omission would be unsafe,

the court must either direct the jury to acquit the defendant of the offence or, if it considers that there ought to be a rehearing, discharge the jury.

(4) This section does not prejudice any other power a court may have to direct a jury to acquit a person of an offence or to discharge a jury.

(5) For the purposes of this section a person's evidence is contaminated where—

    (a) as a result of an agreement or understanding between the person and one or more others, or

    (b) as a result of the person being aware of anything alleged by one or more others whose evidence may be, or has been, given in the proceedings, the evidence is false or misleading in any respect, or is different from what it would otherwise have been.

5.34 This provision comes from the Law Commission, which thought the existing law did not provide sufficient safeguards against the problem of 'contaminated evidence' in such cases. In *R v H* the House of Lords took the position that the question whether the evidence was 'contaminated' was a matter that affected its weight, and therefore a matter for the jury; where the possibility of collusion had been raised at the trial, the proper course was for the judge to leave the case to the jury, with a direction not to accept the evidence unless satisfied that it was reliable and not tainted by collusion. The judge, they said, is entitled 'to rule it out as providing a basis for corroboration only if no reasonable jury could accept it as reliable.'[39] The Law Commission, by contrast, thought that where the judge himself was satisfied that there had been 'contamination' of the evidence, he should be required to stop the case.

5.35 Unfortunately the provision is not clearly drafted—and has the potential to cause difficulty and confusion as a result. One of the obscurities is the meaning of 'contaminated': an expression that section 107(5) does little to clarify. The word 'contaminated' and what is now section 107(5) both originate from the Law Commission's Report,[40] at p 223 of which the following explanation is given:

> By virtue of subsection (5), evidence might be 'contaminated' as a result of: deliberate fabrication of allegations resulting from an agreement between witnesses; concoction of an allegation by one person (no conspiracy); collusion between witnesses to make their evidence sound more credible falling short of concoction of allegations; deliberate alteration of evidence or unconscious alteration of evidence, resulting from having become aware of what the evidence of another will be or has been.

From this, it seems that evidence can be 'contaminated' by accident, as well as by design.

5.36 Although section 107 is very long, its scope is in fact comparatively narrow: as the Court of Appeal pointed out in *Renda*, where it said:

> We are . . . concerned to ensure that section 107 should not be misused. There will, of course, be occasions when counsel is justified in submitting that a conviction would be unsafe because evidence admitted under section 101(1)(c)–(g) proved to be contaminated. That, however, does not provide any justification for a submission which, in truth, is no more than a reiteration of the arguments advanced by counsel against the admission of this evidence. Section 107 deals with a particular situation where the evidence of 'bad character' has been admitted and proves to be false or misleading in the circumstances described in section 107(5).[41]

---

[39] Per Lord Mackay [1995] 2 AC 596, at p612.
[40] *Evidence of Bad Character in Criminal Proceedings* (Law Com no 273, Cm 5257, October 2001).
[41] [2005] EWCA Crim 2826, at §27.

5.37 By section 107(1)(b), the duty that section 107 imposes on the judge to stop the case only arises where 'the court is satisfied . . . that the evidence *is* contaminated.' The court has no duty—and indeed no power—to stop the case merely because it thinks the evidence *may be* affected by collusion or suggestion. Where the court is satisfied that the evidence is contaminated, then it must consider 'the importance of the evidence to the case against the defendant.' If it concludes that its importance is such that a conviction based wholly or partly on such evidence would be unsafe, it must stop the case.

5.38 Where the issue of suggestion or collusion has been raised, but the judge is not persuaded that the bad character evidence has been contaminated in this way, the case should be left to the jury with an appropriate warning; and, similarly, if the judge takes the view that the contamination is not such as to make a conviction on the evidence unsafe.

5.39 Section 107 only applies to a situation where the evidence is evidence of 'bad character' as defined by section 98, and as we have seen, section 98 excludes from the definition of 'bad character' any evidence which 'has to do with the alleged facts of the offence with which the defendant is charged.' In the light of this, it clearly applies where D is prosecuted for an offence against V1, and the prosecution adduce as supportive evidence the similar incidents described by W1 and W2, in respect of whom D has not been charged. But what about the situation where D faces charges in relation to W1 and W2 as well? Is the evidence in relation to W1 and W2 then evidence about 'the alleged facts of the offence,' and therefore outside the definition of 'bad character' in section 98, and hence outside the scope of section 107? By reason of section 112(2), the answer is 'no': section 107 does indeed apply here. By section 112(2):

> Where a defendant is charged with two or more offences in the same criminal proceedings, this Chapter (except section 101(3)) has effect as if each offence were charged in separate proceedings; and references to the offence with which the defendant is charged are to be read accordingly.

5.40 Under section 107, the judge's duty to stop the case arises irrespective of whether there has been a submission by the defence. However, by section 107(1), the scope of the section is expressly limited to jury trials. So it would not apply to a trial before judge alone under Part 7 of the Act.

The Judge's Power to Stop the Case for Other Reasons

5.41 Of course, it must be remembered that the judge at a jury trial has various powers to stop a case at common law, quite apart from the limited power conferred by section 107. In particular, the judge has the power to discharge the jury where a piece of damaging evidence has been let in which should have been excluded; he may exercise this power on his own initiative, or on the application of the defence, and if the defendant is unrepresented the judge must tell him of his right to apply.[42] Where this situation arises, the judge has a discretion: he may decide to discharge the jury, or he may decide to let the trial proceed and warn the jury against acting on the evidence when he sums up. In deciding which course to take, he will have to assess the damage the inadmissible evidence is likely to cause, and this will depend both on the nature of the inadmissible evidence and the strength of the rest of the evidence. In practice, the Court of Appeal will usually respect the judge's decision. In *Arthurton v The Queen*,[43] however, the Privy Council quashed a conviction when, at a trial for unlawful sexual intercourse in which the prosecution case consisted almost entirely of the uncorroborated evidence of the complainant, the jury was improperly informed that a similar accusation had been made against him in the past; here, they thought, the prejudice arising from the inadmissible evidence could not be eliminated by a judicial warning.[44] By contrast, in *Edwards and Rowlands*,[45] the Court of Appeal upheld a conviction where, at a trial for drug offences, evidence of one defendant's previous convictions for offences of minimal relevance had been improperly admitted, the Court of Appeal taking the view that they were 'insignificant in relation to the real issue in the case,' and that the judge had cured the problem by telling the jury to ignore them.[46]

5.42 Whether the judge finds himself in this position depends, of course, on whether the evidence of bad character was admissible or not. Whilst in general terms the admissibility of bad character evidence is something that can and should be resolved ahead of trial, there are some cases in which its relevance and admissibility may depend on matters that may or may not arise in the course of it. Where the judge foresees this, he may decide to delay a ruling on the admissibility of the defendant's previous convictions until towards the end of the prosecution case.

---

[42] See generally *Archbold* (2006) §4-260; *Blackstone's Criminal Practice* (2006) §D12.21.

[43] [2004] UKPC 25, [2005] 1 WLR 949.

[44] As to whether the previous complaint might now be admissible in England as part of the prosecution case, see §5.21–5.24 above.

[45] [2005] EWCA Crim 3244.

[46] To similar effect see also *Enright*, reported together with *Edwards and Rowlands*, n 44 above.

5.43 There are also situations in which the judge can properly stop the case, where after hearing the evidence for both sides he or she believes the totality of the evidence to be so weak that it would not be safe to leave the case to the jury.[47] Earlier in this book it was suggested that, when deciding whether evidence of the defendant's bad character should be admitted, an important consideration is that evidence of this sort should not be used to bolster up a case which is inherently weak (§§1.29–1.32 above). I believe that the same principle should be born in mind at the other end of a trial, when the evidence for both sides has been heard. If evidence of the defendant's bad character was originally admitted to supplement what appeared to be a solid case, and by the end of the trial the other pieces of evidence have been 'blown out of the water,' it would be proper for the judge to stop the case if evidence of the defendant's disposition to commit the sort of offence of which he is accused is the only evidence which remains intact.

Reasons for Decisions

5.44 When courts make rules in relation to evidence of bad character, the CJA 2003 requires them to give reasons. This is provided by **section 110**, which is as follows:

(1) Where the court makes a relevant ruling—

  (a) it must state in open court (but in the absence of the jury, if there is one) its reasons for the ruling;
  (b) if it is a magistrates' court, it must cause the ruling and the reasons for it to be entered in the register of the court's proceedings.

(2) In this section 'relevant ruling' means—

  (a) a ruling on whether an item of evidence is evidence of a person's bad character;
  (b) a ruling on whether an item of such evidence is admissible under section 100 or 101 (including a ruling on an application under section 101(3));
  (c) a ruling under section 107.

Directing Juries

5.45 To guide judges in directing juries, the Judicial Studies Board Specimen Directions have been revised to take account of the character evidence provisions of the CJA 2003: see Specimen Directions 20, 24 and 24A, which are set out in Appendix IV, for completeness, together with Specimen Direction 23 (on the

---

[47] In particular, where it depends on eye-witness identification.

defendant's good character). For the details, reference should be made to the Specimen Directions themselves.

5.46 In outline, Specimen Direction 24 in relation to evidence of the defendant's bad character consists of two elements: first, a general warning against convicting a defendant simply because he is of bad character, and secondly, an explanation to the jury of specific matters in respect of which they may properly find the bad character evidence to be relevant. Most of the seven 'gateways' set out in section 101(1) presuppose a purpose.[48] Where this is so, the judge should first explain to the jury how the evidence is relevant in this respect. Foreshadowing the Court of Appeal decision in *Highton*,[49] Specimen Direction 24 (**see Appendix IV below**) accepts that evidence of the defendant's bad character which is admitted via a 'gateway' that presupposes a particular purpose may also be used in relation to some other issue to which it is relevant as well: for example, evidence admitted via 'gateway (g)' where the defendant has made an attack on another person's charac-ter may shed light not only on the credibility of the defendant when he speaks ill of others, but also on his propensity to commit the type of offence with which he is now charged. Where this is so, the judge should direct the jury on the relevance of the evidence to this issue too.

5.47 In *Chowan*,[50] the Court of Appeal described Judge Mort's direction to the jury in that case as 'impeccable'[51] and commended it as an example. It is set out in full in the Court of Appeal judgment, printed with the other leading cases in Appendix V.

5.48 According to Specimen Direction 23A, a direction about the bad character of a non-defendant should depend on the reason for which the evidence was admit-ted. If it was admitted as necessary to understand the background to the case, or because it is relevant to a specific issue, its relevance in these ways ought to be explained. If the non-defendant is a witness, and the bad character evidence has been admitted in relation to his credibility, the direction should explain that per-sons whose characters are bad may be less likely to tell the truth than those whose characters are good, but it does not follow that they are incapable of doing so.[52]

---

[48] But not gateways (a) and (b); gateway (a), it will be remembered, is where it is admitted by agree-ment and gateway (b) is where it is brought in by the defence.

[49] [2005] EWCA Crim 1985, [2005] 1 WLR 3472, **p 183 below**.

[50] Reported with *Edwards* [2005] EWCA Crim 1813, [2006] 1 CrAppR 3 (31), **p 169 below**, at §77.

[51] Subject to one minor point on which the law was differently stated subsequently in *Hanson* [2005] EWCA Crim 824, [2005] 1 WLR 3169, **p 153 below**.

[52] And even witnesses who lie in one part of their evidence may still be truthful in another: see *EPI Inc v Symphony plc* [2004] EWHC 2945 (Ch), [2005] 1 WLR 3456.

Appendix I

Criminal Justice Act 2003 Part 11, Chapter 1

'Bad character'

98.—References in this Chapter to evidence of a person's 'bad character' are to evidence of, or of a disposition towards, misconduct on his part, other than evidence which—

(a) has to do with the alleged facts of the offence with which the defendant is charged, or

(b) is evidence of misconduct in connection with the investigation or prosecution of that offence.

Abolition of common law rules

99.—(1) The common law rules governing the admissibility of evidence of bad character in criminal proceedings are abolished.

(2) Subsection (1) is subject to section 118(1) in so far as it preserves the rule under which in criminal proceedings a person's reputation is admissible for the purposes of proving his bad character.

Non-defendant's bad character

100.—(1) In criminal proceedings evidence of the bad character of a person other than the defendant is admissible if and only if—

(a) it is important explanatory evidence,

(b) it has substantial probative value in relation to a matter which—

    (i)   is a matter in issue in the proceedings, and

    (ii) is of substantial importance in the context of the case as a whole,

    or

(c) all parties to the proceedings agree to the evidence being admissible.

(2) For the purposes of subsection (1)(a) evidence is important explanatory evidence if—

(a) without it, the court or jury would find it impossible or difficult properly to understand other evidence in the case, and
(b) its value for understanding the case as a whole is substantial.

(3) In assessing the probative value of evidence for the purposes of subsection (1)(b) the court must have regard to the following factors (and to any others it considers relevant)—

(a) the nature and number of the events, or other things, to which the evidence relates;
(b) when those events or things are alleged to have happened or existed;
(c) where—

(i) the evidence is evidence of a person's misconduct, and
(ii) it is suggested that the evidence has probative value by reason of similarity between that misconduct and other alleged misconduct,

the nature and extent of the similarities and the dissimilarities between each of the alleged instances of misconduct;
(d) where—

(i) the evidence is evidence of a person's misconduct,
(ii) it is suggested that that person is also responsible for the misconduct charged, and
(iii) the identity of the person responsible for the misconduct charged is disputed,

the extent to which the evidence shows or tends to show that the same person was responsible each time.

(4) Except where subsection (1)(c) applies, evidence of the bad character of a person other than the defendant must not be given without leave of the court.

Defendant's bad character

101.—(1) In criminal proceedings evidence of the defendant's bad character is admissible if, but only if—

(a) all parties to the proceedings agree to the evidence being admissible,
(b) the evidence is adduced by the defendant himself or is given in answer to a question asked by him in cross-examination and intended to elicit it,
(c) it is important explanatory evidence,
(d) it is relevant to an important matter in issue between the defendant and the prosecution,

(e) it has substantial probative value in relation to an important matter in issue between the defendant and a co-defendant,

(f) it is evidence to correct a false impression given by the defendant, or

(g) the defendant has made an attack on another person's character.

(2) Sections 102 to 106 contain provision supplementing subsection (1).

(3) The court must not admit evidence under subsection (1)(d) or (g) if, on an application by the defendant to exclude it, it appears to the court that the admission of the evidence would have such an adverse effect on the fairness of the proceedings that the court ought not to admit it.

(4) On an application to exclude evidence under subsection (3) the court must have regard, in particular, to the length of time between the matters to which that evidence relates and the matters which form the subject of the offence charged.

'Important explanatory evidence'

102.—For the purposes of section 101(1)(c) evidence is important explanatory evidence if—

(a) without it, the court or jury would find it impossible or difficult properly to understand other evidence in the case, and

(b) its value for understanding the case as a whole is substantial.

'Matter in issue between the defendant and the prosecution'

103.—(1) For the purposes of section 101(1)(d) the matters in issue between the defendant and the prosecution include—

(a) the question whether the defendant has a propensity to commit offences of the kind with which he is charged, except where his having such a propensity makes it no more likely that he is guilty of the offence;

(b) the question whether the defendant has a propensity to be untruthful, except where it is not suggested that the defendant's case is untruthful in any respect.

(2) Where subsection (1)(a) applies, a defendant's propensity to commit offences of the kind with which he is charged may (without prejudice to any other way of doing so) be established by evidence that he has been convicted of—

(a) an offence of the same description as the one with which he is charged, or

(b) an offence of the same category as the one with which he is charged.

(3) Subsection (2) does not apply in the case of a particular defendant if the court is satisfied, by reason of the length of time since the conviction or for any other reason, that it would be unjust for it to apply in his case.

(4) For the purposes of subsection (2)—

(a) two offences are of the same description as each other if the statement of the offence in a written charge or indictment would, in each case, be in the same terms;
(b) two offences are of the same category as each other if they belong to the same category of offences prescribed for the purposes of this section by an order made by the Secretary of State.

(5) A category prescribed by an order under subsection (4)(b) must consist of offences of the same type.

(6) Only prosecution evidence is admissible under section 101(1)(d).

'Matter in issue between the defendant and a co-defendant'

104.—(1) Evidence which is relevant to the question whether the defendant has a propensity to be untruthful is admissible on that basis under section 101(1)(e) only if the nature or conduct of his defence is such as to undermine the co-defendant's defence.

(2) Only evidence—

(a) which is to be (or has been) adduced by the co-defendant, or
(b) which a witness is to be invited to give (or has given) in cross-examination by the co-defendant,

is admissible under section 101(1)(e).

'Evidence to correct a false impression'

105.—(1) For the purposes of section 101(1)(f)—

(a) the defendant gives a false impression if he is responsible for the making of an express or implied assertion which is apt to give the court or jury a false or misleading impression about the defendant;
(b) evidence to correct such an impression is evidence which has probative value in correcting it.

(2) A defendant is treated as being responsible for the making of an assertion if—

(a) the assertion is made by the defendant in the proceedings (whether or not in evidence given by him),
(b) the assertion was made by the defendant—

(i)   on being questioned under caution, before charge, about the offence with which he is charged, or

(ii)   on being charged with the offence or officially informed that he might be prosecuted for it,

and evidence of the assertion is given in the proceedings,

(c) the assertion is made by a witness called by the defendant,

(d) the assertion is made by any witness in cross-examination in response to a question asked by the defendant that is intended to elicit it, or is likely to do so, or

(e) the assertion was made by any person out of court, and the defendant adduces evidence of it in the proceedings.

(3) A defendant who would otherwise be treated as responsible for the making of an assertion shall not be so treated if, or to the extent that, he withdraws it or disassociates himself from it.

(4) Where it appears to the court that a defendant, by means of his conduct (other than the giving of evidence) in the proceedings, is seeking to give the court or jury an impression about himself that is false or misleading, the court may if it appears just to do so treat the defendant as being responsible for the making of an assertion which is apt to give that impression.

(5) In subsection (4) 'conduct' includes appearance or dress.

(6) Evidence is admissible under section 101(1)(f) only if it goes no further than is necessary to correct the false impression.

(7) Only prosecution evidence is admissible under section 101(1)(f).

'Attack on another person's character'

106.—(1) For the purposes of section 101(1)(g) a defendant makes an attack on another person's character if—

(a) he adduces evidence attacking the other person's character,

(b) he (or any legal representative appointed under section 38(4) of the Youth Justice and Criminal Evidence Act 1999 (c. 23) to cross-examine a witness in his interests) asks questions in cross-examination that are intended to elicit such evidence, or are likely to do so, or

(c) evidence is given of an imputation about the other person made by the defendant—

(i)   on being questioned under caution, before charge, about the offence with which he is charged, or

(ii)   on being charged with the offence or officially informed that he might be prosecuted for it.

(2) In subsection (1) 'evidence attacking the other person's character' means evidence to the effect that the other person—

(a) has committed an offence (whether a different offence from the one with which the defendant is charged or the same one), or
(b) has behaved, or is disposed to behave, in a reprehensible way;

and 'imputation about the other person' means an assertion to that effect.

(3) Only prosecution evidence is admissible under section 101(1)(g).

Stopping the case where evidence contaminated

107.—(1) If on a defendant's trial before a judge and jury for an offence—

(a) evidence of his bad character has been admitted under any of paragraphs (c) to (g) of section 101(1), and
(b) the court is satisfied at any time after the close of the case for the prosecution that—

  (i) the evidence is contaminated, and
  (ii) the contamination is such that, considering the importance of the evidence to the case against the defendant, his conviction of the offence would be unsafe,

the court must either direct the jury to acquit the defendant of the offence or, if it considers that there ought to be a retrial, discharge the jury.

(2) Where—

(a) a jury is directed under subsection (1) to acquit a defendant of an offence, and
(b) the circumstances are such that, apart from this subsection, the defendant could if acquitted of that offence be found guilty of another offence,

the defendant may not be found guilty of that other offence if the court is satisfied as mentioned in subsection (1)(b) in respect of it.

(3) If—

(a) a jury is required to determine under section 4A(2) of the Criminal Procedure (Insanity) Act 1964 (c. 84) whether a person charged on an indictment with an offence did the act or made the omission charged,
(b) evidence of the person's bad character has been admitted under any of paragraphs (c) to (g) of section 101(1), and
(c) the court is satisfied at any time after the close of the case for the prosecution that—

  (i) the evidence is contaminated, and

(ii) the contamination is such that, considering the importance of the evidence to the case against the person, a finding that he did the act or made the omission would be unsafe,

the court must either direct the jury to acquit the defendant of the offence or, if it considers that there ought to be a rehearing, discharge the jury.

(4) This section does not prejudice any other power a court may have to direct a jury to acquit a person of an offence or to discharge a jury.

(5) For the purposes of this section a person's evidence is contaminated where—

(a) as a result of an agreement or understanding between the person and one or more others, or

(b) as a result of the person being aware of anything alleged by one or more others whose evidence may be, or has been, given in the proceedings,

the evidence is false or misleading in any respect, or is different from what it would otherwise have been.

Offences committed by defendant when a child

108.—(1) Section 16(2) and (3) of the Children and Young Persons Act 1963 (c. 37) (offences committed by person under 14 disregarded for purposes of evidence relating to previous convictions) shall cease to have effect.

(2) In proceedings for an offence committed or alleged to have been committed by the defendant when aged 21 or over, evidence of his conviction for an offence when under the age of 14 is not admissible unless—

(a) both of the offences are triable only on indictment, and

(b) the court is satisfied that the interests of justice require the evidence to be admissible.

(3) Subsection (2) applies in addition to section 101.

Assumption of truth in assessment of relevance or probative value

109.—(1) Subject to subsection (2), a reference in this Chapter to the relevance or probative value of evidence is a reference to its relevance or probative value on the assumption that it is true.

(2) In assessing the relevance or probative value of an item of evidence for any purpose of this Chapter, a court need not assume that the evidence is true if it appears, on the basis of any material before the court (including any evidence it

decides to hear on the matter), that no court or jury could reasonably find it to be true.

Court's duty to give reasons for rulings

110.—(1) Where the court makes a relevant ruling—

(a) it must state in open court (but in the absence of the jury, if there is one) its reasons for the ruling;
(b) if it is a magistrates' court, it must cause the ruling and the reasons for it to be entered in the register of the court's proceedings.

(2) In this section 'relevant ruling' means—

(a) a ruling on whether an item of evidence is evidence of a person's bad character;
(b) a ruling on whether an item of such evidence is admissible under section 100 or 101 (including a ruling on an application under section 101(3));
(c) a ruling under section 107.

Rules of court

111.—(1) Rules of court may make such provision as appears to the appropriate authority to be necessary or expedient for the purposes of this Act; and the appropriate authority is the authority entitled to make the rules.

(2) The rules may, and, where the party in question is the prosecution, must, contain provision requiring a party who—

(a) proposes to adduce evidence of a defendant's bad character, or
(b) proposes to cross-examine a witness with a view to eliciting such evidence,

to serve on the defendant such notice, and such particulars of or relating to the evidence, as may be prescribed.

(3) The rules may provide that the court or the defendant may, in such circumstances as may be prescribed, dispense with a requirement imposed by virtue of subsection (2).

(4) In considering the exercise of its powers with respect to costs, the court may take into account any failure by a party to comply with a requirement imposed by virtue of subsection (2) and not dispensed with by virtue of subsection (3).

(5) The rules may—

(a) limit the application of any provision of the rules to prescribed circumstances;
(b) subject any provision of the rules to prescribed exceptions;
(c) make different provision for different cases or circumstances.

(6) Nothing in this section prejudices the generality of any enactment conferring power to make rules of court; and no particular provision of this section prejudices any general provision of it.

(7) In this section—

'prescribed' means prescribed by rules of court.

Interpretation of Chapter 1

112.—(1) In this Chapter—

'bad character' is to be read in accordance with section 98;

'criminal proceedings' means criminal proceedings in relation to which the strict rules of evidence apply;

'defendant', in relation to criminal proceedings, means a person charged with an offence in those proceedings; and 'co-defendant', in relation to a defendant, means a person charged with an offence in the same proceedings;

'important matter' means a matter of substantial importance in the context of the case as a whole;

'misconduct' means the commission of an offence or other reprehensible behaviour;

'offence' includes a service offence;

'probative value', and 'relevant' (in relation to an item of evidence), are to be read in accordance with section 109;

'prosecution evidence' means evidence which is to be (or has been) adduced by the prosecution, or which a witness is to be invited to give (or has given) in cross-examination by the prosecution;

'service offence' means an offence under the Army Act 1955 (3 & 4 Eliz. 2 c. 18), the Air Force Act 1955 (3 & 4 Eliz. 2 c. 19) or the Naval Discipline Act 1957 (c. 53);

'written charge' has the same meaning as in section 29 and also includes an information.

(2) Where a defendant is charged with two or more offences in the same criminal proceedings, this Chapter (except section 101(3)) has effect as if each offence were charged in separate proceedings; and references to the offence with which the defendant is charged are to be read accordingly.

(3) Nothing in this Chapter affects the exclusion of evidence—

(a) under the rule in section 3 of the Criminal Procedure Act 1865 (c. 18) against a party impeaching the credit of his own witness by general evidence of bad character,

(b) under section 41 of the Youth Justice and Criminal Evidence Act 1999 (c. 23) (restriction on evidence or questions about complainant's sexual history), or

(c) on grounds other than the fact that it is evidence of a person's bad character.

Armed forces

113.—Schedule 6 (armed forces) has effect.

Appendix II

Criminal Justice Act 2003 (Categories of Offences) Order 2004, SI 2004/3346

Made	*15th December 2004*
Coming into force	*29th December 2004*

The Secretary of State, in exercise of the powers conferred upon him by section 103(4)(b) of the Criminal Justice Act 2003[1] hereby makes the following Order, a draft of which has been laid before and approved by a resolution of each House of Parliament:

1.—(1) This Order may be cited as the Criminal Justice Act 2003 (Categories of Offences) Order 2004 and shall come into force 14 days after the day on which it is made or on the day that sections 98 to 110 of the 2003 Act (Evidence of Bad Character) come into force, whichever is later.

(2) In this Order 'the 2003 Act' means the Criminal Justice Act 2003.

2.—(1) The categories of offences set out in Parts 1 and 2 of the Schedule to this Order are hereby prescribed for the purposes of section 103(4)(b) of the 2003 Act.

(2) Two offences are of the same category as each other if they are included in the same Part of the Schedule.

SCHEDULE

Article 2

PRESCRIBED CATEGORIES OF OFFENCES

PART 1 THEFT CATEGORY

1.—An offence under section 1 of the Theft Act 1968[2] (theft).
2.—An offence under section 8 of that Act (robbery).

---

[1] 2003 c. 44.
[2] 1968 c. 60.

3.—An offence under section 9(1)(a) of that Act[3] (burglary) if it was committed with intent to commit an offence of stealing anything in the building or part of a building in question.

4.—An offence under section 9(1)(b) of that Act (burglary) if the offender stole or attempted to steal anything in the building or that part of it.

5.—An offence under section 10 of that Act (aggravated burglary) if the offender committed a burglary described in paragraph 3 or 4 of this Part of the Schedule.

6.—An offence under section 12 of that Act[4] (taking motor vehicle or other conveyance without authority).

7.—An offence under section 12A of that Act[5] (aggravated vehicle-taking).

8.—An offence under section 22 of that Act (handling stolen goods).

9.—An offence under section 25 of that Act (going equipped for stealing).

10.—An offence under section 3 of the Theft Act 1978[6] (making off without payment).

11.—An offence of—

(a) aiding, abetting, counselling, procuring or inciting the commission of an offence specified in this Part of this Schedule; or
(b) attempting to commit an offence so specified.

PART 2 SEXUAL OFFENCES (PERSONS UNDER THE AGE OF 16) CATEGORY

1.—An offence under section 1 of the Sexual Offences Act 1956[7] (rape) if it was committed in relation to a person under the age of 16.

2.—An offence under section 5 of the Sexual Offences Act 1956[8] (intercourse with a girl under thirteen).

---

[3] Section 9 was amended by sections 139 and 140 of and paragraph 17 of Schedule 6 and Schedule 7 to the Sexual Offences Act 2003 (c. 42); section 26(2) of the Criminal Justice Act 1991 (c. 53) and section 168(2) and paragraph 26 of Schedule 10 to the Criminal Justice and Public Order Act 1994 (c. 33).
[4] Section 12 was amended by section 37(1) of the Criminal Justice Act 1988 (c. 33); section 119(2) and Part I of Schedule 7 to the Police and Criminal Evidence Act 1984 (c. 60); section 37 of the Vehicles (Crime) Act 2001 (c. 3).
[5] Section 12A was inserted by section 2(1) of the Aggravated Vehicle-Taking Act 1992 (c. 11) and was amended by section 285(1) of the Criminal Justice Act 2003 (c. 44).
[6] 1978 c. 31.
[7] 1956 c. 69; section 1 was substituted by section 142 of the Criminal Justice and Public Order Act 1994 (c. 33).
[8] Sections 5 to 7 and 10 to 15 of the Sexual Offences Act 1956 (c. 69); section 54 of the Criminal Law Act 1977 (c. 45); section 1 of the Indecency with Children Act 1960 (c. 33); section 128 of the Mental Health Act 1959 (c. 72) and section 3 of the Sexual Offences (Amendment) Act 2000 (c. 44) were repealed by sections 139 and 140 of and paragraph 11(a) of Schedule 6 and Schedule 7 to the Sexual Offences Act 2003 (c. 42).

3.—An offence under section 6 of that Act[9] (intercourse with a girl under sixteen).

4.—An offence under section 7 of that Act[10] (intercourse with a defective) if it was committed in relation to a person under the age of 16.

5.—An offence under section 10 of that Act (incest by a man) if it was committed in relation to a person under the age of 16.

6.—An offence under section 11 of that Act (incest by a woman) if it was committed in relation to a person under the age of 16.

7.—An offence under section 12 of that Act[11] (buggery) if it was committed in relation to a person under the age of 16.

8.—An offence under section 13 of that Act[12] (indecency between men) if it was committed in relation to a person under the age of 16.

9.—An offence under section 14 of that Act (indecent assault on a woman) if it was committed in relation to a person under the age of 16.

10.—An offence under section 15 of that Act (indecent assault on a man) if it was committed in relation to a person under the age of 16.

11.—An offence under section 128 of the Mental Health Act 1959[13] (sexual intercourse with patients) if it was committed in relation to a person under the age of 16.

12.—An offence under section 1 of the Indecency with Children Act 1960[14] (indecent conduct towards young child).

13.—An offence under section 54 of the Criminal Law Act 1977[15] (inciting a girl under 16 to have incestuous sexual intercourse).

14.—An offence under section 3 of the Sexual Offences (Amendment) Act 2000[16] (abuse of a position of trust) if it was committed in relation to a person under the age of 16.

15.—An offence under section 1 of the Sexual Offences Act 2003[17] (rape) if it was committed in relation to a person under the age of 16.

---

[9] Section 6 was amended by section 10(1) and paragraph 14 of Schedule 2 to the Criminal Law Act 1967 (c. 80).

[10] Section 7 was substituted by section 127(1)(a) of the Mental Health Act 1959 (c. 72).

[11] Section 12 was amended by section 143 of the Criminal Justice and Public Order Act 1994 (c. 33); sections 1 and 2 of the Sexual Offences (Amendment) Act 2000 (c. 44) and section 119 of and Part V of Schedule 6 to the Police and Criminal Evidence Act 1984 (c. 60).

[12] Section 13 was amended by section 2(2) of the Sexual Offences (Amendment) Act 2000 (c. 44).

[13] 1959 c. 72; section 128 was amended by section 129 of and paragraph 29 of Schedule 15 and Schedule 16 to the National Health Service Act 1977 (c. 49); section 148 of and paragraph 15 of Schedule 3 to the Mental Health Act 1983 (c. 20); and section 57 of and paragraph 2 of Schedule 1 to the Registered Homes Act 1984 (c. 23) and section 116 of and paragraph 2 of Schedule 4 to the Care Standards Act 2000 (c. 14).

[14] 1960 c. 33; section 1 was amended by section 39 of the Criminal Justice and Court Services Act 2000 (c. 43) and section 52 of the Crime (Sentences) Act 1997 (c. 44).

[15] 1977 (c. 45); section 54 was amended by section 119(2) and Schedule 7 to the Police and Criminal Evidence Act 1984 (c. 60).

[16] 2000 c. 44.

[17] 2003 c. 42.

16.—An offence under section 2 of that Act (assault by penetration) if it was committed in relation to a person under the age of 16.

17.—An offence under section 3 of that Act (sexual assault) if it was committed in relation to a person under the age of 16.

18.—An offence under section 4 of that Act (causing a person to engage in sexual activity without consent) if it was committed in relation to a person under the age of 16.

19.—An offence under section 5 of the Sexual Offences Act 2003 (rape of a child under 13).

20.—An offence under section 6 of that Act (assault of a child under 13 by penetration).

21.—An offence under section 7 of that Act (sexual assault of a child under 13).

22.—An offence under section 8 of that Act (causing or inciting a child under 13 to engage in sexual activity).

23.—An offence under section 9 of that Act (sexual activity with a child).

24.—An offence under section 10 of that Act (causing or inciting a child to engage in sexual activity).

25.—An offence under section 14 of that Act if doing it will involve the commission of an offence under sections 9 and 10 of that Act (arranging or facilitating the commission of a child sex offence).

26.—An offence under section 16 of that Act (abuse of position of trust: sexual activity with a child) if it was committed in relation to a person under the age of 16.

27.—An offence under section 17 of that Act (abuse of position of trust: causing or inciting a child to engage in sexual activity) if it was committed in relation to a person under the age of 16.

28.—An offence under section 25 of that Act (sexual activity with a child family member) if it was committed in relation to a person under the age of 16.

29.—An offence under section 26 of that Act (inciting a child family member to engage in sexual activity) if it was committed in relation to a person under the age of 16.

30.—An offence under section 30 of that Act (sexual activity with a person with a mental disorder impeding choice) if it was committed in relation to a person under the age of 16.

31.—An offence under section 31 of that Act (causing or inciting a person with a mental disorder impeding choice to engage in sexual activity) if it was committed in relation to a person under the age of 16.

32.—An offence under section 34 of that Act (inducement, threat, or deception to procure activity with a person with a mental disorder) if it was committed in relation to a person under the age of 16.

33.—An offence under section 35 of that Act (causing a person with a mental disorder to engage in or agree to engage in sexual activity by inducement, threat or deception) if it was committed in relation to a person under the age of 16.

34.—An offence under section 38 of that Act (care workers: sexual activity with a person with a mental disorder) if it was committed in relation to a person under the age of 16.

35.—An offence under section 39 of that Act (care workers: causing or inciting sexual activity) if it was committed in relation to a person under the age of 16.

36.—An offence of—

(a) aiding, abetting, counselling, procuring or inciting the commission of an offence specified in this Part of this Schedule; or

(b) attempting to commit an offence so specified.

Appendix III

Criminal Procedure Rules 2005, SI 2005/384

PART 35—EVIDENCE OF BAD CHARACTER

When this applies

35.1—This Part applies in a magistrates' court and in the Crown Court when a party wants to introduce evidence of bad character as defined in section 98 of the Criminal Justice Act 2003.[1]

For the introduction of evidence of bad character in the Court of Appeal see rule 68.21.

Introducing evidence of non-defendant's bad character

35.2—A party who wants to introduce evidence of a non-defendant's bad character or who wants to cross-examine a witness with a view to eliciting that evidence, under section 100 of the Criminal Justice Act 2003 must apply in the form set out in the Practice Direction and the application must be received by the court officer and all other parties to the proceedings—

(a) not more than 14 days after the prosecutor has complied or purported to comply with section 3 of the Criminal Procedure and Investigations Act 1996[2] (disclosure by the prosecutor); or

(b) as soon as reasonably practicable, where the application concerns a non-defendant who is to be invited to give (or has given) evidence for a defendant.

---

[1] 2003 c. 44
[2] 1996 c. 25; section 3 is amended the Regulation of Investigatory Powers Act 2000 (c. 23), Schedule 4, paragraph 7(1). It is further amended by the Criminal Justice Act 2003 (c. 44), section 32 and Schedule 36, Part 3, paragraphs 20 and 21.

Appendix III

Formerly rule 72A(1) of the Magistrates' Courts Rules 1981³ and rule 23E(1) of the Crown Court Rules 1982.⁴

Opposing introduction of evidence of non-defendant's bad character

35.3—A party who receives a copy of an application under rule 35.2 may oppose that application by giving notice in writing to the court officer and all other parties to the proceedings not more than 14 days after receiving that application.

Formerly rule 72A(2) of the Magistrates' Courts Rules 1981 and rule 23E(2) of the Crown Court Rules 1982.

Prosecutor introducing evidence of defendant's bad character

35.4—(1) A prosecutor who wants to introduce evidence of a defendant's bad character or who wants to cross-examine a witness with a view to eliciting that evidence, under section 101 of the Criminal Justice Act 2003 must give notice in the form set out in the Practice Direction to the court officer and all other parties to the proceedings.

(2) Notice under paragraph (1) must be given—

(a) in a case to be tried in a magistrates' court, at the same time as the prosecutor complies or purports to comply with section 3 of the Criminal Procedure and Investigations Act 1996; and

(b) in a case to be tried in the Crown Court, not more than 14 days after—

    (i) the committal of the defendant, or

    (ii) the consent to the preferment of a bill of indictment in relation to the case, or

    (iii) the service of notice of transfer under section 4(1) of the Criminal Justice Act 1987⁵ (notices of transfer) or under section 53(1) of the Criminal Justice Act 1991⁶ (notices of transfer in certain cases involving children),

---

³ S.I. 1981/552; amended by S.I. 2004/2993; there are other amending instruments but none is relevant to this Part.

⁴ S.I. 1982/1109; amended by S.I. 2004/2991; there are other amending instruments but none is relevant to this Part.

⁵ 1987 c. 38; section 4 was amended by the Criminal Justice Act 1988 (c. 33), section 144(1) and (2), the Legal Aid Act 1988 (c. 34), Schedule 5, paragraph 22, the Criminal Justice and Public Order Act 1994 (c. 33), Schedule 9, paragraph 29, the Crime and Disorder Act 1998 (c. 37), Schedule 8, paragraph 65 and the Access to Justice Act 1999 (c. 22), Schedule 4, paragraphs 38 and 39. Section 4 is repealed by the Criminal Justice Act 2003 (c. 44), section 41 and Schedule 3, Part 2, paragraph 58(1), (2) and Schedule 37, Part 4, with effect from a date to be appointed.

⁶ 1991 c. 53; section 53 was amended by the Criminal Justice and Public Order Act 1994 (c. 33), Schedule 9, paragraph 49, the Crime and Disorder Act 1998 (c. 37), Schedule 8, paragraph 93 and the

or
>   (iv) where a person is sent for trial under section 51 of the Crime and Disorder Act 1998[7] (sending cases to the Crown Court) the service of copies of the documents containing the evidence on which the charge or charges are based under paragraph 1 of Schedule 3 to that Act.[8]

Formerly rule 72A(3) of the Magistrates' Courts Rules 1981 and rule 23E(3) of the Crown Court Rules 1982.

Co-defendant introducing evidence of defendant's bad character

35.5—A co-defendant who wants to introduce evidence of a defendant's bad character or who wants to cross-examine a witness with a view to eliciting that evidence under section 101 of the Criminal Justice Act 2003 must give notice in the form set out in the Practice Direction to the court officer and all other parties to the proceedings not more than 14 days after the prosecutor has complied or purported to comply with section 3 of the Criminal Procedure and Investigations Act 1996.

Formerly rule 72A(4) of the Magistrates' Courts Rules 1981 and rule 23E(4) of the Crown Court Rules 1982.

Defendant applying to exclude evidence of his own bad character

35.6—A defendant's application to exclude bad character evidence must be in the form set out in the Practice Direction and received by the court officer and all other parties to the proceedings not more than 14 days after receiving a notice given under rules 35.4 or 35.5.

Formerly rule 72A(5) of the Magistrates' Courts Rules 1981 and rule 23E(5) of the Crown Court Rules 1982.

Methods of giving notice

35.7—Where this rule requires a notice or application to be given or sent it may, with the consent of the addressee, be sent by fax or other means of electronic communication.

Access to Justice Act 1999 (c. 22), Schedule 4, paragraph 47. Section 53 is repealed by the Criminal Justice Act 2003 (c. 44), Schedule 37, Part 4, with effect from a date to be appointed.

[7] 1998 c. 37; section 51 is substituted, together with new sections 51A to 51E, by the Criminal Justice Act 2003 (c. 44), Schedule 3, Part 1, paragraphs 14 and 18, with effect from a date to be appointed.

[8] Paragraph 1 of Schedule 3 was amended by the Access to Justice Act 1999 (c. 22), section 67(1) and Schedule 15, Part 3; it is further amended by the Criminal Justice Act 2003 (c. 44), Schedule 3, Part 1, paragraphs 14, 20(1) and (2), with effect from a date to be appointed.

Formerly rule 72A(8) of the Magistrates' Courts Rules 1981 and rule 23E(8) of the Crown Court Rules 1982.

Court's power to vary requirements under this Part

35.8—The court may—

(a) allow a notice or application required under this rule to be given in a different form, or orally; or
(b) shorten a time-limit under this rule or extend it even after it has expired.

Formerly rule 72A(7) of the Magistrates' Courts Rules 1981 and rule 23E(7) of the Crown Court Rules 1982.

Defendant waiving right to receive notice

35.9—A defendant entitled to receive a notice under this Part may waive his entitlement by so informing the court and the party who would have given the notice.
Formerly rule 72A(6) of the Magistrates' Courts Rules 1981 and rule 23E(6) of the Crown Court Rules 1982.

PART 68 APPEAL TO THE COURT OF APPEAL AGAINST CONVICTION OR SENTENCE

Procedure for the admission of evidence of bad character

68.21—Part 35 applies to the introduction of evidence of bad character in proceedings before the Court of Appeal, except for rule 35.1 and with the following modifications—

(a) a reference to a defendant should be read as a reference to an appellant, and 'non-defendant' and 'co-defendant' read accordingly;
(b) a reference to a court officer should be read as a reference to the Registrar; and
(c) an application under rule 35.2 (non-defendant's bad character) must be received, and a notice under rule 35.4 or 35.5 (defendant's bad character) must be given, not more than 28 days after—

   (i) leave to appeal is given, or
   (ii) notice of appeal is given, if leave is not required.

Formerly rule 9D of the Criminal Appeal Rules 1968.

EVIDENCE OF BAD CHARACTER

(CRIMINAL PROCEDURE RULES, PART 35)

Application for leave to adduce non-defendant's bad character under s.100 Criminal Justice Act 2003 *(Criminal Procedure Rules, rr 35.2, 68.21)*	
Details required	*Notes*
1. Details of applicant Name: Address: Name of prosecuting agency (if relevant)	
2. Case details Case reference numbers: Date the trial or proceedings is due to start/or started: Name of defendant(s): Charges:	*Give brief details of those charges to which this application applies.*

3. Details of this application
 	
Please provide the following details
  (a) the particulars of the bad character evidence including how it is to be adduced or elicited in the proceedings (including the name of the relevant non-defendant and all other relevant witnesses); and
  (b) the grounds for the admission of evidence of a non-defendant's bad character under section 100 of CJA 2003.
	s.100 Criminal Justice Act 2003
	
	Please attach any relevant documentation.

4. Extension of time Are you applying for an extension of time for service? (yes/no) If so please provide details.	
Signed: Dated	

[Note: Formerly set out in the Schedule to the Magistrates' Courts (Amendment) Rules 2004 (SI 2004/2993) relating to rule 72A of the Magistrates' Courts Rules 1981 and form BC1 of the Crown Court (Amendment No.3) Rules 2004 (SI 2004/2991) relating to rule 23D of the Crown Court Rules 1982 and form 21 of the Criminal Appeal (Amendment No.2) Rules 2004 (SI 2004/2992) relating to rule 9D of the Criminal Appeal Rules 1968].

Notice of intention to adduce bad character evidence under s.101 Criminal Justice Act 2003

(Criminal Procedure Rules, rr 35.4(1), 68.21)

Details required	Notes
1. Details of party giving notice Name: Address: Name of prosecuting agency (if relevant)	
2. Case details Case reference numbers: Date the trial or proceedings is due to start/or started: Name of defendant(s): Charges:	*Give brief details of those charges to which this application applies.*
3. Details of this Notice To the named defendant: You are hereby given notice that bad character evidence, particulars of which are detailed below, is to be adduced or elicited in these proceedings. The particulars of that bad character evidence are as follows:	*In this section include:* *a) a description of the bad character evidence and how it is to be adduced or elicited in the proceedings (including the names of any relevant witnesses); and* *b) the grounds for the admission of evidence of the defendant's bad character under section 101 of the Criminal Justice Act 2003. Please attach any relevant documentation.*
4. Extension of time Are you applying for an extension of time for service? (yes/no). If yes, state your reasons.	
Signed: Dated:	

[Note: Formerly set out in the Schedule to the Magistrates' Courts (Amendment) Rules 2004 (SI 2004/2993) relating to rule 72A of the Magistrates' Courts Rules 1981 and form BC2 of the Crown Court (Amendment No.3) Rules 2004 (SI 2004/2991) relating to rule 23D of the Crown Court Rules 1982 and form 22 of the Criminal Appeal (Amendment No.2) Rules 2004 (SI 2004/2992) relating to rule 9D of the Criminal Appeal Rules 1968].

Details required	Notes
Application to exclude evidence of the defendant's bad character under ss 101, 108(2) Criminal Justice Act 2003 *(Criminal Procedure Rules, rr 35.6, 68.21)*	
1. Details of the defendant Name: Address: Date of Birth: If you are in custody, please give your Prison Index No. and address where detained:	
2. Case details Case reference numbers: Date the trial or proceedings is due to start/or started: Charges: Date that you were served with the notice of the intention to adduce bad character evidence in these proceedings:	
3. Details of the application This section must include the following information: (a) why the admission of the bad character evidence would have such an adverse effect on the fairness of the proceedings that the court should not admit it.	*Note that an application to exclude this evidence under section 101(3) of the Criminal Justice Act 2003 can only be made if you have been notified of a party's intention to adduce this evidence under subsection 101(1)(d) (it is relevant to an important matter in issue between the defendant and the prosecution) or subsection 101(1)(g) (that the defendant has made an attack on another person's character).*
(b) details as to the length of time between the matters to which the bad character evidence relates and the matters which form the subject of the offence charged.	*Section 101(4) of the 2003 Act.*
(c) if you are applying for the exclusion of this evidence on grounds other than section 101(3) of CJA 2003, please set out such objections.	

(Criminal Procedure Rules, rr 35.6, 68.21)

4. Extension of time	
Are you applying for an extension of time for service (yes/no) If so, state your reasons	
Signed:	
Date:	

[Note: Formerly set out in the Schedule to the Magistrates' Courts (Amendment) Rules 2004 (SI 2004/2993) relating to rule 72A of the Magistrates' Courts Rules 1981 and form BC3 of the Crown Court (Amendment No.3) Rules 2004 (SI 2004/2991) relating to rule 23D of the Crown Court Rules 1982 and form 23 of the Criminal Appeal (Amendment No.2) Rules 2004 (SI 2004/2992) relating to rule 9D of the Criminal Appeal Rules 1968].

Appendix IV

Judicial Studies Board Specimen Directions

20. Similar facts

The following specimen directions are designed to be of assistance in three 'classic' similar fact situations. In *DPP v P* 93 CrAppR 267, 279 Lord Mackay LC said: 'Once the principle has been recognised that what has to be assessed is the probative force of the evidence in question, the infinite variety of circumstances in which the question arises, demonstrates that there is no single manner in which this can be achieved.' The directions below involve illustrations of specific offences. They do not cover all similar fact situations. They are given by way of general guidance only, and must of course be carefully adapted to suit the needs of each individual case. Note that evidence leading to previous acquittals may be admissible as similar fact evidence in a subsequent trial: *R v Z* [2000] 2 CrAppR 281.

A. Where there is no direct evidence that the defendant committed the offence charged or any of the 'similar offences' (as in the cases of *Makin v Attorney General for New South Wales* [1894] AC 57 PC and *R v Smith* 11 CrAppR 229).

There is no direct evidence that the defendant [killed A or that he did so with intent to kill or cause him really serious harm]. There is evidence that he had the opportunity to do so, but that, in itself, is far from sufficient to enable you to be sure that he did.

You have, however, heard evidence suggesting the commission of [a number of] other similar offences, all of which the defendant had the opportunity to commit.

If (where it is not admitted) you are sure that the events to which the witnesses have testified took place, you must look at the whole of this evidence and ask yourselves: is the relationship between the circumstances of these offences/occurrences (eg in time, place and (. . . state other circumstances highlighting in particular unusual characteristics)) so close that you are sure that they must be a series of similar offences committed by the same person?

If that is so, looking at the case against this defendant is it possible that he can have an innocent explanation for the fact that [all of those bodies of children were found buried in gardens of houses in which he had carried on a business of fostering children] [three women whom he had married under false names had all made wills in his favour and drowned in their baths shortly afterwards]; or is the only reasonable explanation that these [children] [women] were killed by the defendant [or with his assistance or encouragement]?

If, but only if, you are sure that there is no credible innocent explanation you may take the whole of this evidence into account in deciding whether you are sure that [the defendant killed, or was a party to the killing with intent of A].

B. Where there is no direct evidence that the defendant committed the offence charged but there is independent evidence that he committed other 'similar offences' (as in *R v Straffen* 36 CrAppR 132).

There is no direct evidence that the defendant [killed A or that he did so with intent to kill or cause really serious harm]. However, there is [evidence that] [the defendant has admitted that] he killed B and C. You have also heard evidence as to the circumstances in which those offences were committed.

The prosecution say that the circumstances of the offence which is presently charged and which you must decide so closely resemble those of the other [two] [earlier] [later] offences that the only reasonable conclusion is that all three offences are the work of one person, and that it therefore follows that the defendant is guilty of the offence charged. (Here state the circumstances). You must therefore consider three questions:

1. Are you sure that the defendant committed offences B and C? If you are not sure of that, the evidence relating to those offences is of no value, and you must ignore it. If, however, you are sure that he did commit these offences, go on to consider:
2. Are you sure that the circumstances of those offences were as alleged by the prosecution? If you are not sure of that ignore them. Equally if you are not sure that any particular alleged circumstance existed, ignore it. If you are sure that all, or some of those circumstances existed, go on to consider:
3. Are you sure that the circumstances in which offences B and C were committed so closely resemble the circumstances which you are sure existed in the present case that you can have no doubt that the three offences must have been the work of one person, i.e. the defendant? [It is suggested on behalf of the defendant that it is possible that the resemblance between the circumstances of these offences might be purely coincidental. If you think that there is any realistic possibility that the resemblance between the circumstances of the offences might be no more than a coincidence, and that the offence might have been committed by someone else, the evidence is of no value and you must ignore it.]

C. Where there is direct testimony that the defendant committed the offence and the question is whether the witness (W) who says that he did was speaking the truth. X and Y testify to similar offences on other occasions.

1. Ask yourselves: Are sure that W, X and Y did not put their heads together to make false accusations against the defendant? If you are not sure of that, the evidence of X and Y is of no value, and you must ignore it. If you are sure that there was no collaboration of that kind, you are entitled to consider the evidence of X and Y in deciding whether W was speaking the truth [and vice versa if e.g. three offences are charged].

2. You must then ask: Is it reasonably possible that the three persons, independently making the similar accusations which you have heard, could all be either lying or mistaken? If you think that is incredible then you may well be satisfied that W was speaking the truth. In answering this question you must consider two important aspects of the evidence:

   (i) The degree of similarity between the accusations. The greater the degree of similarity, the more likely it is that independent witnesses are speaking the truth, for you may think it would be a remarkable coincidence if they hit upon the same lies or made the same mistakes as to matters of detail. On the other hand, the less the degree of similarity, the less weight should be given to this evidence; and

   (ii) Whether W, X or Y may have been consciously or unconsciously influenced in their evidence through hearing of complaints made by others. If you think it is possible that they, or any of them, may have been influenced in making the accusation at all, or in the detail of their evidence, you must take that into account in deciding what weight, if any, you give to their evidence.

Notes

1. The leading case relating to the principles to be applied in similar fact cases is *DPP v P* 93 CrAppR 267. In relation to the issue of collusion, see *R v Ryder* 98 CrAppR 242 and *R v H* 99 CrAppR 178. In relation to identification, see *R v Brown and others* [1997] Crim LR 502 and *R v John W* [1998] 2 CrAppR 289.

2. Much assistance will also be derived from *R v Wharton* [1998] 2 CrAppR 289 and *R v Musquera* [1999] Crim LR 857 (and commentary). In the former case, the Court of Appeal considered when a 'sequential' approach and when a 'cumulative' approach to similar fact evidence would be appropriate.

Archbold (2003) 13–1 page 1301 *et seq.*
Blackstone (2003) F12.3 page 2148 *et seq.*

23. Defendant's character—good

Wherever there is any doubt as to whether both limbs of the character direction apply, or wherever it is thought that it may be necessary in the particular circumstances to modify a 'character direction', it is desirable to canvass the proposed direction with counsel before their closing speeches. In *R v Durbin* [1995] 2 CrAppR 84, 91, the court laid down guidelines for cases in which it might be appropriate to give a modified direction. The court stressed the importance of the principle that 'The jury should not be directed to approach the case on a basis which . . . is artificial or untrue.'

Generally, however, this direction should not be watered down: see eg Note 5 overleaf.

You have heard that the defendant is a man/young man of good character [not just in the sense that he has no convictions recorded against him, but witnesses have spoken of his positive qualities]. Of course, good character cannot by itself provide a defence to a criminal charge, but it is evidence which you should take into account in his favour in the following way/s:

First limb

If a defendant does not give evidence and he has not made any statement to the police, or other authority or person which is admitted in evidence, ignore 1 below.

1. (If a defendant has given evidence) In the first place, the defendant has given evidence, and as with any man of good character it supports his credibility. This means it is a factor which you should take into account when deciding whether you believe his evidence.
2. (If a defendant has not given evidence, but has eg made a statement to the police or has answered questions in interview, see Note 2, below). In the first place, although the defendant has chosen not to give evidence before you, he did, as you know give [an explanation to the police]. In considering [that explanation] and what weight you should give it, you should bear in mind that it was made by a person of good character, and take that into account when deciding whether you can believe it.

Second limb

2. In the second place, the fact that he is of good character may mean that he is less likely than otherwise might be the case to commit this crime now. (In cases where it is necessary to give the Delay direction, see direction 37, para 4.)

I have said that these are matters to which you should have regard in the defendant's favour. It is for you to decide what weight you should give to them in this case. In doing this you are entitled to take into account everything you have heard about the defendant, including his age, [. . .] and [. . .]. (Obviously the importance of good character will vary from case to case, and becomes stronger if the defendant is a person of unblemished character of mature years, or has a positively good character, and at this stage the benefit of this to a defendant whose good character justifies it may be pointed out to the jury, with words such as:

Having regard to what you know about this defendant you may think that he is entitled to ask you to give [considerable] weight to his good character when deciding whether the prosecution has satisfied you of his guilt).

Notes

1. See *R v Vye, Wise and Stephenson* 97 CrAppR 134; *R v Aziz and others* [1995] 2 CrAppR 478. In *Aziz* the House of Lords referred to the 'veritable sea-change in judicial thinking in regard to the proper way in which the judge should direct the jury on the good character of the defendant' and to the recognition that 'the good character of a defendant is logically relevant to his credibility and the likelihood that he would commit the offence in question.' Also see: *R v Fulcher* [1995] 2 CrAppR 251 and *R v Hickmet* [1996] Crim LR 588.

2. In the case of *R v Napper* [1996] Crim LR 591, Lord Taylor CJ held that the requirement to give a '*Vye*' direction is unaffected by the situation arising when it may be appropriate to give an Inference direction under Section 35 of the Criminal Justice and Public Order Act 1994 (see post, page 39.1). See also *R v Kanuga* [1998] 2 Archbold News 3, CA.

3. If the judge rules that a defendant should be treated as a man of good character even though strictly speaking he is not (for example because he has spent convictions), the full direction on good character should be given to the jury: *R v Miller and others*, unreported (97 /02841/X4). See also *R v M (Ian)* [1999] 6 Archbold News 3.

4. For the application of this direction to a case in which a defendant had cautions but no convictions, see *R v Martin* [2000] 2 CrAppR 42.

5. A good character direction should be given in the form of an affirmative statement rather than a rhetorical question (*R v Lloyd* [2002] CrAppR 355) and should not be qualified by suggesting that its significance in relation to propensity is less when the offence is spontaneous (*R v Fitton* [2001] 3 Archbold News 2).

Archbold (2003) 4–406 page 482 *et seq.*
Blackstone (2003) F13.1 page 2177 *et seq.*

24. Defendant's character—bad

[**Author's note** In April 2006, when this book was sent to the printers, this Specimen Direction was being revised to take account of *Hanson and others* [2005] EWCA Crim 824, [2005] 2 CrAppR 299, and the other cases leading cases interpreting the bad character decided during 2005 that are set out in Appendix V of this book. The date when the revised version will be officially promulgated was not then known. For further information, readers are advised to consult the Judicial Studies Board website.]

Unusually, this specimen direction has been issued before the provisions to which it relates, namely sections 98 to 112 of the Criminal Justice Act 2003 have come into force, and thus before there has been any authoritative interpretation of them. This has been done in the belief that some guidance will be welcomed, given the fundamental changes brought about by the new provisions, and the frequency with which they are likely to arise in practice. The writers will keep under review the need for any amendments to reflect future practical experience and judicial development.

1. In this case you have heard evidence that the defendant has a bad character in the sense that he [has criminal convictions] [has otherwise mis-conducted himself]. It is important that you should understand why you have heard this evidence, and how you may use it. As I will explain in more detail later, you must not convict him only because he has a bad character (see Note 2).

2. You have heard of his bad character because (as appropriate—see Note 3):

   (a) all parties to the proceedings have agreed to it;
   (b) the defendant has told you about it [and/or] asked questions [by his barrister/solicitor] that brought it up;
   (c) it may help you to understand other evidence in the case [namely . . .] and the case as a whole (see Note 4);
   (d) it may help you to resolve an issue that has arisen between the defendant and the prosecution [namely . . .] (see Note 4);
   (e) it may help you to resolve an issue that has arisen between the defendant and his co-defendant [X] [namely . . .] (see Note 4);
   (f) it may correct a false impression [said to have been] (see Note 5) given by the defendant [namely . . .];
   (g) the defendant has made an attack on the character of [Y] [namely . . .].

3. (Only if one or more of cases (c) to (f) above apply and, if case (f) applies, it is accepted that the defendant has given a false impression:) You may therefore use the evidence of the defendant's bad character for the particular purpose[s] I have just indicated, if you find it helpful to do so (see Note 6).

4. (Only if case (f) alone applies, and it is disputed that the defendant has given a false impression:) If you are not sure that the defendant has given you that false impression, you should disregard the evidence of his bad character altogether. But if you are sure, you may use that evidence to correct the false impression, if you find it helpful to do so.

5. (In any case:) You may [also] use the evidence of the defendant's bad character in the following ways:

   (a) If you think it right, you may take it into account when deciding whether or not the defendant's evidence to you was truthful (see Note 7). A person with a bad character may be less likely to tell the truth, but it does not follow that he is incapable of doing so. [Indeed, the defendant argues that his character means that he is more likely to be telling the truth.] You must decide to what extent, if at all, his character helps you when judging his evidence.

(and/or)

(b) If you think it right, you may [also] take it into account when deciding whether or not the defendant committed the offence[s] with which he is now charged (see Note 7). (Here summarise any arguments that arise in this connection (see Note 8) and give any direction that may be appropriate where the prosecution rely on other similar offences or misbehaviour (see Notes 9 and 10)). You must decide to what extent, if at all, his character helps you when you are considering whether or not he is guilty. But bear in mind that his bad character cannot by itself prove that he is guilty. It would therefore be wrong to jump to the conclusion that he is guilty just because of his bad character. [Indeed, the defendant argues that his character means that he is less likely to be guilty]. (See Note 11).

Notes

1. The section references in these Notes are to the Criminal Justice Act 2003.

2. In the rare case in which there is no direct evidence that the defendant committed the offence charged, and the prosecution rely solely on evidence of bad character in the form of evidence that the defendant has committed other similar offences (as in *R v Straffen* 36 Cr. App. R. 132) the final sentence of paragraph 1 should be omitted.

3. See s. 101(1).

4. The words 'important' in ss. 101(1)(c), (d) and (e) and 'substantial' in ss. 101(1)(e) and 102(b) have been omitted. The judge will have found these adjectives appropriate when deciding to admit the evidence; but it is then for the jury to make its own assessment of the importance and value of the issues and evidence.

5. The passage in square brackets should be omitted if it is not disputed that the defendant has given a false impression. The writers consider that if the judge rules that the evidence should be admitted under s.101(1)(f) in a disputed case, it will ultimately be for the jury to decide whether or not the defendant has given a false impression. The situation is similar to that in which the judge rules that a confession is admissible, but the jury ultimately decides whether or not it is voluntary and/or reliable. Hence the form of paragraphs 3 and 4 of this direction.

6. Should a case ever arise in which one or more of (c) to (e) apply and (f) also applies and it is disputed that the defendant has given a false impression, it is suggested that the following be added to paragraph 3: 'But obviously you could not use the evidence to correct a false impression unless you were sure that the defendant had actually given a false impression.'

7. The writers' view is that evidence of bad character may be admitted to impugn (or bolster) the credibility of a defendant, and/or to show that the defendant is more (or less) likely to be guilty, through any of the 'gateways' provided by section 101(1), depending of course on the evidence and issues in the particular case.

8. The prosecution may, for example, rely on the defendant's propensity to commit offences of a certain kind as showing that he is more likely to be guilty. The defence may, for example, rely on points of distinction between his previous convictions and the offence charged as showing that he is less likely to be guilty.

9. In a case of the kind referred to in Note 2 above, a direction based on the specimen at page 20.2 of these Directions should be incorporated at this point and the passage from 'But bear in mind . . .' to '. . . just because of his bad character' in paragraph 5(b) of this direction should be omitted.

10. If there is direct evidence that the defendant committed the offence charged from a witness or witnesses whose truthfulness is in issue, and the prosecution rely also on evidence of bad character in the form of evidence that the defendant committed other similar offences, a direction based on the specimen at page 20.3 of these Directions should be incorporated at this point.

11. This paragraph may need to be adapted suitably if a defendant introduces evidence of a co-defendant's bad character pursuant to s.101(1)(e), with a view to establishing that the co-defendant is more likely to be guilty of an offence charged against both, and/or is less likely to be telling the truth.

24A. Non-defendant's character—bad

A. 1. In this case you have heard that [Z] has a bad character in the sense that he has criminal convictions [has mis-conducted himself].

2. You have heard this because [as appropriate] (see Note 1):

(a) It may help you to understand other evidence in the case [namely . . .] and the case as a whole (see Note 2);
(b) It may help you to resolve an issue that has arisen [namely . . .] (see Note 2);
(c) All parties have agreed to it.

3. (Only if cases (a) and/or (b) above apply:) You may therefore use the evidence of the [Z's] bad character for the particular purpose[s] I have just indicated, if you find it helpful to do so (see Note 3).

4. [Here explain any more general use to which the jury may put the evidence of bad character in the particular case. This may, for example, be when they are considering whether the non-defendant committed the offence with which the defendant is charged, if that issue arises. It may be when they are considering whether the non-defendant (if a witness) has told the truth, in which case the jury should be directed that a person of bad character may be less likely to tell the truth, but it does not follow that he is incapable of doing so. In any case, it will be necessary to direct the jury that it is for them to decide the extent to which the evidence of bad character helps them, if at all. The form of the appropriate direction will vary considerably from case to case.] (see Note 3).

Notes

    1. See s100(1). All section references in these notes are to the Criminal Justice Act 2003.

    2. The words 'important,' 'importance' and 'substantial' in ss100(1) and (2) have been omitted. The judge will have found these adjectives appropriate when deciding to admit the evidence, but it is then for the jury to make its own assessment of the importance and value of the issues and the evidence.

    3. It may also be necessary to refer to some or all of the matters referred to in s100(3), depending of course on the issues and evidence in each case.

Appendix V

Leading Cases

R v Hanson, R v Gilmore; R v P [2005] EWCA Crim 824, [2005] 1 WLR 3169, [2005] 2 CrAppR 21 (299), CA, 22 March 2005; Rose LJ (Vice-President), Hughes and Hallett JJ

A. Nicol QC, J. Lindsay, P.Bradley and S Tierney for the applicants
B. Houlder QC, G. Bridge, S. Powis and M. Maxwell-Burnside for the Crown

The Vice President, Rose LJ:

1. All members of the constitution have contributed to this judgment.

2. We have heard these three applications together because they raise similar questions in relation to the admissibility of evidence of a defendant's bad character under the recently introduced provision in sections 98 to 113 of the Criminal Justice Act 2003. These abolish the long established common law rules governing the admissibility of evidence of bad character and introduce a raft of new provisions.

3. Before turning to the individual cases, it is first convenient to set out our conclusions in the light of the helpful submissions made to us by counsel as to the way in which trial judges should approach their task when confronted by a prosecution application to adduce such evidence. These comments are not intended to be a comprehensive treatise on the new provisions. Their primary focus is on the issues raised in these applications.

4. The starting point should be for judges and practitioners to bear in mind that Parliament's purpose in the legislation, as we divine it from the terms of the Act, was to

assist in the evidence based conviction of the guilty, without putting those who are not guilty at risk of conviction by prejudice. It is accordingly to be hoped that prosecution applications to adduce such evidence will not be made routinely, simply because a defendant has previous convictions, but will be based on the particular circumstances of each case.

5. Section 101(1) provides seven possible gateways through which evidence of a defendant's bad character is admissible. The ones likely to be most commonly relied upon by the prosecution are (d), where the evidence is relevant to an important matter in issue between the defendant and the prosecution, (f), where the evidence is to correct a false impression given by the defendant and (g), where the defendant has made an attack on the character of another person who will often, though not always, be the victim of the alleged crime, whether alive or dead.

6. The present applications are concerned only with the Crown wishing to rely upon evidence of previous convictions rather than other evidence of bad character. By section 103(1) matters in issue for the purpose of section 101(1(d) include:

(a) the question whether the defendant has a propensity to commit offences of the kind with which he is charged, except where his having such a propensity makes it no more likely that he is guilty of the offence;

(d) the question whether the defendant has a propensity to be untruthful, except where it is not suggested the defendant's case is untruthful in any respect.

By section 103(2) a defendant's propensity to commit offences of the kind with which he is charged may be established (without prejudice to any other way of doing so), by evidence of conviction of an offence of the same description or category as the one with which he is charged, but by section 103(3), this does not apply if the Court is satisfied that this would be unjust 'by reason of the length of time since the conviction or for any other reason'. The Criminal Justice Act 2003 (Categories of Offences) Order 2004, Statutory Instrument 2004 No 3346, prescribes offences in the categories of theft and sexual offences against persons under the age of 16.

7. Where propensity to commit the offence is relied upon there are thus essentially three questions to be considered:

1. Does the history of conviction(s) establish a propensity to commit offences of the kind charged?
2. Does that propensity make it more likely that the defendant committed the offence charged?
3. Is it unjust to rely on the conviction(s) of the same description or category; and, in any event, will the proceedings be unfair if they are admitted?

8. In referring to offences of the same description or category, section 103(2) is not exhaustive of the types of conviction which might be relied upon to show evidence of propensity to commit offences of the kind charged. Nor, however, is it necessarily sufficient, in order to show such propensity, that a conviction should be of the same description or category as that charged.

9. There is no minimum number of events necessary to demonstrate such a propensity. The fewer the number of convictions the weaker is likely to be the evidence of propensity. A single previous conviction for an offence of the same description or category will often

not show propensity. But it may do so where, for example, it shows a tendency to unusual behaviour or where its circumstances demonstrate probative force in relation to the offence charged (compare *DPP v P* [1991] 2 AC 447 at 460E to 461A). Child sexual abuse or fire setting are comparatively clear examples of such unusual behaviour but we attempt no exhaustive list. Circumstances demonstrating probative force are not confined to those sharing striking similarity. So, a single conviction for shoplifting, will not, without more, be admissible to show propensity to steal. But if the modus operandi has significant features shared by the offence charged it may show propensity.

10. In a conviction case, the decisions required of the trial judge under section 101(3) and section 103(3), though not identical, are closely related. It is to be noted that wording of section 101(3)—'must not admit'—is stronger than the comparable provision in section 78 of the Police and Criminal Evidence Act 1984—'may refuse to allow'. When considering what is just under section 103(3), and the fairness of the proceedings under section 101(3), the judge may, among other factors, take into consideration the degree of similarity between the previous conviction and the offence charged, albeit they are both within the same description or prescribed category. For example, theft and assault occasioning actual bodily harm may each embrace a wide spectrum of conduct. This does not however mean that what used to be referred as striking similarity must be shown before convictions become admissible. The judge may also take into consideration the respective gravity of the past and present offences. He or she must always consider the strength of the prosecution case. If there is no or very little other evidence against a defendant, it is unlikely to be just to admit his previous convictions, whatever they are.

11. In principle, if there is a substantial gap between the dates of commission of and conviction for the earlier offences, we would regard the date of commission as generally being of more significance than the date of conviction when assessing admissibility. Old convictions, with no special feature shared with the offence charged, are likely seriously to affect the fairness of proceedings adversely, unless, despite their age, it can properly be said that they show a continuing propensity.

12. It will often be necessary, before determining admissibility and even when considering offences of the same description or category, to examine each individual conviction rather than merely to look at the name of the offence or at the defendant's record as a whole. The sentence passed will not normally be probative or admissible at the behest of the Crown, though it may be at the behest of the defence. Where past events are disputed the judge must take care not to permit the trial unreasonably to be diverted into an investigation of matters not charged on the indictment.

13. As to propensity to untruthfulness, this, as it seems to us, is not the same as propensity to dishonesty. It is to be assumed, bearing in mind the frequency with which the words honest and dishonest appear in the criminal law, that Parliament deliberately chose the word 'untruthful' to convey a different meaning, reflecting a defendant's account of his behaviour, or lies told when committing an offence. Previous convictions, whether for offences of dishonesty or otherwise, are therefore only likely to be capable of showing a propensity to be untruthful where, in the present case, truthfulness is an issue and, in the earlier case, either there was a plea of not guilty and the defendant gave an account, on arrest, in interview, or in evidence, which the jury must have disbelieved, or the way in which the offence was committed shows a propensity for untruthfulness, for example, by

the making of false representations. The observations made above in paragraph 9 as to the number of convictions apply equally here.

14. As to section 101(1)(g), pre-2003 Act authorities will continue to apply when assessing whether an attack has been made on another person's character, to the extent that they are compatible with section 106.

15. If a judge has directed himself or herself correctly, this Court will be very slow to interfere with a ruling either as to admissibility or as to the consequences of noncompliance with the regulations for the giving of notice of intention to rely on bad character evidence. It will not interfere unless the judge's judgment as to the capacity of prior events to establish propensity is plainly wrong, or discretion has been exercised unreasonably in the *Wednesbury* sense: *Associated Provincial Picture Houses v Wednesbury Corpn.* [1948] 1 KB 223 (compare *Makanjuola* (1995) 2 CrAppR 469 at 473E).

16. Furthermore, if, following a ruling that evidence of bad character is admissible, a defendant pleads guilty, it is highly unlikely that this Court will entertain an appeal against conviction (see *Chalkley and Jeffries* [1998] QB 848, 859A, 860A, 861G, 864G).

17. In cases of the kind we are considering, it is the Crown which begins the process of applying to adduce evidence of bad character. It must specify the relevant gateways. The form of application (BC2), prescribed by Rule 23E, inserted into the Crown Court Rules 1982 by Statutory Instrument 2004 No 2991 (L18)[1] requires that the Crown set out 'a description of the bad character evidence and how it is to be adduced or elicited in the proceedings including the names of any relevant witnesses.' Form BC 3, similarly prescribed for the use of the defence, calls for particulars of why it is contended that the evidence ought not to be admitted. It follows from what we have already said that, in a conviction case the Crown needs to decide, at the time of giving notice of the application, whether it proposes to rely simply upon the fact of conviction or also upon the circumstances of it. The former may be enough when the circumstances of the conviction are sufficiently apparent from its description, to justify a finding that it can establish propensity, either to commit an offence of the kind charged or to be untruthful and that the requirements of section 103(3) and 101(3) can, subject to any particular matter raised on behalf of the defendant, be satisfied. For example, a succession of convictions for dwelling-house burglary, where the same is now charged, may well call for no further evidence than proof of the fact of the convictions. But where, as will often be the case, the Crown needs and proposes to rely on the circumstances of the previous convictions, those circumstances and the manner in which they are to be proved must be set out in the application. There is a similar obligation of frankness upon the defendant, which will be reinforced by the general obligation contained in the new Criminal Procedure Rules 2005 to give active assistance to the court in its case management (see rule 3.3). Routine applications by defendants for disclosure of the circumstances of previous convictions are likely to be met by a requirement that the request be justified by identification of the reason why it is said that those circumstances may show the convictions to be inadmissible. We would expect the relevant circumstances of previous convictions generally to be capable of agreement, and that, subject to the trial judge's ruling as to admissibility, they will be put before the jury by way of admission. Even where the circumstances are genuinely in dispute, we would expect the minimum indisputable facts to be thus

---

[1] For the relevant part of the Criminal Procedure Rules 2005, see Appendix III above.

admitted. It will be very rare indeed for it to be necessary for the judge to hear evidence before ruling on admissibility under this Act.

18. Our final general observation is that, in any case in which evidence of bad character is admitted to show propensity, whether to commit offences or to be untruthful, the judge in summing-up should warn the jury clearly against placing undue reliance on previous convictions. Evidence of bad character cannot be used simply to bolster a weak case, or to prejudice the minds of a jury against a defendant. In particular, the jury should be directed: that they should not conclude that the defendant is guilty or untruthful merely because he has these convictions; that, although the convictions may show a propensity, this does not mean that he has committed this offence or been untruthful in this case; that whether they in fact show a propensity is for them to decide; that they must take into account what the defendant has said about his previous convictions; and that, although they are entitled, if they find propensity as shown, to take this into account when determining guilt, propensity is only one relevant factor and they must assess its significance in the light of all the other evidence in the case. We do not purport to frame a Specimen Direction but the Judicial Studies Board may wish to consider these observations in relation to their helpful Specimen Direction No 24 on bad character.

19. We turn, now, to consider each of the applications.

Hanson:

20. On 26th January 2005, at Bradford Crown Court, following a pre-trial ruling by Mr Recorder Babb, this applicant pleaded guilty to theft, a plea acceptable to the Crown as an alternative to the single count of burglary in the indictment. He was sentenced to 9 months' detention in a young offender institution. He applies for leave to appeal against conviction and the Registrar has referred that application to the Full Court.

21. The circumstances were that, between about 2.00 and 3.30 pm on Saturday 24th July 2004, a carrier bag containing approximately £600 in cash was stolen from Paul James' bedroom within the private living quarters at a public house in Halifax. The applicant had been drinking in the bar during the early afternoon. At some stage, after 2.00 pm, but before 3.30, he had been given permission to enter the kitchen behind the bar, to make up a bottle for his child.

22. The Crown's case was that a stairway from the kitchen was the only effective means of access to Mr James' bedroom. It was the prosecution case that the applicant was the only person with the opportunity to enter the bedroom and steal the money at that time. Furthermore, the statement of the landlord, Mr Calland, was of considerable significance. He described the applicant asking his mother to lend him some money. She said she did not have any. Later, Mr Calland noticed the applicant go through into the back of the public house. He did not question it, 'as his mum lived upstairs'.

23. About an hour after he had asked his mum for some money, the applicant came to the bar and ordered some drinks for himself and a group of four or five others for which he paid with a £10 note. About an hour later he ordered another round and this time he paid with a £20 note.

24. In interview by the police, the applicant denied the offence. He claimed that he had not gone upstairs and there was, in any event, another means of access to Mr James' room.

He said that he and Mr James did not get on and this was why he had been accused of responsibility for the disappearance of the money. The police established that there was another means of gaining access to the bedroom, via another staircase and door, but the Crown's case was that the door had been locked and there were no signs of it being tampered with.

25. The applicant having earlier pleaded not guilty to the burglary count, the matter came on for trial on 26th January 2005. Prior to the jury being sworn, the Crown sought leave for details of the applicant's previous convictions for dishonesty to be admitted, pursuant to section 101(1)(d). The Crown submitted that the convictions were relevant to an important matter in issue between the defence and prosecution, namely, whether the applicant had a propensity to commit offences of this kind and whether he had a propensity to be untruthful within 103(1)(b).

26. Counsel for the applicant in the Court below, as before us, resisted the application, maintaining that the applicant's previous convictions for dishonesty did not demonstrate a propensity to commit burglary, and did not demonstrate a propensity to be untruthful as opposed to dishonest. The defence further submitted that, even if the conditions required by gateway (d) were met, the evidence should be excluded under section 103(3). The Recorder ruled that there was no doubt that the applicant had a bad character, within the meaning of sections 98 and 112 of the Act. He was satisfied, under gate way (d), that evidence of that bad character was relevant to propensity to commit offences of the kind with which he was charged. He had regard to the length of time between the applicant's previous convictions and the matters forming the subject of the offence before the court, as required under section 101(4). The application to admit on the basis that the applicant had a propensity to be untruthful, the Recorder concluded, had been less easy to determine and he said that he would have lacked sufficient information to determine that the applicant was shown to have a propensity to be untruthful. He therefore refused to admit the evidence via that route. The admissions of previous convictions was always likely to have an affect on the fairness of proceedings. But to accede to the defence submission to exclude the applicant's bad character would be tantamount to saying that if a defendant's record was bad enough it would always be excluded, whereas a defendant with one or two convictions was likely to have his bad character put before the jury. The Recorder concluded that admissibility of the evidence of the applicant's bad character, under (d), would not have such an adverse effect on the fairness of the proceedings that it ought not to be admitted.

27. No issue was raised before the Recorder in relation to the adequacy of the prosecution's notice of intention to rely on the previous convictions, although, in fact, no written notice had been given. Although the Recorder was not invited to admit in evidence the applicant's convictions when he was aged under 14, and the offences of dishonesty relied on by the prosecution were all within the theft category in Part 1 of the Schedule to the categories of offences order, he looked at the previous dishonesty offences globally, without considering, or apparently being invited by counsel to consider, the relevance to propensity of the individual convictions. In this respect, for the reasons given earlier, he was in error. For example, convictions for handling and aggravated vehicle taking, although within the theft category, do not, in our judgment, show, without more pertinent information, propensity to burgle as indicted or to steal, to which the applicant pleaded guilty. The applicant's robbery conviction, albeit also within the theft category, might, had it been analysed,

have been regarded as being so prejudicial as to adversely affect the fairness of the proceedings in relation to the offence charged. But the applicant had a considerable number of convictions for burglary and theft from a dwelling, which were plainly properly admissible to show propensity to commit an offence of the kind here charged. The other evidence against the applicant was powerful, particularly that of Mr Calland, which we have rehearsed.

28. If, as the Recorder anticipated, appropriate directions were given to the jury, the convictions would not have had such an adverse effect on the fairness of the proceedings that they ought not to be admitted. Accordingly, although, as it seems to us, the Recorder's ruling could and should have been more narrowly confined, it was in substance correct. The Recorder was also correct to rule that the convictions for dishonesty were not, without more information, admissible to show propensity to be untruthful. It cannot generally be a sound objection to admissibility that the defendant has a very large number of previous convictions capable of showing propensity. This, as it seems to us, merely makes the evidence more compelling.

29. In the event, following the ruling and legal advice, the applicant unambiguously pleaded guilty to theft. As explained earlier, a plea of guilty is generally a bar to an appeal against conviction. We are wholly unpersuaded by Mr Nicol, by reference to *Bailey, Brewin and Ghangi* [2001] EWCA 733, the comment on that decision in Archbold news on 27th June 2001, paragraph 13 in Lord Bingham's speech in *Attorney-General's Reference (No 2 of 2001)* [2004] 2 AC 72, or otherwise, that the circumstances of the applicant's plea of guilty afford him any basis for appealing against his conviction. No unfairness resulted from the Recorder's ruling. The conviction was safe. It was for those reasons that we yesterday refused his application for leave to appeal against conviction.

Gilmore

30. On 11th February 2005, at Wood Green Crown Court, following a trial before Mr Recorder Etherington QC, this applicant was convicted of theft and sentenced to four months' imprisonment. His application for leave to appeal against conviction has been referred to the Full Court by the Registrar.

31. The facts were these. Between 22nd and 29th July 2004 a fax machine and two adult videos, which belonged to the complainant, were stolen from his locked garden shed in Enfield. On 29th July, at about 12.30 in the morning, police noticed the applicant in a road nearby, carrying a bag filled with electrical items and a torch. The applicant told the police that he had found the bag and torch next to some rubbish bins in the alleyway directly behind the complainant's garden and he believed it to be rubbish. He had taken the bag to see if the electrical items worked. The police then noticed that the complainant's shed door had been broken into and they alerted the complainant. He confirmed that the bag recovered from the applicant contained his property, which had been stored in the shed.

32. The prosecution case was that the applicant had stolen those items, or had taken them from the alleyway knowing perfectly well that they belonged to somebody else. The defence case was that the applicant had seen the property in the alleyway and climbed over a gate to take it, believing it to be abandoned as rubbish. The applicant gave evidence in his defence.

33. The issue for the jury was therefore whether the applicant had stolen the property from the shed or whether he had found it abandoned in the alleyway. If they found that it

had not been abandoned, then they had to be sure that the appellant knew the property belonged to somebody else.

34. The appellant gave evidence and that evidence included a reference to the three convictions for shoplifting to which he said he had pleaded guilty. It is to the Recorder's ruling, admitting evidence in relation to those convictions, that this application is directed. The first of those three offences was committed on 4th March 2004 and conviction followed the following day. The second offence was committed on 21st March and the third on 13th April. The convictions in relation to the second and third offences took place on 30th June. The material before the Recorder, at the time of his ruling, indicated that the defendant had pleaded guilty to two of those three offences.

35. No written notice of intention to rely on the previous convictions was given in accordance with the Crown Court (Amendment No 3) Rules of 2004. Objection was taken by the defence to the Crown's failure to provide such notice. But it was conceded by the defence that there was no prejudice in dealing with the application to extend the time limits.

36. The Recorder, on 10th February 2005, took into account, as he was entitled to, that it was only since 14th January 2005, and the decision of this Court, differently constituted in *Bradley* [2005] EWCA Crim 20, [2005] 1 CrAppR 397, that it had been appreciated that the provisions of this part of the 2003 Act applied to trials taking place after 15th December 2004, whether or not the proceedings were instituted before that date.

37. The rules provide in 23E(7) that the Crown Court may allow oral notice and shorten or extend time limits if it is in the interests of the justice to do so. In our judgment, the Recorder's exercise of discretion, in relation to notice, bearing in mind in particular the conceded absence of prejudice, was impeccable.

38. It is correct, as Mr Nicol submits, that the Recorder in his ruling identified the dates of conviction of the three offences rather than the dates of commission of the offences. In the present case, having regard to the respective dates which we have rehearsed, that is of no significance. All three of these shoplifting offences were committed within a six week period, ending 3 months before the date of the offence charged. The Recorder was fully entitled to conclude that the offences showed a recent persistent propensity to steal. He was also entitled to conclude, bearing in mind, in particular, that the material before him showed pleas of guilty to two of the three offences and there was no further information about the offences before him, that none of them showed a propensity to be untruthful. There was substantial evidence against the applicant apart from the convictions. He had been found, after midnight, in a dark alley, leading to the garden in which was the shed from which the goods had been stolen. He had a torch in his possession. His explanation was that he had found the goods stacked by rubbish and had seen them there two days before. In our judgment, the previous convictions were plainly relevant to the issue of whether his possession of the goods, in those circumstances, was innocent or criminal. They established propensity to steal, and that propensity increased the likelihood of guilt. There is not, nor could there be, any criticism of the way in which the Recorder dealt with these matters in his summing-up. There is no arguable ground that Gilmore's conviction is unsafe. It was for these reasons that his application for leave to appeal against conviction was refused.

P

39. On 24th January 2005 at Wolverhampton Crown, following a trial before His Honour Judge Eades, the applicant was convicted on counts 1 and 2 of indecent assault on a female and on counts 3, 5 and 6 of rape. He was acquitted on count 4 of anal rape. On 4th March he was sentenced, in total, to an extended sentence of 10-and-a-half years, the custodial term of which was 8 years and the extended period of licence two-and-a-half years. He applies for leave to appeal against conviction and that application has been referred to the Full Court by the Registrar.

40. In July 1993 the applicant had pleaded guilty to indecent assault on an 11 year old girl and had been sentenced to two years' probation.

41. The facts were that the applicant met his wife, the complainant's mother, before that conviction. The complainant and her twin brother were born in May 1994, and there was another sister born in 1996.

42. When the complainant was born, the applicant was living at a bail hostel. Some time later, at his instigation, his wife moved in with his mother. At about Christmas 1996, he was allowed back to live with the family as a result of him having entered into a contract with social services whereby he undertook never to be alone with his children or to dress or bathe them, or to do anything that might trigger his fantasies, to which, in a moment, we shall return. The other members of the family agreed to that.

43. On 4th July 2002, the complainant was interviewed on video by police officers, following concerns on the part of the social services that their agreement with the applicant had been broken. At that time the complainant made no allegation of sexual impropriety against the applicant. The following month the complainant and her siblings were removed from the family by the social services and were placed with foster parents.

44. In March 2004 the complainant girl made a series of revelations to her foster mother which led to the police investigating. In consequence, on 11th May 2004 the applicant was arrested. In interview, he gave an account which foreshadowed the evidence which he was to give before the jury. The details of the offences are immaterial for present purposes. It suffices to say that count 1, of indecent assault, related to an occasion in the applicant's car, when the girl said he had inserted his finger into her vagina; count 2, of indecent assault, had occurred, she said, in the applicant's mother's bedroom. Again, the applicant had inserted his finger into her vagina. Counts 3 and 4, of rape (and it will be recalled that the applicant was acquitted on count 4) had occurred, the girl said, downstairs in the living room. Counts 5 and 6, of rape, had occurred in the applicant's bedroom, when the complainant's twin brother was on a Playstation.

45. The prosecution case was based, in part, on the evidence of the complainant but, in significant part also, on the medical evidence of injuries to her hymen and vagina which were described as being consistent with digital or penile penetration, the latter being slightly the more likely. There was no anal damage found. The prosecution also relied on the applicant's previous conviction, in 1993, as showing a propensity, making it more likely that he had committed these offences.

46. The defence case was that the complainant had made up the allegations in order to procure the applicant's removal from the family home, which would have enabled the girl

to leave her foster parents and move back home. Any injuries, according to the defence, must have been caused either accidentally or by someone else.

47. The defendant gave evidence that he had fantasies about girls of 9 years and upwards which had continued since the time of his previous conviction and they could be triggered by a variety of events. He denied any form of sexual misbehaviour towards the complainant. The issue for the jury was therefore the credibility of the complainant and the applicant, in the context of the medical evidence.

48. The Crown sought to have the applicant's 1993 conviction admitted under gateways (d), (f) and (g). The judge ruled it was admissible under (d) and (g) but not under (f). No objection before the judge was taken by the defence in relation to the lack of written notice by the prosecution of intention to rely on the conviction.

49. The crucial question before us is whether the judge was entitled to admit evidence of the 1993 conviction. He concluded, correctly, that the earlier offence was of the same description and the same category, within the Criminal Justice Act 2003 (Categories of Offences) Order 2004 (SI 2004/3346),[2] as the offences charged. He expressly took into account the length of time since the previous offence and said that 'a defendant's sexual mores and motivations are not necessary affected by the passage of time.' He said that the passage of time was not here sufficient to make the admission of the evidence unjust. He concluded that it had significant probative value, and its admission would not adversely affect the fairness of the proceedings. He therefore admitted the evidence under (d). He also admitted it under (g) on the basis that what the defendant had said in interview was a false allegation giving rise to an attack on the complainant's character within section 106(1)(c)(i) and (2)(b). He declined to admit the evidence under (f), to correct a false impression, because of the defendant's assertion that the complainant had a motive to have the defendant removed from the matrimonial home. In that respect the judge was right. The suggestion made in interview did not amount to the giving of a false impression, which, as section 105(1) makes clear, must be 'about the defendant'.

50. In our judgment, the judge's conclusions as to (d) and (g) are unassailable. We do not accept Mr Nicol's submission that the judge imposed a burden on the defence in relation to lapse of time. Nor is the fact that the conviction was spent under the Rehabilitation of Offenders Act 1974 relevant. What the defendant said in interview was an attack on the girl's character. It is true, as Mr Nicol reminded us, that the interview took place some months before the 2003 Act came into force. He submitted that the conviction, therefore, had to be excluded under section 101(3), on the ground that, at the time of the interview, an attack or imputation on a prosecution witness, made only in interview, would not have triggered the provisions of section 1(3) of the Criminal Evidence Act 1898. Whether or not this argument was put before the trial judge, we do not accept it. The law of admissibility in a trial is that in force at the time of trial. There is no question of the defendant being tried for conduct which was not a crime at the time of its commission. Nor do we accept that the evidence had to be excluded because the defendant was not warned at the time of the interview of the possible consequences of what he said. Anyone who makes a self-serving assertion of significance in interview can expect the Crown to seek to adduce, at the sub-

---

[2] Set out in Appendix II above.

sequent trial, relevant and admissible evidence to refuse it. In this case, that included the evidence of the defendant's earlier conviction.

51. Mr Nicol was also critical of the summing-up. There was undoubtedly an error by the judge as to why the evidence had been admitted. But this was corrected. Mr Nicol makes a further criticism of the judge's direction on credibility. We have not heard full argument as to whether it is right or indeed necessary to give a credibility direction where evidence of bad character has been admitted under this Act, nor as to whether the nature of the direction should be dependent on the gateway through which the evidence has been admitted. But, in this case, the defendant's credibility was so inextricably bound up with whether he had committed the offences that no sustainable criticism can be made of this aspect of the summing-up.

52. Mr Nicol also criticised the judge's failure to warn the jury that the fact that the social services had taken the girl away in 2000 was not of itself evidence that the defendant had breached his agreement with the social services. It was not, in our judgment, incumbent on the judge to give such a warning. But, in any event, its absence cannot possibly render the verdicts unsafe. The jury cannot have failed to appreciate that their deliberations should focus on the credibility of the defendant and the complainant, in the context of the medical evidence. That this happened is demonstrated by their acquittal on count 4 alleging anal rape.

53. There is no reason to regard P's conviction as, even arguably, unsafe. It was for these reasons that we refused him leave to appeal.

Applications for leave to appeal refused.

R v Bovell; R v Dowds [2005] EWCA Crim 1091, [2005] 2 CrAppR 27 (401), CA, 25 April 2005; Rose LJ (Vice-President), Gibbs and Stanley Burnton JJ

J Anders and M Hurst for the applicants
B Houlder QC, V Vyas and S Knight for the Crown

The Vice-President, Rose LJ:

1. These two applications for leave to appeal against conviction have been referred to the Full Court by the Registrar. Although they are unrelated, we have heard them together because they provide further examples of the application of the bad character provisions in sections 98 to 113 of the Criminal Justice Act 2003 which were considered by this Court, differently constituted, in *R v Hanson, Gilmore and P* [2005] EWCA Crim 824.[3]

2. These cases afford no basis for further general guidance, but we think it desirable to mention two additional matters. First, it is necessary for all parties to have the appropriate information in relation to convictions and other evidence of bad character, whether in relation to the defendant or to some other person, in good time. That can only be achieved if the rules in relation to the giving of notice are complied with. It is worth mentioning that

[3] See p 153 above.

the basis of plea in relation to an earlier conviction may be relevant where it demonstrates differences from the way in which the prosecution initially put the case. In other words, a mere reference to the statement of a complainant in an earlier case may not provide the later court with the material needed to make a decision as to the admissibility of the earlier conviction. Secondly, it is apparent that difficulties may arise in relation to the preservation and storage of information, having regard to the present provisions of paragraph 5.8 in the Current Code of Practice made under Part II of the Criminal Procedure and Investigation Act 1996. That provides for the retention of relevant material until a convicted person is released from custody, or discharged from hospital, in cases where the court imposes a custodial sentence or a hospital order, or, in all other cases, for 6 months from the date of conviction.

3. It is not feasible for this Court, today, to propose any amendment of that provision. But consideration as to whether it should be amended in the light of the obligations arising from the bad character provisions of the Criminal Justice Act 2003 ought, as it seems to us, to be given, in particular by the prosecuting authorities.

4. We turn to the case of Bovell. He was convicted at Woolwich Crown Court, on 27th January 2005, following a trial before His Honour Judge Moss, of wounding with intent. The following day he was sentenced to five-and-a-half years' imprisonment and an order for forfeiture of golf clubs was made under section 1(2) of the Prevention of Crime Act 1953.

5. In outline, the facts were that, on 5th September 2004, the applicant was involved in an altercation with a shopkeeper, Singh Harjinder Nazran, outside his shop. The culmination of the incident was that Mr Nazran was stabbed three times, twice to the leg and once in the buttock. The applicant ran away before the police arrived. The prosecution case was that the applicant had deliberately stabbed Mr Nazran, intending serious harm.

6. The defence case was that it was the applicant who had been attacked by Mr Nazran and he, the applicant, was acting in self-defence.

7. Mr Nazran gave evidence that the incident occurred after 7 o'clock in the evening. He knew the applicant. The applicant asked for credit. Mr Nazran refused. A little later, the applicant returned. He was aggressive. So much so that the complainant put his daughter, who was with him, inside the shop. The applicant was accompanied by his girlfriend, who had a golf club. The applicant walked up to him, seized the golf club from his girlfriend, which she immediately snatched back, and came towards the complainant face-to-face. According to the complainant, the applicant was ranting and raving and stabbed him in the top part of his left thigh. At first he felt nothing, but, as he turned to get a piece of wood, his leg gave way. Thereupon he was stabbed in the buttock by the applicant.

8. At hospital there were found to be two cuts in his leg. They were stitched together and the wound in his buttock was also stitched.

9. The defence sought to adduce before the jury, under section 100 of the Criminal Justice Act 2003, evidence of the bad character of Mr Nazran. The material then available was a conviction for handling stolen goods in October 1993, when the complainant was 20, for which he was fined and a conviction for robbery, committed in 1993, for which he had been sentenced to 4 years' imprisonment, following a guilty plea. The details of that offence of robbery then provided were that Mr Nazran had attacked his victim, placed a bag over his head, threatened him and stolen his property.

10. The defence submitted that these convictions were relevant and admissible, in accordance with section 100(1)(b), that is to say, they had substantial probative value. It was said that they showed Mr Nazran's propensity to act violently and also went to his credibility.

11. The trial judge concluded that he could not imagine a jury giving any weight to the previous convictions at all. They were over a decade ago, and neither of them involved, on the information then before the court, a weapon. He was not persuaded that they had substantial probative value and he declined to permit evidence in relation to them to be adduced. It is that aspect of the matter which is at the heart of the present application and to it we shall shortly return.

[12. and 13. The court described further evidence called by the prosecution, which corroborated Mr Nazran's account.]

14. The applicant, in evidence, said that he had gone to the shop initially to buy a drink. He was a few pence short and asked if he could owe the balance. The complainant had sworn at him. He, the applicant, had sworn back and called the complainant a 'drunken idiot'. He had gone to his girlfriend's to get the money he needed. He went back to the shop followed by his girlfriend, who had a golf club, although he did not. He had reached for the golf club because he was afraid of the complainant's dog, but she had snatched it back. Someone had hit him from behind and on the side and he suspected that that was Mr Doal. He had been winded by that. He was slumped over and heard a knife drop. He picked it up and waved it around in front of him at leg height, to frighten the complainant, not to harm him. He did not intend to make any contact with the complainant. He just wanted to stop the hitting. He saw blood on the knife and the complainant running away. He panicked and ran away himself, throwing away the knife. He denied, in cross-examination, having had the knife with him. It had, he said 'just appeared'.

15. The grounds of appeal challenge the judge's refusal to accede to the defence application to put the complainant's previous conviction and a caution before the jury. As a result of disclosure which has taken place in connection with this appeal, it appears that in the robbery, (committed in 1993, but for which the complainant was not tried until 1996 or 1997) the complainant, had carried a knife. That, as is apparent from the ruling which he gave, was not something which the judge knew about.

16. The submission is made by Mr Anders, on behalf of the applicant, that, had he known about that, the judge might very well have reached a different decision and permitted the jury to hear the evidence in relation to the complainant's robbery conviction.

17. It has also emerged that, in May 2001, the complainant was accused of violence and, in consequence, charged with an offence of wounding with intent, contrary to section 18 of the Offences Against the Person Act. That was a matter which was not known at the time of trial. It is now known that the charge was not, ultimately, pursued. On the day on which he made the allegation against the complainant in the present case, the victim stressed that he did wish to proceed. Two days later, it appeared that there was a dearth of witnesses of the incident about which he complained. Four days after the allegation had been made, the officer in the case expressed concern about the credibility of the victim. The matter was not pursued because the victim, in a written statement, on 18th June, withdrew the allegation against the present complainant, for reasons which, even now, are not known.

18. The submission made by Mr Anders, in relation to that section 18 charge is that it gave rise to evidence within section 100(1) which was substantially probative in relation to

165

the allegation made against this applicant. Therefore, it is said, had the judge known of the material now available, both in relation to the carrying of a knife in the robbery offence in 1993, and the events of 2001, he would have admitted evidence of both those matters in relation to the character of the complainant. Mr Anders submits that, that being so, it is impossible for this Court to be sure of the safety of the conviction. It might be that had the jury known of these matters, their verdict would have been different.

19. In response, on behalf of the Crown, Mr Houlder QC submits that, so far as the 1993 robbery is concerned, the judge's conclusion may or may not have been different had he known of the knife. So far as the events in 2001 are concerned, Mr Houlder submits that they do not give rise to evidence, still less of evidence of substantial probative value, within the terms of section 100(1)(b), and the learned judge, even had he known about those matters, could and would not properly have permitted them to be elicited before the jury.

20. In any event, Mr Houlder submits, had material of either of the kinds now relied on, in relation to the complainant's bad character, been admitted by the judge, it would have been inevitable that the judge would have acceded to a prosecution request, either to adduce evidence of, or to cross-examine the applicant about, his previous convictions. They, as is apparent from his record, were numerous in relation to dishonesty and, more specifically, he had been imprisoned in 1997 for possessing an offensive weapon in a public place and, in September 2001, he had been imprisoned for three separate offences of common assault. Those matters, submitted Mr Houlder, demonstrated not just dishonesty but a propensity to use violence and the possession of an offensive weapon. Had that material been before the jury, who had also known of the complainant's 1993 conviction for robbery and the accusation of section 18 wounding in 2001, their verdict would have been no different. There is no ground to question the safety of the conviction when there is also borne in mind the significant other evidence in the case, in particular, confirmation of the complainant's account by both Mr Doal and Miss Drummond. The jury had seen all the witnesses and, of particular significance, one of the wounds sustained by the victim was to his left buttock which, Mr Houlder submits, is an unlikely source of wounding if the applicant had been acting as he claimed, either accidentally or in self-defence. Furthermore, the applicant admitted that he himself used insulting words towards the complainant and the complainant's cousin. The jury would, inevitably, have come to the same conclusion. In any event, submits Mr Houlder, the events in 2001 would not have been admitted in evidence by the trial judge, even had he known about them.

21. As it seems to us, it may be that the judge's decision with regard to the admissibility of the robbery offence, in 1993, might have been different had he known that the complainant had then been carrying a knife. It is to be noted, however in relation to that offence, that, notwithstanding he was only prosecuted for it some years later, when fingerprint evidence come to light, the complainant immediately admitted his guilt. This would have been relevant to the judge's decision. It seems to us to be unlikely in the extreme that the judge, had he known of the events in 2001, would have admitted the allegation of a section 18 offence made against the complainant. We say that, first, because we entertain considerable doubt as to whether the mere making of an allegation is capable of being evidence within section 100(1). As the allegation was, in the circumstances which we have identified, withdrawn, our doubt on this aspect is increased.

22. It is apparent from the circumstances, as we have summarised them, that if there was to be any question of the section 18 allegation being admitted before the jury, it would necessarily have given rise to investigation of the other subsequent matters, including the aspersions on the credibility of the victim, the want of independent confirmation of his account, and the fact that he had withdrawn the allegation. An excursion into those satellite matters is, as it seems to us, precisely the sort of excursion which, as was suggested in paragraph 12 of the judgment in *Hanson*, a trial judge should be discouraged from embarking upon. All of this adds to the unlikelihood of the judge permitting evidence of the 2001 events even if they had been known about at trial.

23. As it seems to us, even if the judge had admitted the complainant's conviction for robbery and even if, which for the reasons we have given, we think highly unlikely, he had admitted the allegation of section 18 wounding, we are entirely unpersuaded that that might have affected the jury's verdict. We say that in part because of the inevitable consequences of the jury learning of the applicant's record and in part because of the other powerful evidence against the applicant.

24. Despite Mr Anders' able submissions, we are unpersuaded that it is arguable that Bovell's conviction is unsafe.

25. We turn to Dowds. On 28th January 2005, at Nottingham Crown Court, following a trial before Miss Recorder Dix-Dyer, he was convicted of burglary and he was subsequently sentenced to 2 years' detention in a young offender institution. A co-accused called Travis Leleu, had pleaded guilty on 26th January and he received a similar sentence.

26. The facts were that, at about 8 o'clock on the evening of 30th August 2004, a house in Beeston was burgled. Entry was gained by the co-accused using a key. There was no evidence that anything had actually been stolen; indeed, the Crown's case was that, in consequence of that entry, the applicant had left some items there, in particular, an orange and brown shoe box containing trainers and a poster. It appeared that the co-accused was claiming squatter's rights and had left a bag of his own in the premises.

27. The applicant had been seen, by someone living near the burgled house, carrying the box, prior to leaving it in the premises.

28. It was the prosecution case that the burglary enterprise was joint, involving both the applicant and the co-accused. The applicant's defence was that he had never gone into the house and he had no idea how the items connected to him had come to be inside.

29. The applicant had, on two previous occasions, pleaded guilty to an offence of burglary. It is at the heart of this appeal whether the learned Recorder ought properly to have permitted evidence in relation to those convictions, dating from when the applicant was aged 16 and 18 (he now being 19) to be before the jury.

30. It was conceded at trial by Mr Hurst, then as now appearing for the applicant, that in the course of giving evidence, the applicant made an attack on another person's character, within section 101(1)(g) of the Act. That came about in the following way. In the course of his evidence in-chief, Mr Hurst asked the applicant a question, which in his submission to us, he described as intended to elicit part of the background, but which in fact elicited from the applicant an answer which Mr Hurst had not been expecting. The answer was, in effect, that, on the day before the burglary of which the applicant was accused, his co-accused, Leleu, had committed another burglary.

31. The submission which Mr Hurst makes is that, notwithstanding this was undoubtedly an attack on another person's character, the learned Recorder, in the exercise of her discretion, when addressing the fairness of the proceedings under section 101(3) ought not to have admitted evidence of the applicant's two convictions for burglary. The sole basis advanced by Mr Hurst for the claim of unfairness in admitting the evidence is that the defendant's motive in giving the answer which he did may not have been to attack the co-accused.

32. As it seems to us, there are two difficulties with that proposition. First, in our judgment, it cannot have been Parliament's intention that, in order to assess 'adverse effect on the fairness of the proceedings', a trial judge should conduct some sort of investigation on the voir dire or otherwise as to why a defendant gave the answer which he did. Impact on the fairness of the proceedings must be assessed, in our judgment, by reference to matters other than what the particular defendant's intention in giving an answer may or may not have been. Secondly, having regard to the account of the applicant's evidence set out in detail, in particular, at pages 20 and 21 of the transcript of the summing-up, it is difficult to the point of impossibility to accept that the defendant's motive in giving the answer which he gave was not to cast an aspersion upon his co-accused. The applicant gave an account of what occurred, including his co-accused kicking in the door of the premises, and he, the applicant, storming off because he did not like what the co-accused was doing. For a person with two fairly recent previous convictions for burglary, that is an account which, to put it no higher, would not seem to sustain the suggestion that the applicant's reason for the answer he gave was not to be critical of the accused. That is particularly so, bearing in mind that the whole thrust of the applicant's defence was that only the co-accused was involved in this burglary and he, the applicant, was not. It is, in that context, perhaps worth commenting that evidence in relation to the applicant's bad character would, as it seems to us, have been admissible, under section 101(1)(f), to correct a false impression given by the defendant. It is unnecessary further to explore that aspect of the matter. But it suffices to say that, in our judgment, despite Mr Hurst's submissions, there is no basis for suggesting that the learned Recorder exercised her discretion under the statute in a way which was other than correct. That being so, Dowds' application does not, in our judgment, afford any arguable ground for challenging the safety of his conviction. Accordingly his application is, likewise, dismissed.

Applications for leave to appeal refused.

R v Edwards; R v Fysh; R v Duggan; R v Chohan [2005] EWCA Crim 1813, [2006] 1 CrAppR 3 (31), CA, 29 June 2005; Rose LJ (Vice-President), Holland and Richards JJ

F Arshad, J Lynn, J McCrindell and J Samuels for the applicants
B Houlder QC and A Bassano for the Crown

The Vice-President, Rose LJ:

1. These four cases have been listed and heard together because they provide further examples to add to those previously considered by this Court in *Hanson and Others* [2005] EWCA Crim 824, **p 153 above** and *Bovell and Dowds* [2005] EWCA Crim 1091, **p 163 above** of the admissibility of bad character under sections 98 to 113 of the Criminal Justice Act 2003.

2. Because of grounds which have been advanced in the cases of Fysh and Duggan in particular, in relation to alleged non-compliance in the respective summings-up with observations made by this Court in paragraph 18 of *Hanson*, it is convenient, before turning to the individual cases, to make some general observations in relation to that part of that judgment.

3. The guidance proffered in paragraph 18 of *Hanson* as to what a summing-up should contain was, as is apparent from the last sentence of the paragraph, not intended to provide a blueprint, departure from which will result in the quashing of a conviction. What the summing-up must contain is a clear warning to the jury against placing undue reliance on previous convictions, which cannot, by themselves, prove guilt. It should be explained why the jury has heard the evidence and the ways in which it is relevant to and may help their decision, bearing in mind that relevance will depend primarily, though not always exclusively, on the gateway in section 101(1) of the Criminal Justice Act 2003, through which the evidence has been admitted. For example, some evidence admitted through gateway (g), because of an attack on another person's character, may be relevant or irrelevant to propensity, so as to require a direction on this aspect. Provided the judge gives such a clear warning, explanation and guidance as to use, the terms in which he or she does so can properly differ. There is no rigid formula to be adhered to. That said, there is, in the case of Chohan, a summing-up by Judge Mort which seems to us to be almost impeccable and which could serve as a model in many cases where evidence of bad character is admitted. We shall rehearse the relevant passage in that summing-up when dealing with Chohan's application.

4. We turn, first, to the case of Edwards. On 24th February 2005, at Manchester Crown Court, following a trial before Mr Recorder Finestein, this applicant was convicted on two counts of common assault, on counts 1 and 2, and of having a bladed article in a public place on count 4. He was acquitted on count 3, of having an offensive weapon. He was sentenced to 2 months' imprisonment on each of the counts of common assault consecutively to each other, and to a further 8 months consecutively for possession of a bladed article. His total sentence was therefore 12 months' imprisonment, and an order was made under section 143 of the Powers of Criminal Courts (Sentencing) Act 2000 for forfeiture of the knife. His applications for leave to appeal against conviction and sentence were referred to the Full Court by the Registrar.

5. The facts were these. On 30th April 2004 two police officers stopped the applicant, who was driving a motor vehicle along Queen's Road, Manchester. They asked to see his licence and searched his car. They discovered a bottle of ammonia, which gave rise to count 3, in relation to which, as we have said, he was acquitted. The officers sought to arrest the applicant. A scuffle ensued. The officers and the applicant sustained minor injuries. The applicant was taken to a police station where he voluntarily handed over a lock-knife, which gave rise to count 4. It was the prosecution case that the applicant had assaulted the officers while they were lawfully seeking to arrest him and that he had no good reason for being in possession of the lock-knife. It was the defence case that the police officers had carried out an unprovoked assault on the applicant. He claimed to have a good reason for being in possession of the lock-knife, namely, he had used it on a fishing trip a couple of days previously, and had then completely forgotten about it.

6. The first of the officers to give evidence, Police Constable Smithwaite, described the applicant swearing at him and being generally obstructive when he, the officer, reached his car. There was a struggle inside the car as the other officer, Constable Bryson, went to get the keys. Then there was a struggle outside the car, during which the officers restrained the applicant by getting him onto the floor. The officer admitted in cross-examination that, during this altercation, he had himself sworn at a passer-by. Constable Bryson gave a similar account of the aggressive and uncooperative nature of the applicant's behaviour. A further officer described the knife as being located, not as the applicant claimed on his belt, but down the front of his trousers inside his jeans.

7. In interview, the applicant essentially said nothing in response to questions; he read a prepared statement, denying the offences and saying he had been mistreated by the police.

8. At the outset of the trial, the prosecution sought to adduce evidence of the applicant's previous convictions for robbery and dwelling-house burglary in 1992 in relation to the issue of credibility pursuant to section 101(1)(d). The Recorder ruled, at that stage, that, due to the age of the offences, it would not be right to allow that material to go before the jury. However, during the course of the prosecution case, the defence mounted a severe attack on the prosecution witnesses. Accordingly, the prosecution case made a further application to introduce evidence of bad character, under gateway (g), because of that attack.

9. On behalf of the defence, Miss Arshad accepted that the defendant had attacked the character of the two prosecution witnesses. But she invited the Recorder to exclude the evidence under section 101(3) on the basis that, by reason of the length of time, it would be unjust for the evidence to be admitted, bearing in mind that the offences were 13 years old; and their prejudicial effect, it was said, would outweigh their probative value. The Recorder ruled that, in view of the sustained attack on the character of the police, the jury was entitled to know about the 1992 conviction and he would direct the jury to give such weight to them as they saw fit.

10. The applicant gave evidence. He said that he was gratuitously and offensively treated by the police, whereas he had not been guilty of any bad conduct towards them. They had assaulted him and had caused him pain in the manner they applied and pulled down the handcuffs. Constable Smithwaite had told a passer-by to 'fuck off'. He said the lock-knife was not his. Two days earlier it had been handed to him by a friend, on a fishing expedition to cut the lines. He had hooked the knife onto his jeans (the ones which he was wearing at the time of his arrest). It had been there for two days, and he had simply forgotten about it.

He called his friend to confirm that he was the source of the knife. A young woman also gave evidence of the manner of application of the handcuffs by the police officers.

11. In passing sentence, the Recorder said that the applicant had behaved in a wholly aggressive way in assaulting the police, acting in their duty. Fortunately, the injuries were not serious, but the offences were so serious that only a custodial sentence was appropriate.

12. The appellant, who is 34 years of age, has a large number of previous convictions since 1991, mainly for driving and theft related offences. But, in 1992, as we have indicated, he was convicted of robbery and burglary from a dwelling and also assault occasioning actual bodily harm.

13. The submission which is made to this Court by Miss Arshad, on behalf of the appellant, is confined to a single ground of appeal, namely, that the previous 1992 convictions ought not to have gone before the jury. She submits that, when he ruled against the first application to admit that evidence under gateway (d), the Recorder had expressed the view that to admit that evidence would have so adverse an effect on the fairness of the proceedings that it ought not to be admitted at that stage. It is apparent from the transcript of the first ruling on 21st February that the Recorder, having referred to the offences being committed 13 years ago, said:

> to allow that in at this stage would seem to be on balance to have such an adverse effect on the fairness of the proceedings that the court ought not to admit it.

He went on to say:

> I have to balance the type of conviction that would go before the jury as against the allegation that the defendant faces, and in the context of this case, there are offensive weapons, be it CS gas or a knife and incidents of effectively common assault on police officers, and to allow that in for these offences it seems to me would have an adverse effect on the fairness of the proceedings, but more fundamental as I have indicated, I think it is the age of the conviction which plainly must be taken into account, and, having regard to the balancing act that I have to do, . . . I think it is perfectly clear on the authorities that these should not be allowed in, and so I do not allow them in.

That conclusion as to the impact of the 1992 matters on the fairness of the proceedings, Miss Arshad submits, was a finding which bound the Recorder when the later application was made, following the attack upon the prosecution witnesses.

14. As it seems to us, the difficulty with that submission is that the fairness of the proceedings and the impact on it of admitting the evidence, has to be gauged at the time at which the application is made and by reference to the gateway under which admissibility is sought. At the initial stage there had been no attack on the character of the prosecution witnesses. In that regard, when dealing with the matter at the time of the second application, the Recorder, as appears from the transcript, said this:

> I have come to the conclusion that there is a difference now between the prosecution arguments, the difference being a sustained attack upon the character of the police, and it seems to me that, even though these convictions are of a serious nature and of some age, the jury are entitled to know about this conviction, that I think they would be misled seriously if they did not know of this matter.

In our judgment, that was a conclusion which was not only open to the Recorder, it is one which he was, in the circumstances as we have described them, right to reach.

15. The second submission made by Miss Arshad is that, in admitting the evidence under gateway (g) because of its relevance to credibility and permitting the jury to know of a conviction in relation to the defendant's capacity to tell the truth, the learned Recorder adopted the wrong approach. He ought, Miss Arshad submits, to have admitted, rather than this conviction for a very serious offence of dishonesty, different convictions to be found in the applicant's record in more recent years.

16. The difficulty with that submission, as it seems to us, is that the convictions in more recent years included four convictions for offences of violence. Had the Recorder admitted those, it might well have been said that they had a significantly prejudicial effect against the defendant when he was facing charges of using violence: an impact which far outweighed the probative value of those offences. It is therefore, in our view, an impossible contention that the learned Recorder was wrong to admit an offence of dishonesty, but not to admit offences of violence. In those circumstances, there is, as it seems to us, no arguable ground of appeal in relation to conviction so far as Edward's is concerned. That application is refused.

[17. and 18. The court allowed the appeal against sentence.]

19. We turn to the case of Fysh. On 9th February 2005 at Norwich Crown Court, following a trial before His Honour Judge Worsley, this appellant was convicted of having an offensive weapon, on count 2, and common assault on count 3. On 23rd March he was sentenced to nine months on count 2 and five months concurrently on count 3. The total sentence was therefore 9 months' imprisonment. He appeals against conviction by leave of the single judge.

20. The facts were these. On 18th September 2004 the appellant went to the home in South Lynn of a man called Nicholas Moore. The appellant's friend drove him there in a Rover car, but remained in the car throughout. The appellant knocked on Mr Moore's door. He answered. The appellant accused Mr Moore of assaulting his son. Voices were raised. Mr Moore and his wife said that the appellant struck Mr Moore with some form of cosh, made from a sock containing something hard. Two 999 calls were made during the incident. The first by Mrs Moore, in which she at first described the weapon as a baseball bat, but, later in the conversation, said it was a sock containing, possibly, coins. There was a similar confusion in a second similar call.

21. The woman police constable called to the incident described Mr Moore as having an injury to the right side of his face, by his eye. There was redness, swelling and a small cut but she conceded that she had got the location wrong when she was cross-examined.

22. The appellant was known to the Moore family as, twenty years earlier, he had been engaged to Mr Moore's sister.

23. When the appellant was arrested and interviewed he said nothing. He was, however, picked out on identity parades by four witnesses. It was the prosecution case that the appellant had a cosh of the character which we have described and, when he confronted Mr Moore at his house, he deliberately struck out at him twice, and one of those blows struck Mr Moore's eye causing injury. It was the defence case that the appellant had been at Mr Moore's home on this day, but he had not touched Mr Moore with a weapon or anything else.

24. The judge indicated that, whether the appellant gave evidence or not, he would have to consider whether bad character was admissible, and he contemplated that it might be, under gateways (g) and/or (d) of section 101. He also indicated that he would not go back beyond 1986, in relation to the appellant's record, in the event that he allowed evidence to be admitted of previous convictions.

25. The evidence for the prosecution came from Mr Moore and Mrs Moore and from Stephen Coe and Spencer Canon who had been sitting in the kitchen of the Moores' house. Mr and Mrs Moore and Stephen Coe all described the appellant as using a weapon of the kind which we have described or, so far as Stephen Coe is concerned, he said he saw it raised above the appellant's head, though he did not actually see him strike Mr Moore. Spencer Canon also referred to the appellant holding what he described, initially, as a rounders bat, but later, after discussion with others, he realised was an old sock.

26. The Crown applied to adduce previous convictions of the appellant, not by any means all of them, but those starting with a conviction for common assault in 1999. The application also related to an offence of theft by shoplifting, in May 2002, making a false statement in order to obtain benefit or payment, including three offences taken into consideration, in August 2002, battery, in March 2002 and a further offence of theft by shoplifting in August 2002.

27. The learned judge ruled that these convictions were evidence of bad character, admissible under one of the gateways, in particular, gateways (d) and (g) and he concluded that there was no basis for excluding those convictions from being admitted.

28. The learned judge concluded that propensity to untruthfulness was an issue under gateway (d).

29. The submission which is made by Mr Lynn, on behalf of the appellant is that the judge was wrong to permit this evidence to be adduced. Mr Lynn points out that there was some confusion at the time of trial in February as to the rules applicable. The new Criminal Procedure Rules had not come into force and the old Crown Court rules, in particular rule 23 E3, appeared to govern the position. Those rules have now been replaced since April 2005 by the new Criminal Procedure Rules.[4]

30. In the light of the applicable rules Mr Lynn submits, first, that no notice was given by the prosecution of their intention to rely upon these convictions and there was no reason why appropriate notice could not have been given. By reason of the absence of notice, Mr Lynn submits that there was prejudice to the defence in two respects. First, there was a lack of time for him to prepare an argument against admissibility under the new statutory provisions. He accepts that he did not seek from the judge an adjournment, and that the judge said that, if he needed time further to consider the matter, he could have it. As it seems to us, there can have been no prejudice on this basis.

31. The second basis for prejudice, Mr Lynn submits, is that the facts were not agreed because no notice had been given and no adequate pre-trial enquiries had, in consequence, been made. The defendant was cross-examined about the facts of one of these offences. Mr Lynn submits the defendant was embarrassed in consequence, because the explanation which he had to give in relation to one of the offences was that it did not involve entry into

[4] See Appendix III above.

someone else's home, and the victim of the offence was his girlfriend. Clearly, it is unfortunate that there was cross-examination in those circumstances.

32. As this Court has previously pointed out, (see *Bovell and Dowds* para 2) it is important that provisions in relation to notice are observed so that adequate enquiries can be made on both sides as to the circumstances of offences, in so far as those circumstances may be relevant when the question of the admissibility of previous convictions arises. But, in the circumstances of this case, we are unpersuaded that the unfortunate cross-examination to which we have referred was such as, even arguably, to render the appellant's conviction unsafe. We say this in view of the limitation placed by the learned judge on the number of the appellant's abundant previous convictions which could be placed before the jury and having regard to the nature of the evidence against the appellant which, on any view, was substantial and came from a number of sources.

33. The second ground which was advanced in oral submissions by Mr Lynn was that the learned judge, in admitting previous convictions for offences of dishonesty, failed to consider the question of whether such offences gave rise, in the terms of the statute, to a propensity to be untruthful (see section 103 (1)(b)). As this Court has previously pointed out, dishonesty does not necessarily equate with a propensity to be untruthful. It may be that the offences of theft by shoplifting, had the appeal centred on that aspect of the matter alone, could properly be regarded as not showing a propensity to be untruthful, rather than merely dishonesty. That cannot, however, be said in relation to the offences of benefit fraud, committed on four occasions.

34. Mr Lynn accepted that, in any event, if the evidence was properly admissible under gateway (g), as well as under gateway (d), there could not be the same objection to the admissibility of the offences of dishonesty. Mr Lynn submitted that the judge's basic consideration, as he put it, in relation to admissibility was under gateway (d). He submits that if the convictions had not been admitted, there was a real likelihood that the appellant would have been acquitted. It is, at that point, convenient to refer to the observation made by the judge in the course of his ruling as to bad character. He said this:

So far as gateway (g) is concerned, yes, it is an inevitable consequence of the defendant's case that the prosecution witnesses have to be attacked by counsel as having made this up and put their heads together, as was put squarely to them, and rightly to them, by Mr Lynn, cooked up a story, invented a malicious and unpleasant story, a fraud.

As it seems to us, once it is accepted, as it was in the court below and is here, that the attack on the prosecution witnesses amounted to an allegation of conspiracy to put their heads together, in order falsely to implicate the appellant, the judge's ruling under gateway (g) was, as he described it himself 'inevitable.' In our judgment, there is no substance in the grounds of appeal so far as Fysh is concerned.

35. We add this, by reference to one of the written grounds not supported in oral submission before us today by Mr Lynn, that there is no sustainable criticism to be made of the terms in which the learned judge summed up this matter to the jury. It is correct that he did not have the advantage, if such it be, of this Court's judgment in *Hanson*, in relation to the distinction between a propensity to untruthfulness and dishonesty. In the course of his summing-up he equated the two. But the judge's summing-up followed, closely, the Specimen Direction given by the Judicial Studies Board, in December 2004, in relation to

the admissibility of evidence of bad character and the blemish upon it which we have identified it does not give rise to any reason for regarding the appellant's conviction as unsafe. Fysh's application is therefore refused.

36. We turn to the case of Duggan. On 4th March 2005, at Snaresbrook Crown Court, following a trial before Mr Recorder Marshall, this applicant was convicted of wounding with intent to cause grievous bodily harm and sentenced to 5 years' imprisonment. His application for leave to appeal against conviction and sentence was referred to the Full Court by the Registrar. The incident giving rise to the charge occurred on the evening of 25th April 2004, in the Walkabout Public House on Upper Street, Islington. There was an altercation between the applicant and a woman called Susan Green. She sustained an injury from glass to the outside of her right hand, a deep laceration of her right middle finger, a black eye and a bruised jaw.

37. It was the prosecution case that the applicant had deliberately punched the complainant in the face, whereupon she had raised her hands in protection and the applicant then thrust a glassed object towards her, injuring her hand. The defendant's case was that the complainant had thrust a pint glass towards his face and, as he raised his hand to protect himself, the bottle he was holding had collided with the glass, so that injuries were caused to the complainant's hand. He said that his arm must have inadvertently connected with the complainant's face, causing the bruising. The central issue was self-defence in the context of which of the two was the aggressor.

38. The evidence from Susan Green was that, on her way back from buying a round of drinks, she was bumped into from behind so her drink spilled. She tapped the applicant on the shoulder and spoke to him, but he was offhand. She asked whether he was going to apologise and he effectively spat out the word 'no' and threw his drink in her face. She thereupon threw her drink on him. At that stage, he punched her in the face with a clenched fist, straight to the eye. She was shocked. She held up her hands to protect herself; her glass by this stage had gone out of her hands. She could not say what the man had in his hands and she was not able to say precisely what happened after that. She denied in cross-examination that her hand injury was sustained when she was punched in the face. The two incidents were separate and her hand had been injured after she had been punched. She had done nothing violent. Evidence confirmatory of her account was given by Beth Howells, who said that it might have been 10 to 12 seconds after the punch that she saw the attack with the glass.

39. A Policewoman Constable came to the scene. When she arrived, the applicant was being aggressive and shouting at the door staff: 'You're a fucking cunt'. She warned him about his behaviour and he shouted: 'Your mother blows fucking Pakis'. She arrested him for a public order offence. Details were taken by another officer, in relation to the assault on Susan Green and the applicant was arrested for that. He continued to be racially abusive. When he was told he was being arrested for a racially aggravated public order offence, he claimed, falsely as he later said, to be a member of the British National Party and proud of it. He continued with similar insults and refused to give his name. He declined the services of a solicitor and did not answer any questions in interview.

40. He gave evidence that he had been drinking and watching football during the day. He had eight beers over three or four hours but was not drunk. The atmosphere in the pub had been 'lovely.' The complainant had bumped into him rather than the other way round.

She had moved her glass to his face and he was afraid she was going to glass him, so he brought up his arm to protect himself. He had a bottle of beer in his hand, which must have broken the complainant's glass. He assumed, although he had not felt it, that his arm must have carried on and must have hit her on the face. He had been asked to leave by a bouncer.

41. He said in relation to his previous convictions, as to the rulings about which we shall in a moment come, that he always pleaded guilty. He was not in fact a member of the BNP but he did not dispute what the police officer said he had said. He claimed that he was upset because he was being arrested for nothing at all. He described himself as a gentleman. Both of the witnesses against him were lying.

42. The learned judge ruled, in relation to the admission of evidence of bad character, that although the Crown's application was out of time, and that no notice in accordance with the rules had been given, it was in the interests of justice that the application should succeed because no prejudice had resulted to the defence from the lack of notice.

43. The Recorder said that the applicant's convictions for assault and theft, in 1998, and for an offence contrary to section 5 of the Public Order Act 2003 were clearly bad character within the meaning of section 98. In addition the applicant had pleaded guilty to a racially aggravated section 5 Public Order Act offence, which arose from the events following his arrest for the wounding of Miss Green. That offence also, in the Recorder's judgment, came within the definition of bad character. He rejected a defence submission that that evidence came within the exception in section 98(b) as being 'misconduct in connection with the investigation . . . of that offence.'

44. The Recorder ruled that the applicant's behaviour, after the offence, was admissible as being relevant to his demeanour and state of mind at the time of the offence. It was clearly capable of informing the jury of what was happening so soon after the crucial events. There was no prejudice in admitting the evidence, such as to lead to exclusion under section 78 of the Police and Criminal Evidence Act and therefore the evidence was admissible.

45. The Crown sought to admit the previous convictions under gateway (d), on the basis that the matters in issue between the parties were who attacked whom and whether the applicant was telling the truth in relation to self-defence. The Recorder ruled that the convictions for violence or disorder were relevant to the issue of self-defence. They showed a clear pattern of attacking people, so that the Crown could properly adduce the evidence to establish propensity. The Recorder said he was not satisfied that the applicant's honesty was a substantial issue, so that his conviction for theft ought to be admitted.

46. Having referred to section 101(3) and (4) the Recorder said he was satisfied that the evidence would not have such an adverse effect on the fairness of the proceedings that it ought to be excluded: on the contrary, it was capable of informing the jury of precisely what they needed to know. Although the first assault was committed when the applicant was 16, it could not be said to be one-off in view of his more recent offending in November 2002. Although the offences were not of the same description or category, for the purposes of section 103(2) and (4), that did not preclude admissibility.

47. There was an issue about whether the earlier conviction was for assaulting occasioning actual bodily harm or, as the applicant maintained, for common assault. That is one of the aspects which give rise to this application for leave to appeal. We shall return to it a little later. The learned Recorder ruled that the underlying facts in relation to the conviction in 1998, for which no memorandum of conviction was then available, should not be admitted.

[48. and 49. The court discussed matters relevant to sentence.]

50. On behalf of the applicant, Mr McCrindell advances a number of grounds of appeal in seeking to challenge the applicant's conviction. First, he says, rightly, that it was not until the morning of the trial that antecedents were obtained and there had been no previous notice of an intention to rely on the applicant's previous convictions. Mr McCrindell refers to paragraph 2 in the judgment of this Court in *Bovell and Dowds*, which stressed the importance of the rules being adhered to, so that, in particular, the defence are in a position to deal with the matters on which the prosecution rely, and both sides can make such enquiries as may be necessary with regard to the circumstances of convictions sought to be relied on. Mr McCrindell points out, rightly, that, if the rules had been complied with, everyone would have been clear as to exactly what evidence was to go before the jury.

51. So far as the admissibility of the convictions is concerned, Mr McCrindell stresses the difficulties arising from the want of notice in investigating the nature of what was said to be an assault occasioning actual bodily harm. It is apparent from the memorandum of conviction, which has been obtained since trial, that the offence of which the applicant was previously convicted, which was the subject of dispute (it is to be noted the only subject of dispute) was common assault, not assault occasioning actual bodily harm. So far as that is concerned, however, the learned judge directed the jury that it was probably best to assume for safety 'that it was a conviction of common assault.'

52. So far as the applicant's aggressive behaviour after the incident and following the arrival of the police officers is concerned, Mr McCrindell makes no complaint about want of notice in relation to that because statements from prosecution witnesses served on the defence described that conduct on which the prosecution wished to rely. The want of notice in relation to the convictions, as it seems to us, did not give rise to any prejudice so far as the defence were concerned. Clearly, it may well have been prejudicial had the matter proceeded wrongly on the basis that the offence was assault occasioning actual bodily harm, rather than merely common assault. But, by virtue of the direction given by the Recorder in his summing-up, it is apparent that the case did not proceed on that basis.

53. The second ground advanced by Mr McCrindell is that the material before the court, on the basis of which the bad character evidence was admitted, was of poor quality, in that it was derived from the Police National Computer. The difficulty with that submission, as it seems to us, is that there was nothing in dispute by the defence, in relation to the material from the Police National Computer, apart from the nature of the assault to which we have already referred. There is, in consequence, no substance in that ground.

54. The third ground advanced by Mr McCrindell is that the bad character evidence should not have been admitted. In particular, in that regard, he refers to the speech of Lord Phillips of Worth Matravers in the civil, similar fact, case of *O'Brien v Chief Constable of South Wales Police* [2005] UKHL 26, [2005] 2 AC 354. At paragraphs 12 and 52 Lord Phillips observed that the statutory provisions with which this Court is presently concerned 'require an enhanced relevance in order to ensure that the ambit of the trial remains manageable.' As it seems to us, there was an enhanced relevance in relation to the earlier convictions and the events after these offences, so far as the applicant's behaviour is concerned. In our judgment, such matters were capable of establishing propensity to violence relevant to the crucial issue as to who was the aggressor.

55. There are further grounds, 4, 5 and 6, in relation to the use of unchallenged racist language. But for the reasons which we have already indicated, the learned Recorder was entitled to conclude that they showed a high level of aggression on the applicant's part, immediately following the incident giving rise to the section 18 offence.

56. Ground 7 is a further complaint about reliance on the Police National Computer with which we have sufficiently dealt.

57. Grounds 8 to 12 are critical in various respects of the summing-up. It is said that, in Mr McCrindell's words, 'this went a little bit too far', when the learned Recorder said that the prosecution case was that the applicant was an aggressive man who had been aggressive on this night. Something which goes a little bit too far, even if it does—and we are not persuaded that it does—is an insubstantial basis on which to suggest that a summing-up is so defective as to render a conviction arguably unsafe.

58. Mr McCrindell relies on the observations made in paragraph 18 of this Court's judgment in *Hanson*, and submits that further directions in accordance with that judgment ought to have been given. Of course, that judgment was not available at the time of the Recorder's summing-up, and we have already, at the beginning of this judgment, referred to the way in which paragraph 18 in *Hanson* should be understood.

59. The further criticism is made that, in the summing-up, the Recorder's use of the phrase 'you have been permitted to hear of these convictions,' in the context of an explanation by the Recorder as to why those convictions were before the jury, was terminology which might induce in the jury's mind a belief that the Recorder himself had already decided that the convictions were determinative of issues which the jury had to decide. We are wholly unpersuaded that that is a possible interpretation of that passage in the summing-up. In our judgment, without descending into further detail, there is no substance in any of the criticisms of the summing-up. Accordingly, leave to appeal against conviction is refused.

[60. and 61. The court allowed the defendant's appeal against sentence.]

62. We come, finally, to the application of Chohan. On 8th February 2005, at Manchester Crown Court, following a trial before His Honour Judge Mort, this applicant was convicted on count 1 of robbery, on count 2 of possession of an imitation firearm while committing a schedule 1 offence and on count 3 of possession of an imitation firearm with intent to cause fear of violence. He was sentenced to 10 years' imprisonment on count 1 and to 3 years' imprisonment concurrently on each of counts 2 and 3. The total sentence was therefore 10 years' imprisonment. His application for leave to appeal against conviction has been referred to this Court by the Registrar.

63. The facts were these. A couple of days prior to the incident which formed the basis of the three counts, an 89 year old man called Sidney Marsh was visited at home by the applicant, who claimed that his mother had been robbed and he was looking for the culprits. He said he had written their descriptions on a piece of paper which he gave to Mr Marsh.

64. On 19th May 2003 Mr Marsh was again at home, in Solway Close, Oldham. The applicant arrived and shouted through the window: 'I've found those lads.' He walked into the kitchen, shook the complainant by the shoulders, produced what appeared to be a gun, pointed it at Mr Marsh's chest and said: 'I want a fiver.' Mr Marsh went to get a £5 note and the man took his wallet from him. That gave rise to counts 1 and 2. Astonishingly, when his

robber had left his home, this 89 year old victim gave chase. He told a neighbour he had been robbed. Two women neighbours gave chase for a short while and confronted the man, who pointed a gun at them, giving rise to count 3. They backed off. He made good his escape.

65. The identification of the robber as the applicant rested upon a prosecution witness called Donna Marsh. She happened to be nearby, in Lee Street, when, she said, the applicant, whom she knew as 'Tony,' ran past her. The issue, essentially, was whether she was right. The two women neighbours who had given chase, although they gave descriptions of the man they chased, were unable to pick him out on an identification parade.

66. Donna Marsh described seeing the man running away. She had a clear view of him. She turned and said 'Hello.' He replied. She knew him as Tony. He was an Asian man, about 30, five feet eight or nine, stocky and wearing a hat. She had his face in sight for a minute or so. He had a gun in his hand. At this time, that is May 2003, she had known him for about a year. Her evidence (and to the circumstances in which it was admitted in this form we shall come in a moment), was that she had seen him a lot, indeed every other day for a year or so, because she bought heroin from him. She was taking heroin three or four times a day. She used to meet him at the bottom of Lee Street, the street in which he was when she saw Mr Marsh's assailant running away. She also met him at The Junction pub.

67. On 25th August 2004 she picked out the applicant on a VIPER parade as being the man she had seen the previous May. The reason why there had been so long a lapse of time between the offence of robbery and the VIPER parade was because, for most of that period, from a time starting two days after the commission of this offence, the applicant had been out of this country.

68. She said that she had not wanted to say that she was a heroin user. That was why, in the first statement which she made to the police, she only referred to knowing the applicant from seeing him around and in a pub. She thought she had mentioned the gun in her first statement, but it was not there. She said she had no reason to invent her evidence.

69. There were submissions made to the learned judge in relation to two different categories of evidence namely Donna Marsh the appellant's previous convictions. In relation to Donna Marsh she made a second statement on 8th January 2005 describing the basis on which she was able to recognise the applicant, namely the frequency of their encounters during heroin dealings. The prosecution sought to adduce it, under gateway (c) of section 101(1), that is to say, that it was 'important explanatory evidence': explanatory, of course, in relation to the basis of her identification.

70. The judge ruled that, in such a case, it was inevitable that the jury, who would have to be directed as to the caution necessary in identification by reference to *Turnbull* [1977] QB 224, would have to consider the circumstances in which the witness claimed to be able to identify the defendant. It would, the judge concluded, be difficult properly to understand other evidence in the case without knowing the background of the heroin dealings which, he concluded, went to the heart of matters.

71. The wording of section 101(3) of the Act, whereby the court must not admit evidence under gateways (d) or (g) if it appears that it would have such an adverse effect on the fairness of the proceedings that the court ought not to admit it, suggested, the judge said, that section 78 of the Police and Criminal Evidence Act was not applicable in relation to gateways (d) and (g). But, he concluded, even if he was wrong, he would not exercise his

discretion in this case to exclude the evidence, bearing in mind the vital importance to the identification by Donna Marsh of the explanatory evidence.

72. Submissions were also made in relation to the applicant's previous convictions, of which there are a considerable number. The application related to a robbery/assault with intent to rob, in 1992, and three burglaries in 2000. The Crown sought to adduce that evidence as to those convictions under gateway (d) on the basis that they were relevant to an important matter in issue, namely, a propensity to commit the type of offence with which the applicant was charged. They fell under subsection(1)(a), in that they were of the same description or category as the offence charged and, therefore, were admissible, subject to section 103(3), in relation to the length of time since the conviction, or any other matter, which rendered them inadmissible. The judge concluded that, despite the lapse of time, it was not unjust to admit the robbery conviction in 1992, bearing in mind the applicant's continuing criminality thereafter and the fact that it was a serious robbery at knife-point, which was material in the present case. Furthermore, the three burglaries in 2000 were relevant because they involved very similar methods of operation, namely gaining entry, by falsity, into the homes of the elderly. The judge concluded that it would not have such an adverse effect on the fairness of the proceedings that they ought not to be admitted. Furthermore, so far as the robbery in 1992, was concerned, although that offence was old, it demonstrated a propensity to commit offences involving the use of a weapon against a householder.

73. The defendant in evidence said that he had not been at Mr Marshall's house on 19th May, nor had he had a gun. He had never been a drug dealer. He had gone to Pakistan soon after the offence because his wife's mother was there and she had been taken ill. He said that, in interview, he had not known what was meant by the name Donna Marsh: he only knew her by her first name. He claimed to have recognised her when he came to court. He had known her for several years, as they were both heroin users. He claimed, and it is to be emphasised that this was denied by Donna Marsh, that he had had a sexual relationship with her. He suggested that she must have lied about seeing him running away from the robbery because he had not told her that he had remarried.

74. On behalf of the applicant, Mr Samuels submits that the judge was wrong to admit Donna Marsh's second statement describing the heroin dealing with the applicant. Mr Samuels accepted, rightly, that only a fraction of the applicant's record went before the jury by reason of the judge's ruling. He submits that it would have been possible to edit the statement in relation to the heroin dealing, in order to disclose a frequency of encounters, without disclosing the reason for those encounters. The prejudice arising from the allegation of heroin dealing was such that the judge ought not to have admitted the statement in the form which he did. It is to be noted that whereas initially the defence based upon a challenge to the frequency of the association between the applicant and Donna Marsh, it later changed to a claim of deliberate dishonesty by her, promoted by malice.

75. In our judgment, the circumstances of this case, in relation to identification, were such that no sustainable criticism can be made of the judge's decision to admit in evidence the witness Donna Marsh's second statement. Only if that was done, as it seems to us, would it be possible for her sensibly to explain, not least, in the face of the different defences emanating from the applicant, the basis of her ability to identify him in the circumstances which she did.

76. So far as the admission of the 1992 robbery and the three dwelling-house burglaries in 2000 are concerned, Mr Samuels was frank enough to concede that the circumstances of the three burglaries were, as he put it, 'uncomfortably close' to the offence charged. As it seems to us, that was a reason not for excluding the evidence of those convictions but for admitting it. The judge's exercise of discretion, in relation to the admission of these convictions was, as it seems to us, impeccably performed. No suggestion is made that he took into account inappropriate considerations or failed to take into account appropriate considerations. Accordingly, the application for leave to appeal against conviction on behalf of Chohan fails.

77. Before leaving the case of Chohan, it is, as we foreshadowed at the beginning of this judgment, perhaps helpful to refer to the summing-up of His Honour Judge Mort in Chohan's case:

In this case you have heard evidence that Mr Chohan has a bad character, in the sense that he has got criminal convictions and you have heard, it is alleged, that he otherwise misconducted himself by supplying heroin to Donna Marsh. It is important that you understand why you have heard this evidence and how you can use it. As I will explain in more detail later, you must not convict Mr Chohan only because he has got a bad character. You have heard of this bad character because, first of all, in relation to the allegation that he was supplying drugs to Donna (and bear in mind it is her allegation that that is the position) it may help you to understand other evidence in the case, namely how is it that Donna Marsh was so confident that the man running past her on Lee Street, running away from Mr Marsh and from the two women, was the defendant. The reason being because she was seeing him several times a day when acquiring drugs from him. So it may help you to consider the accuracy and reliability of her identification and it may help you to understand the case as a whole. You have heard, in relation to the previous convictions, of his bad character and it may help you to resolve an issue that has arisen between the defence and the prosecution, namely the question whether he has a propensity or a tendency or an inclination to commit offences of the kind with which he is charged. If you think it is right, you may take the previous convictions into account, in deciding whether or not Mr Chohan committed the offences with which he is now charged. The prosecution rely on the robberies in 1992 because they show that he has a tendency to use weapons to threaten violence to steal and two instances have been given to you where a sheath knife was used, one in order to steal and one whereby theft actually took place and it is said, ten years on, now he is using a handgun. The prosecution rely on the burglaries in 2000 because they say that they show that the defendant has a tendency to use bogus explanations to trick his way into older people's homes in order to steal from them . . . So the prosecution's case there is that it is, on this occasion, a combination of pretending to be looking for people who have robbed his mother, asking for a pen and paper to write down the description of the alleged robberies and then using the pretext, coming back and saying: 'We have found them' going in, producing the gun and stealing wallet. So the Crown are saying here there is a tendency to commit robberies with a weapon and to target the elderly with bogus explanations and, therefore, they say it makes it more likely that he is guilty of the offence. The defence, on the other hand, say, first of all, these robberies were ten years ago, he described himself, 'I was about

16 or 17 at the time, the burglaries were three years old, I always pleaded guilty to offences that I had been arrested for' and it is, in fairness to the defence, a matter which you can take into account, deciding what impact the convictions had on his truthfulness. Mr Samuels put it in a well known phrase from Casablanca of 'rounding up the usual suspects' and that is what obviously you must be very careful about . . .

If you do conclude that, at the time of these offences in May, 2003, Mr Chohan did have a propensity to commit offences of that type, namely robberies with weapons or targeting the elderly with bogus explanations to get entry into the property, then you can consider whether it makes it more likely that he committed the offences in May, 2003. You have to decide to what extent, if at all, his character helps you when you are considering whether or not he is guilty. You must not convict simply because of his convictions, nor mainly because of them. The propensity or tendency amounts to some additional evidence pointing to guilt, but please bear in mind, even if he did have such a tendency, it does not necessarily prove that he would commit further offences or that he has committed these offences.

You are also entitled to consider the evidence of Mr Chohan's previous convictions in the following way. If you think it right, you may take into account, when deciding whether or not his evidence to you was truthful, because a person with convictions for dishonesty may be less likely to tell the truth, but it does not follow that he is not capable of telling the truth. Indeed, Mr Chohan says, 'The fact that on the previous occasions I have been arrested and I have always held my hands up means that, when I plead not guilty, I am likely to be telling the truth' and you decide to what extent his character helps you when judging his evidence. So that is the extent to which the evidence of his previous convictions may be used for the particular purposes I have just indicated, if you find it helpful.

That approach is not only, rightly not criticised by Mr Samuels in this case, but, subject to one refinement in relation to the distinction drawn between propriety of dishonesty and propriety to untruthfulness in para 13 of *Hanson*, it provides an impeccable summing-up which may well afford useful guidance in other cases where summing up the significance of previous convictions.

78. For the reasons which we have given, Chohan's application for leave to appeal against conviction is refused.

79. Although we have not, in the course of this judgment, referred expressly to the written submissions provided for the Court's benefit by Mr Houlder QC, on behalf of the Crown, we are greatly indebted to him for the submissions which he made in relation to each of these cases.

Edwards: appeal against sentence allowed, application for leave to appeal against conviction refused.
Fysh: appeal against conviction dismissed.
Duggan: appeal against sentence allowed, leave to appeal against conviction refused.
Chowhan: application for leave to appeal against conviction refused.

R v Highton; R v Van Nguyen; R v Carp [2005] EWCA Crim 1985, [2005] 1 WLR 3472, [2006] 1 CrAppR 7 (125) CA, 28 July 2005; Lord Woolf (Chief Justice), Moore-Bick and Richards JJ

P Du Feu, M Goldwater and T Munyard for the applicants
F Horlick, W Baker and P.Ashman for the Crown

Lord Woolf CJ:
This is the judgment of the Court.

The general position

1. We are hearing these three appeals together because they each concern the bad character provisions contained in the Criminal Justice Act 2003 (the '2003 Act'), Part XI, Chapter 1, sections 98–113. There are already 3 previous decisions of this Court dealing with these provisions. The cases are those of *Hanson* [2005] EWCA Crim 824 (**p 153 above**), *Bovell and Dowdes* [2005] EWCA Crim 1091 (**p 163 above**) and *Edwards, Fysh, Duggen and Chohan* [2005] EWCA Crim 1813 (**p 169 above**). The principal issue which arises on these appeals is whether evidence admitted under section 101(1)(g) as a result of an attack by the defendant on another person's character is admissible as evidence of a propensity to commit offences of the kind with which the defendant is charged, or is only admissible in relation to his credibility, that is, as evidence tending to show that he is likely to be untruthful. That issue did not arise in those earlier appeals and this judgment is the first judgment relating to it.

2. The issue arises because section 101 of the 2003 Act identifies 7 different gateways, at least one of which must be complied with before evidence of a defendant's bad character is admissible in criminal proceedings. However, the 2003 Act does not expressly identify the purpose for which the bad character evidence can be used if it passes through one of those gateways and is therefore admissible. Two different interpretations are contended for by counsel appearing for the appellants and the Crown. The appellants contend that the purposes for which admissible evidence of bad character can be used are confined by the terms of the gateway through which the evidence is admitted. The Crown, on the other hand, contends that once the evidence becomes admissible by passing through any gateway, it can be used for any purpose for which bad character evidence is relevant in the particular case.

3. The dimensions of the issue are apparent when the relevant provisions of the sections of the 2003 Act are considered.

[4.–7. The court set out sections 98, 101, 102 and 103 in full, together with parts of section 112 and paraphrased sections 104, 105 and 106.][5]

8. If [. . .] we return to section 103(1), it is to be noted that it deals with propensity. The argument before us was as follows: as subsection 101(1)(d) is the only gateway that is referred to in section 103(1), the reference it contains to propensity makes it clear that it is only if the evidence is admitted under section 101(d) that bad character evidence can be used to show a propensity on the part of the defendant to commit the offences of which he is charged or a propensity to be untruthful.

---

[5] These provisions are set out in Appendix I above.

9. In our view, however, the force of this argument is diminished for a number of reasons. First, section 103(1) prefaces section 103(1)(a) and (b) with the word 'include.' This indicates that the matters in issue may extend beyond the two areas mentioned in this subsection. More importantly, while this argument can be advanced in relation to section 101 (d), it can also be advanced in respect of the other parts of sub-section (1), in particular in relation to section 101(1)(a) and (b). In addition, section 101(1) itself states that it is dealing with the question of admissibility and makes no reference to the effect that admissible evidence as to bad character is to have. We also consider that the width of the definition in section 98 of what is evidence as to bad character suggests that, wherever such evidence is admitted, it can be admitted for any purpose for which it is relevant in the case in which it is being admitted.

10. We therefore conclude that a distinction must be drawn between the *admissibility* of evidence of bad character, which depends upon it getting through one of the gateways, and the *use* to which it may be put once it is admitted. The use to which it may be put depends upon the matters to which it is relevant rather than upon the gateway through which it was admitted. It is true that the reasoning that leads to the admission of evidence under gateway (d) may also determine the matters to which the evidence is relevant or primarily relevant once admitted. That is not true, however, of all the gateways. In the case of gateway (g), for example, admissibility depends on the defendant having made an attack on another person's character, but once the evidence is admitted, it may, depending on the particular facts, be relevant not only to credibility but also to propensity to commit offences of the kind with which the defendant is charged.

11. This approach underlines the importance of the guidance that was given in the case of *Hanson and others* as to the care that the judge must exercise to give the jury appropriate warnings when summing up. (We refer in particular to para 18 of that judgment and para 3 of the judgment of *Edwards* and its commendation of the summing up of Judge Mort in the case of *Chohan*). In *Edwards* The Vice-President, Lord Justice Rose said:

> What the summing up must contain is a clear warning to the jury against placing undue reliance on previous convictions, which cannot, by themselves, prove guilt. It should be explained why the jury has heard the evidence and the ways in which it is *relevant* to and may help their decision. Bearing in mind that *relevance* will depend primarily, though not always exclusively, on the gateway in section 101(1) of the Criminal Justice Act 2003, through which the evidence has been admitted. For example, some evidence admitted through gateway (g), because of an attack on another person's character, may be relevant or irrelevant to propensity, so as to require a direction on this aspect. (para 3) (emphasis added)

12. Protection is also provided for the defendant at the stage of admissibility by the terms of section 101(3) if the admission of the evidence could cause unfairness, and by the reference in section 103(3) to convictions which it would be unjust to admit as evidence of a propensity to commit offences of the kind with which he is charged because the Court is satisfied, 'by the reason of the length of time since the conviction or for any other reason' that it would be unjust for sub-section 103(2) to apply. In this context, there is a very close relationship between the requirements of fairness and the general requirement of the rules of evidence that, unless evidence is relevant, it should not be admitted.

13. Those provisions protect against unfairness arising out of the admission of bad character evidence under section 101(1)(d) or (g). The question also arises as to whether reliance can be placed on section 78 of Police and Criminal Evidence Act 1984 ('PACE'). The application of section 78 does not call directly for decision in this case. We, therefore, do not propose to express any concluded view as to the relevance of section 78. However, it is right that we should say that, without having heard full argument, our inclination is to say that section 78 provides an additional protection to a defendant. In light of this preliminary view as to the effect of section 78 of PACE, judges may consider that it is a sensible precaution, when making rulings as to the use of evidence of bad character, to apply the provisions of section 78 and exclude evidence where it would be appropriate to do so under section section 78, pending a definitive ruling to the contrary. Adopting this course will avoid any risk of injustice to the defendant.

14. In addition, as section 78 serves a very similar purpose to Article 6 of the European Convention on Human Rights, following the course we have recommended should avoid any risk of the court failing to comply with Article 6. To apply section 78 should also be consistent with the result to which the court would come if it complied with its obligation under section 3 of the Human Rights Act 1998 to construe sections 101 and 103 of the 2003 Act in accordance with the Convention.

The appeal of Highton

The facts

15. Having given this general guidance, we turn to the appeal of Edward Paul Highton ('Highton'). Highton is now 24 years of age. On 28 February 2005, at Oxford Crown Court, he was unanimously convicted of two counts of kidnapping, two offences of robbery and one count of theft. He was sentenced to four and a half years' imprisonment on each count to run concurrently. Highton's application for leave to appeal against conviction was referred directly to this Court by the Registrar. We give Highton leave to appeal. Highton had a co-accused, Dean Wilson. He was also convicted of the counts on which Highton was convicted. In addition, he pleaded guilty to a separate offence of theft. He received a total of six and a half years' imprisonment.

16. The prosecution's case was that on 29 September 2004, the two victims, Stephen Duckett and Alan McPherson, were kidnapped by Dean Wilson in Milton Keynes and forced to drive to Highton's house in Oxford. At that house, they were robbed at knifepoint and thereafter, taken to a cash point where Highton withdrew and stole £330 from Duckett's account. It was said by the Crown that Highton and Wilson were engaged in a joint enterprise.

17. The defence's case was that the two victims went to Oxford voluntarily to buy drugs. Neither the robberies nor the kidnapping took place, and the cash was stolen by the dealer from whom the victims were trying to buy the drugs. They said that the victims had originally lied to the Police in their statements, stating that Highton had been present in Milton Keynes at the alleged kidnapping, which they stated was at random by two strangers. Not surprisingly in these circumstances the credibility both of the defendants and of the complainants, that is to say who was speaking the truth, was one of the main issues at the trial.

18. Wilson and Highton both had previous convictions, details of which were allowed to go before the jury. Wilson had convictions for various offences of dishonesty and for offences of violence, including convictions for two robberies in 2002. Highton also had convictions for offences of dishonesty and for offences of violence, including four offences of assault occasioning actual bodily harm, one of causing grievous bodily harm, two relating to the possession of offensive weapons, and one of affray, all in the period 1998 to 2004.

19. The grounds of appeal were:

(a) that the judge wrongly admitted the appellant's previous convictions under section 101(g) of the 2003 Act.
(b) that he also wrongly directed the jury as to the significance of the appellant's conviction in relation to the issue of propensity.

Our conclusions

20. There was no answer to the contention that this was a case that fell within section101(1)(g). Mr Du Feu based his argument upon section101(3). He argued that the judge should exclude evidence as to Highton's previous convictions as a matter of discretion under that subsection. Against the co-defendant, Wilson, the prosecution also relied on section101(1)(d). section 101(1)(d) was never clearly relied upon by the prosecution against Highton. Furthermore, at the end of the argument, Judge Jack said with regard to Highton 'he is not at risk from a propensity argument'.

21. However, when the judge came to sum up, he unfortunately does not appear to have recalled his exchange with Mr Du Feu, since when dealing with the evidence as to bad character he told the jury:

Well, plainly that is a substantial attack on the prosecution witnesses' character, and in those circumstances, the law says that it is only right that you should hear what character those who are making such an attack bear. But you also heard about their characters because it may help you to resolve an issue in the case, which is this: the prosecution argue that the *defendants* have a propensity to commit offences of the sort that you are considering. You may therefore use the evidence of the defendant's bad character in relation to those two matters which explains why you have heard about it, but only if you find it helpful to do so.

22. The evidence having been properly admitted through the section 101(1)(g) gateway, for the reasons we have explained, it can be, in the appropriate circumstances, relied upon as evidence of a propensity to commit offences of the kind with which the defendant is charged as well as as evidence going to the defendant's credibility. However, in the course of the exchange which took place between the judge and Mr Du Feu during argument, the judge led counsel and the appellant to believe that he would not direct the jury that they could take his previous convictions into account when deciding whether he was guilty of the offences with which he was charged. In those circumstances, the judge was in error in summing up in the terms that he did.

23. This was not a case where the judge was required to exclude the previous convictions under section 101(3). Mr Du Feu candidly acknowledged that he did not ask the judge to

exclude the evidence, but any such application would have been doomed to fail. It may be worth pointing out, however, that the exclusion of evidence under the provisions of section 101(3) depends on there being an application by the defendant. If no such application is made, no criticism can be made of the judge for failing to act of his own motion under this section.

24. The appellant's previous convictions, which included convictions for offences of violence and for the possession of offensive weapons, did provide evidence of a propensity to commit offences of the kind with which he was charged. In addition, the judge did direct the jury carefully as to the limits of the value of character evidence. In the result, therefore, we have come to the conclusion that, while the judge did make the error that we have identified in this summing up, the error was not such as to make the verdicts of the jury unsafe. Accordingly, Highton's appeal is dismissed.

The appeal of Dong Van-Nguyen

The background to the appeal

25. On 16 February 2005, at the Crown Court of Manchester before His Honour Judge Ensor, Dong Van-Nguyen was convicted of cultivating a controlled drug, namely a plant of the genus cannabis. He was sentenced to 30 months' imprisonment. In addition, an order was made for the forfeiture and the destruction of the cannabis. We gave Mr Van Nguyen leave to appeal, his application for leave having been referred to the Court by the Registrar.

26. Mr Van Nguyen was jointly indicted with his brother. The brother pleaded guilty to the same offence.

27. 19 Halliwell Street West, in Manchester, is the property of a Housing Association. The tenancy was in the name of the appellant's father, who had become a tenant on 15 April 2004.

28. On 15 May 2004, the appellant had a visit from a Police Constable Ludlow who was investigating the appellant's complaint of having had £10 stolen in a public lavatory. The police constable did not enter the premises but spoke to the appellant on the doorstep.

29. On 11 August 2004, the police called again at the premises. On this occasion, it was to search for a wanted man who used to live at the premises. The reason for the visit was unconnected with this appeal. When the police arrived, they saw the appellant run upstairs to the loft. He remained there until he was approached by officers.

30. Upon entry into the house, the police found a large quantity of cannabis and other material. They also found a total of 193 cannabis plants in various stages of maturity. A large number were little more than seedlings, but there were 85 large mature plants which the police estimated would have yielded 1.3 kg of cannabis at a value of between £3,800 and £6,400 pounds. The plants were in the dining room and in one of the upstairs bedrooms. These rooms had been converted into growing rooms and had been fitted with lighting, heating equipment, fans, silver foil and various electrical equipment. In addition, two empty containers of methadone were found. But fingerprints of the appellant were not found on any of the cannabis plants or the equipment used in the cultivation process. Fingerprints of the appellant's brother were, however, found. It was the appellant's case that he had no knowledge that the plants were cannabis plants, he was not involved in the cultivation and he had been living in the premises for only 3 weeks. However, in the circumstances, he could hardly deny he was aware that plants that were controlled drugs

were being grown in the premises and did not do so. This meant that the only live issue in the cases was whether the appellant was engaged in the cultivation of the plants. Was this joint enterprise or was it solely the activity of the brother?

31. At the outset of the trial, Mr Goldwater, who appeared on behalf of the appellant, made an application to His Honour Judge Ensor, the trial judge, to exclude evidence of an interview which had taken place between the appellant and the police. This was evidence that indicated that he took heroin and used methadone. Mr Baker, on behalf of the prosecution, contended that the evidence was relevant and admissible at common law and admissible under the provisions of section 101(1)(d) of the 2003 Act. He argued that the important issue to which it was relevant, was whether the appellant knew that the plants were cannabis, and the fact that the appellant was very conversant with the drug scene made it more likely that he would know that they were cannabis. He contended that there was an obvious link between those who took drugs of any kind and those who took cannabis. The judge accepted the prosecution's submissions and allowed the evidence to be given.

32. As a result of the evidence being admitted, during the course of the defendant's cross examination, the prosecution suggested that his heroin addiction meant that he would be desperate for money to fund his habit and that was the reason for his becoming involved in the cultivation of cannabis.

33. In addition, the appellant had previous convictions consisting of 4 offences of shoplifting in 2001. The prosecution served notice to introduce these convictions under the provisions of section 101. The introduction was not resisted and in the event they were introduced by the appellant himself when he gave evidence. This was no doubt because the appellant wished to establish that he had no convictions for drug offences. However, the prosecution suggested that the shoplifting offences were carried out to fund his addiction. There was no evidence to support this assumption. There was no evidence, for example, that the goods which were stolen had a significant re-sale value.

34. The appellant was also cross-examined on the basis that his connections with drug dealers through his purchases of heroin would mean that he had ready means of access to persons who could dispose of the cannabis crop.

35. Finally, the prosecution relied on the complaint which the appellant made of being robbed of £10 and which resulted in Police Constable Ludlow making the initial call to the house. The prosecution alleged the robbery demonstrated that the defendant, at the time, had been trying to buy drugs in the toilet. This it was suggested, showed that he was the sort of person who did heroin deals in the lavatories of public houses and that the person from whom he was buying heroin could be the dealer in the cannabis that was being cultivated.

36. Mr Goldwater contended with some justification that, since the appellant accepted that he thought the plants were probably some form of controlled drug, the offence for which he was charged did not depend on it being established that he knew the drug that was being grown was cannabis. What was critical was that the appellant was engaged in the cultivation of cannabis.

The summing up

37. The very experienced trial judge summed up to the jury that they had to be satisfied that 'cannabis was being cultivated, the defendant played a part in the cultivation and that

he knew it was cannabis.' He also made it clear that the case for the prosecution was that this was a joint enterprise between the appellant and his brother. The judge also gave a perfectly adequate direction about the relevance of lies which the appellant had undoubtedly told.

38. Mr Goldwater's complaint about the trial and the summing up following the initial ruling is that, because of the emphasis that was being placed upon the fact that the appellant was a heroin consumer, the real issue was being lost sight of. The issue was not whether he knew that the plants were cannabis but solely whether he was engaged in the cultivation of the plants which he accepted he appreciated were probably some form of drug. He submits accurately that the judge failed to give the jury any assistance as to how to approach the defendant's admission that he was a heroin user, its relevance or the weight to be attached to it.

Conclusion

39. In our view Mr Goldwater's submission is well-founded. Once the appellant had admitted that he thought the plants were a controlled drug of some kind and thereby ruled out any possibility of a defence under section 28(3) of the Misuse of Drugs Act 1971, it did not matter for the purposes of proving the offences whether he knew they were cannabis. The only issue was whether he was involved in growing them and we do not think that any knowledge he might have had of the precise nature of the plants was likely to shed much light on that question. In our view, therefore, the judge was wrong to hold that the evidence was relevant to an important issue between the defendant and the prosecution so as to render it admissible under section 101(1)(d).

40. Another criticism that is made of the judge's ruling was that he did not take into account section 101(3), namely the adverse affect on the fairness of the proceedings. By section 110 of the 2003 Act, the court must give reasons for any ruling on the admissibility of evidence under section 101 and on any application made under section 101(3) to exclude evidence on the grounds of unfairness. In the present case the judge's ruling clearly dealt with the question of admissibility, but he made no mention of section 101(3) in the ruling, nor did he give any reasons for holding that it would not be unfair to admit it. However, it had been the subject of argument and we do not accept that the admission of evidence that the appellant was a heroin addict was unduly prejudicial, provided that the jury was given a proper direction about its place in the case as a whole. The judge may have been technically wrong to regard the situation as one where the evidence could be admitted under section 101(1)(d) as relating to an important matter in issue, but it certainly assisted in understanding the issues in the case.

41. There is the further problem that, having allowed the evidence of the appellant's heroin addiction to be put before the jury, its relevance was not explained to the jury. In our judgment, there is force in Mr Goldwater's submission that the fact that a person is addicted to heroin does not mean that he is more likely to recognise a cannabis plant than someone who is not addicted to heroin. More importantly, the fact that he is addicted and therefore a user of drugs in their processed form, is not evidence he was engaged in their cultivation or even that he has an enhanced ability to identify a particular controlled drug.

42. What is unfortunate about the trial is that once the evidence of the appellant's heroin addiction was placed before the jury, it became the centre of focus of the trial. It was a major

subject of cross-examination and played a disproportionate part in the trial, not least because of the nature of the cross-examination of the appellant when he gave evidence.

43. The fact was that the only evidence that the appellant was engaged in cultivation was that he lived in the house were cultivation was taking place and behaved as though he had something to hide when the police arrived at the house. Having regard to this, it was incumbent upon the judge to clearly explain to the jury that the appellant's heroin addiction was no more than background to the offence alleged. A warning of its limited relevance did not appear in the summing up, which indeed contained no guidance on the use to which the evidence might be put. It should have done so because the focus of the trial was distorted as a result of the cross-examination which took place and the emphasis on the appellant's addiction. Accordingly, we have come to the conclusion that this conviction is unsafe.

The appeal of Anthony Carp

The background

44. On 9 February 2005 at the Crown Court at Taunton, Anthony Carp was convicted of 2 counts of common assault. He was sentenced in respect of the first assault to two months' imprisonment suspended for 2 years and in relation to the second offence, he was sentenced to 4 months' imprisonment, consecutive to the sentence on count 1, suspended for 2 years. He was also ordered to pay £400 towards the costs of the prosecution.

The facts

45. The victim of both assaults had cohabited with the appellant for many years. At the time of the two alleged incidents, and for some time previously, she and the appellant had been living together in the appellant's house. There is no doubt that the relationship at times was stormy. The appellant had obtained an injunction against the complainant as he claimed that she had been violent towards him.

46. On New Year's Eve 2003, the couple had an argument in a public house. They both made their separate ways home where the row continued. The complainant alleged that she was slapped by the appellant who also punched her in the face. This was the first assault. On 9 January 2004, there was another incident in the home in which the complainant alleged that she had been assaulted by the appellant who had punched her in the face. On both occasions, the complainant had been drinking.

47. It was the appellant's case that he had acted in self defence.

48. At the start of the prosecution's evidence, the defence applied under section 100 of the 2003 Act to cross-examine the complainant about her violent background. The Recorder granted the application. At the commencement of the appellant's case, the Recorder also ruled that a number of the previous convictions of the appellant could be admitted in evidence under section 101(1)(g). They included a number of offences of violence (including wounding with intent, assault occasioning actual bodily harm, and assault on a police officer) in the period 1982 to 1993; offences of theft, handling and deception dealt with in 1993; and two drink-related driving offences (failing to provide a specimen, and driving with excess alcohol) in 2000 and 2004.

49. In his evidence, the appellant admitted that he had been a tearaway in the past but he did not attack women. A baby-sitter who was regularly employed by the complainant and the appellant gave supporting evidence of an incident in September 2003. On that occasion the complainant had returned home very drunk. She abused the appellant and physically assaulted him by hitting him on the head with a cordless phone and slapping him.

50. The appellant now appeals against his conviction by leave of the single judge. In support of the appeal, he relies on 3 grounds:

(i)   that evidence of the convictions admitted under the section 101(1)(g) is relevant only in relation to credibility, as would have been permissible if the case were being determined under the old law.
(ii)   that if evidence of previous convictions admitted under section 101(1)(g) can be relevant to propensity in either sense, the judge should not have admitted evidence of the convictions for theft and deception;
(iii) the Recorder failed properly to direct the jury as to the relevance of previous convictions or to warn them of the dangers of placing too much reliance on them.

51. At the start of the presentation of the case for the prosecution, counsel for the defence applied under section 100 of the 2003 Act to cross-examine the complainant about her violent background. That background included a significant psychiatric history, incidents of self-harm, at least one incident of violence towards the appellant and the grant of an injunction restraining the complainant from using violence against the appellant. The application under section 100 was granted by the Recorder. As the evidence of the complainant's character was admitted under section 100, an application by the prosecution under section 101(1)(g) of the 2003 Act was irresistible and the Recorder ruled that the previous convictions were admissible.

52. In his summing up, the Recorder said, having referred to the complainant's conduct:

You also heard that the defendant has previous convictions for a number of offences of violence, last being April 1993; a number of offences of dishonesty, last of those also being in 1993; and two drink related offences, which took place during the time of the defendant's relationship with Miss Byron. This has been given in evidence because the defendant has attacked the character of Miss Byron and it is right in those circumstances that you should know the character of the person making the attack as well.

You may use the evidence of the defendant's bad character, his previous convictions in the following ways. First, if you think it is right you may take it in to account when deciding whether or not the defendant's evidence is truthful. A person with previous convictions for dishonesty may be less likely to tell the truth but of course it doesn't follow that he is incapable of doing so. You must decide to what extent if at all his character helps you when judging his evidence. If you think it is right you can also take into account when deciding whether or not the defendant committed the offences—with which he is now being charged—his previous convictions.

These allegations are of violence and Miss Byron has also said that she had been drinking when he had allegedly committed these offences. You have got to decide to what extent if at all his convictions help you when you are considering whether or not he is guilty, but bearing in mind that his bad character itself cannot prove anything, it cannot

191

prove anything. It cannot prove his guilt on its own. It would therefore be wrong to jump to the conclusion that he is guilty just because of his bad character.

Conclusion

53. Since the appellant had attacked the character of the complainant, evidence of his bad character became admissible under section 101(1)(g), subject only to the judge's duty to exclude it under section 101(3) if he considered that to admit it would render the proceedings unfair. Here the convictions which were relied on did not occur so long ago that it could be said that in the circumstances the evidence was so prejudicial that it must have been wrong for the evidence to be admitted. The Recorder exercised his discretion and there is no basis upon which this Court can properly interfere with the exercise of the Recorder's discretion.

54. As we have already made clear, the fact that the evidence of the appellant's bad character was admitted under section 101(1)(g) does not prevent the evidence from being used for purposes other than establishing the appellant's credibility. It could be used to show that he was more likely to commit the offences with which he was charged. That is to say, the evidence could be used to show a propensity on his part to commit the sort of assaults with which he was charged, subject to the question of relevance and the evidence not being unduly prejudicial.

55. The appellant relies on paragraphs 7–13 of the judgment of the Vice-President Rose LJ in *Hanson*. We do not consider that the guidance given by Rose LJ in these paragraphs is inconsistent with the approach adopted by the Recorder, but it is necessary to deal with one particular aspect of the appellant's case which arises out of what was said in paragraph 13 of the judgment in that case.

56. Although the second ground of appeal in this case is apparently directed to the admissibility of the appellant's previous convictions, it is apparent from counsel's skeleton argument and the advice on appeal that what it is really directed to is the use of which that evidence may properly be put. Mr Munyard submitted that the Recorder was wrong to direct the jury that they could take the appellant's bad character into account when deciding whether his evidence was truthful without any further qualification. In *Hanson* the court pointed out that convictions for dishonesty (and the same applies to convictions for other kinds of offences) do not necessarily provide reliable evidence of a propensity to be untruthful: it all depends on the nature and circumstances of the conviction. Accordingly, it is said, the Recorder should have warned the jury that they could not place any weight on the fact that the appellant had previous convictions when considering whether they could believe what he said.

57. Since the appellant's previous convictions included three offences of obtaining by deception in addition to offences of theft, this is not a particularly meritorious point. In our view his convictions for obtaining by deception were evidence of a propensity to be untruthful and in that context his convictions for theft added little. (The Recorder did not suggest that previous convictions for offences of violence were relevant in this context). It would have been better, therefore, if the Recorder had given the jury more detailed guidance on the relevance of the appellant's convictions to the issue of his truthfulness, but in the circumstances of this case we do not think that his failure to do so affected the outcome of trial so as to render his convictions unsafe.

58. In the course of argument Mr Munyard submitted on behalf of the appellant that the Recorder was wrong to have admitted evidence of his two drink-related driving offences. The Recorder was asked to exclude them in the exercise of his powers under section 101(3), but he decided that in all the circumstances they were relevant to the offences with which the appellant was charged and that it would not be unfair for them to be admitted. We can see no grounds on which the exercise of his discretion in this matter can properly be challenged.

59. In paragraph 18 of the judgment in *Hanson*, Vice-President Rose LJ emphasises the need for warnings to be given to a jury not to place undue reliance on previous convictions. In particular, the jury should be directed that they should not conclude that the defendant is guilty or untruthful merely because he has convictions. Looking at the language used by the Recorder, we find that the Recorder gave the necessary warnings in a manner which adequately brought home to the jury the need to take proper care when deciding how much weight, if any, to place on the appellant's previous convictions. In particular he dealt separately with issues of truthfulness and guilt and indicated how different convictions might be relevant to those issues. We therefore do not accept that there is any substance in any of the grounds of appeal relied upon by the appellant and dismiss his appeal.

Appeals of Highton and of Carp dismissed.
Appeal of Van Nguyen allowed.

R v Renda; R v Ball; R v Akram; R v Osbourne; R v Razaq and Razaq [2005] EWCA Crim 2826, CA, 10 November 2005; Judge LJ (President), Bean J and Sir Charles Mantell

A. Felix, J. Hillis, W.N. Goldstein, L. Jones, R. Cifonelli and J. Stone for the appellants
G. Ong, R. Newbury, M. Lavery, M. Parry-Evans and R. Whittaker for the Crown

The President, Sir Igor Judge LJ:

General

1. These six appeals were listed together, and heard consecutively over two days. Each required consideration of one or more practical problems arising from the 'bad character' provisions in Part II, Chapter 1, of the Criminal Justice Act 2003.

2. It will not be necessary or useful for us to set out these provisions in the judgment. In coming to our conclusions, in each case we had an overall view of the structure of this chapter together with the specific legislation said to apply directly to the point in issue. In addition, we shall not spell out all the detailed evidence in support of either sides' case. We only focus attention on those parts of the evidence relevant to our decisions.

3. We have some general observations. Several of the decisions or rulings questioned in these appeals represent either judgments by the trial judge in the specific factual context of the individual case, or the exercise of a judicial discretion. The circumstances in which this Court would interfere with the exercise of a judicial discretion are limited. The principles

need no repetition. However we emphasise that the same general approach will be adopted when the Court is being invited to interfere with what in reality is a fact specific judgment. As we explain in one of these decisions, the trial judge's 'feel' for the case is usually the critical ingredient of the decision at first instance which this Court lacks. Context therefore is vital. The creation and subsequent citation from a vast body of so-called 'authority,' in reality representing no more than observations on a fact-specific decision of the judge in the Crown Court, is unnecessary and may well be counterproductive. This legislation has now been in force for nearly a year. The principles have been considered by this Court on a number of occasions. The responsibility for their application is not for this Court but for trial judges.

4. Finally, even if it is positively established that there has been an incorrect ruling or misdirection by the trial judge, it should be remembered that this Court is required to analyse its impact (if any) on the safety of any subsequent conviction. It does not follow from any proved error that the conviction will be quashed.

5. In the context of these appeals, although other points arose from time to time, it would be useful to set out the provisions which are of direct relevance in each individual appeal.

6. Renda

(a) Creation of a false impression by a defendant (s101(1)(f) and s105(1))
(b) Withdrawal of a false impression (s105(3))
(c) Reprehensible behaviour other than the commission of an offence (s112(1))
(d) Discharge of the jury for 'contamination' (s107)

7. Ball
Evidence 'given' of an imputation made during questioning under caution (s101(1)(g) and s106(1)(c))

8. Akram
Complainant's bad character (s100)

9. Osbourne

(a) Bad character of complainant and defendant's witness (s100)
(b) Duty to give reasons (s110(1))

10. Razaq and Razaq
Complainant's bad character and limits to cross-examination (s 100)

Renda

11. This is an appeal by Raymond Renda against a conviction for attempted robbery on 13th May 2005 at the Inner London Crown Court before HHJ Van Der Werff and a jury.

12. At the date of the hearing of the appeal he had not been sentenced. He appeals with leave of the single judge.

13. The facts are straightforward. At about 2 am on 10th November 2003, the complainant, Robert Flint, was walking home along Mile End Road in Stepney Green London. At about the same time the appellant left a nearby public house, and was walking along Mile End Road in the opposite direction. Their paths crossed, and the appellant stood beside Mr

Flint and asked him for money. When Mr Flint responded that he did not have any, and carried on walking, the appellant then fell in to walk beside him, continually pressing him for money. The appellant put his right hand into his jacket pocket saying, 'What is this I have got in my pocket?.' Hardly surprisingly, Mr Flint began to feel frightened, and the appellant continued to follow him, ordering him to turn into Whitehorse Lane, which, as it happened, was the street in which Mr Flint lived. As Mr Flint walked up the path to his flat the appellant followed him, still asking him for money, and, under an archway, seized hold of him by the neck, swinging him round and pushing him against the gate, saying 'Give me your money now.' Mr Flint pushed the appellant away, and into a hedge, and ran to his front door, but before he had time to open the door, the appellant returned and pushed him against the wall with his hand on his neck.

14. Two police officers in a passing police car saw what they believed to be a fight, and stopped, and separated the combatants. Mr Flint immediately complained that the appellant had followed him home and tried to rob him. The appellant denied that he had done anything at all, asserting that he was on his way home from the pub and that the allegation must be some sort of joke. When interviewed the appellant declined to answer any questions, but submitted a prepared statement in which he denied that he had attempted to rob the complainant: rather, after making a false accusation, the complainant had attacked him.

15. The issue at trial was therefore straightforward. The jury had to decide whether any offence at all had been committed, and their decision largely depended on their judgment of Mr Flint's veracity, and, if he gave evidence, the veracity of the appellant.

16. The issues in this appeal arise from the appellant's evidence. He sought to enhance his credibility by asserting that he had been a serving soldier in HM Armed Forces, who had, while so employed, sustained a serious head injury, which had resulted in long-term brain damage. He said that at the date of his arrest he was in regular employment as a security guard.

17. The Crown was in possession of evidence to show that although it was true that the appellant had served in the armed forces, his serious head injury had not been sustained while he was in the course of his duties, but while he was on holiday, driving his own vehicle. Although it was also true that he had been employed in a security capacity, checking 'passes,' this had been short-term employment only. He was no longer in gainful employment. If this evidence was correct, the appellant was seeking to convey a misleading impression about his life and history.

18. The additional material available to the Crown included the defendant's antecedent history and police computer print-outs, and a report prepared by a psychiatrist instructed by the Crown. This material showed not only that there had been a number of reported crimes of violence for which the appellant was alleged to have been responsible, but that on an earlier occasion, in July 2001, when he was found unfit to plead to a count of assault occasioning actual bodily harm, the jury was satisfied as a fact that the appellant had approached someone from behind and struck him about the head with a large wooden table leg. The case had been disposed of by way of an absolute discharge.

19. Our attention was drawn to some earlier authorities, which considered the impact of s 1(3)(ii) of the Criminal Evidence Act 1898. However it is unnecessary to refer to them in this judgment. It is most unlikely to be useful to refer to authorities which were no more than factual examples of occasions when it was decided that an individual defendant had

put his character in issue. For the purposes of s101(1)(f) the question whether the defendant has given a 'false impression' about himself, and whether there is evidence which may properly serve to correct such a false impression within s105(1)(a) and (b) is fact-specific. In the present case the appellant was plainly seeking to convey that he was a man of positive good character.

20. When the appellant was cross-examined he continued to maintain that he had been in regular employment as a security guard, and that he had not been dismissed from that employment. He did however concede that when he described himself as a security guard, his duties amounted to no more than checking passes. He agreed that he had not sustained his head injury during the course of his military duties as a soldier, but while he was on holiday in a car accident. In short, in cross-examination, he was forced to concede the truth.

21. It was submitted that in these circumstances the appellant should be treated as having withdrawn or disassociated himself with any false assertion relating to the claim that he had sustained injury while in the course of his duties. Accordingly s105(3) should apply, and it was therefore no longer appropriate to treat him as having given evidence which was 'apt to give the ... jury a false or misleading impression about' him. We do not agree. Our reason is simple. There is a significant difference between the defendant who makes a specific and positive decision to correct a false impression for which he is responsible, or to disassociate himself with false impressions conveyed by the assertions of others, and the defendant who in the process of cross-examination is obliged to concede that he has been misleading the jury. A concession extracted in cross-examination that the defendant was not telling the truth in part of his examination-in-chief will not normally amount to a withdrawal or disassociation from the original assertion for the purposes of s105(3).

22. The Crown sought leave to ask questions about this incident of violence. Judge Van Der Werff decided that it would not be prudent or right for the Crown to explore, through the appellant's own testimony, the details of his psychiatric history, not least because the appellant himself might not be in a position to deal with it properly. He made a preliminary ruling that the Crown was entitled to ask questions about the appellant's military service, the circumstances of the accident, and his subsequent employment. It was appropriate for the jury to understand that the appellant had been charged with assault occasioning actual bodily harm, and that although he was found unfit to plead, he was also found by the jury to have committed the physical act of assault. The case was disposed of by way of an absolute discharge.

23. The judge was very concerned that the jury should not labour under a false impression about the appellant. He rejected a submission that the Crown should not be allowed to adduce the facts of the assault because proper notice had not been given. Counsel for the Crown submitted that these matters had arisen for consideration during the appellant's evidence, so that it was impractical to have given any notice. The judge ruled that the Crown could ask about the facts of the assault which were relevant to the issue of credibility.

24. Before us it was argued that the judge's rulings were wrong. An absolute discharge following a finding that the defendant was unfit to plead did not constitute a criminal conviction, nor did it constitute 'reprehensible behaviour' amounting to misconduct for the purposes of the 'bad character' provisions in Part II of the Criminal Justice Act 2003. We agree that the appellant was not 'convicted' of a criminal offence. We also accept that as a matter of ordinary language, the word 'reprehensible' carries with it some element of

culpability or blameworthiness. What however we are unable to accept is the mere fact that the appellant was found unfit to plead some 18 months after an apparent incident of gratuitous violence has occurred, of itself, connotes that at the time of the offence his mental acuity was so altered as to extinguish any element of culpability when the table leg was used in such a violent fashion. On the face of it, this was reprehensible behaviour, and there was no evidence before Judge Van Der Werff to suggest otherwise.

25. Accordingly, this material was available to help refute the false impression as of positive good character given by the appellant in his evidence-in-chief. Recognising as the judge did, that this was not an entirely straightforward issue, he was at pains to explain to the jury the precise status of the earlier court proceedings, and in particular, how the process encompassed in the phrase 'not fit to plead' works, and what it involves, and that the appellant was not convicted, and indeed had no convictions. He also explained that its relevance in this particular case was confined to helping the jury decide whether the appellant had tried to present himself as a 'rather better man' than he actually was, and whether he was in truth, as the jury might consider he was seeking to convey, deserving of sympathy. If they were sure that he had tried to give a false impression about himself, then the jury was entitled to see how it affected the way in which they should approach the evidence about events on 10th November 2003. All that was fairly done.

26. The remaining point arising in this appeal arises from a submission that the judge should have stopped the case because the evidence had become contaminated. The point arose in this way. When the issue of the table leg incident was first raised, counsel for the appellant conceded that the finding by the jury amounted to a conviction. After further research she concluded, rightly, that it was not. Accordingly she sought the discharge of the jury on the basis that the evidence before it was 'contaminated' for the purposes of s107.

27. We can deal briefly with this submission. For the reasons we have given, the evidence was not in fact 'contaminated.' We are however concerned to ensure that s107 should not be misused. There will, of course, be occasions when counsel is justified in submitting that a conviction would be unsafe because evidence admitted under s101(1)(c)–(g) proved to be contaminated. That however does not provide any justification for a submission which, in truth, is no more than a reiteration of the arguments advanced by counsel against the admission of this evidence. S107 deals with a particular situation where the evidence of 'bad character' has been admitted and proves to be false or misleading in the circumstances described in s107(5). Unless the case falls squarely within that statutory provision, the Court of Appeal Criminal Division is the appropriate court in which the correctness of the judge's decision should be questioned.

28. For these reasons, this appeal will be dismissed.

Ball

29. This is an appeal by Nathan Ball against his conviction on two counts of rape on 18th April 2005 in the Crown Court at Sheffield before His Honour Judge Keen QC and a jury. The two counts related to incidents of penetration of the mouth and sexual intercourse with the same woman on 21st January 2005.

30. This unpleasant incident needs very little narrative explanation. Prior to 21st January 2005 the complainant and the appellant had been involved in a very casual sexual

relationship. Consensual sexual intercourse had taken place after heavy alcohol consumption in circumstances devoid of any hint of affection.

31. On 21st January the pair were drinking in the same public house. There was evidence of some very unpleasant language by the appellant generally and at least in part insulting of the complainant. In any event, they left the premises together. They started to make their way to the rear of a nearby supermarket, and began intimate touching each other. In the course of this foreplay the complainant fell over and hurt her knee. The appellant was unsympathetic and became aggressive. According to the complainant, she was no longer willing to have sexual intercourse with him, and she made her position absolutely clear. Nevertheless he forced her to take his penis in her mouth, and then proceeded to sexual intercourse. When it was over she reported that the appellant had said to her, 'What are you going to do now, go off and get me done for rape? Look at you, you're nowt but a slag'.

32. The appellant's case was that this sexual activity took place with the complainant's consent. She appeared to be entirely happy afterwards, but she may have become aggrieved because she thought or understood from what people were saying that the appellant was using her. Perhaps she recollected or heard about the appellant's earlier disparaging remarks about her in the public house, and this provoked her to make a false allegation of rape. In short, the complainant was lying, motivated by a wish for vengeance.

33. No further summary of the conflicting and mutually contradictory accounts of the incident is needed. We must however refer to the contents of the interviews between the appellant and the police. The appellant told the police that most of the men in the local public house had had sexual intercourse with the complainant. He criticised the complainant's sexual promiscuity in very disparaging terms. She was easy. 'She's a bag really, you know what I mean, a slag.' This echoed the comment attributed to the appellant by the complainant after sexual intercourse.

34. When the appellant gave evidence, the Crown submitted that his bad character arising from previous convictions and breaches of court orders, should properly be deployed in cross-examination. The judge rejected a number of different bases advanced by the prosecution, including in particular, that he should admit this evidence simply on the basis of the direct attack on the complainant's credibility based on the appellant's instructions that the allegations of rape were fabricated. If we may say so, the judge's approach to this part of the case seems to have been impeccable.

35. However, the judge was troubled by the attack made against the complainant by the defendant in the course of the police interviews. In effect, the appellant asserted that the complainant had behaved or was disposed to behave in a reprehensible way. Accordingly an attack had been made on the complainant's character for the purposes of s101(1)(g), as explained and expanded in s 106, and in particular s106(1)(c). Evidence was given 'of an imputation about the other person made by the defendant—(i) on being questioned under caution, before charge'. The judge considered whether to exclude the evidence under s101(1)(3) on the basis that its admission would have an adverse effect on the fairness of the proceedings. He concluded that cross-examination about the appellant's bad character should be permitted.

36. Although a number of minor matters were raised in argument, we need only address the complaint directed by Mr Hillis at the judge's ruling that the appellant could be cross-examined about his previous convictions. No criticism is made of the way in which the judge dealt with these issues in his summing up. The complaint is directed at his ruling.

37. Mr Hillis began his argument by submitting that a major difficulty in this case arose from the impact of s41 of the Youth Justice and Criminal Evidence Act 1999, which although restricting evidence or questions by the defence about a complainant's sexual history, did not extend to the prosecution. We agree that this is a feature of s 41, but it does not advance the argument further. The appellant chose to make the observations reported by the police. If what he said was relevant and served to support the allegation of rape, this evidence was admissible, and for the purposes of s106(1)(c) was indeed 'given.' The answers by the appellant in his interview purported to be exculpatory in nature (there was no rape: it was consent) but were said by the Crown, with every justification, to provide evidence which indicated an attitude to the complainant which at least carried with it the implication that the appellant believed that she would have agreed to sexual intercourse with him, and any other man, at any time and in any circumstances, and that if and when she purported to be unwilling to have sexual intercourse, any such refusal should be disregarded as quite meaningless. In reality, therefore, and somewhat unusually, answers which might have been treated as exculpatory alone, and possibly not admissible on that basis, formed part of the prosecution case adduced by the Crown. The highlight, at its most stark, was the epithet, 'slag', used by the appellant in the interviews to describe the complainant which echoed what she claimed he had said to her after sexual intercourse had finished. The Crown also contended that the remark about rape attributed to him by the complainant was inconsistent with a genuine belief that she was consenting to what happened.

38. In our judgment this evidence was properly before the jury as part of the prosecution case. It did not represent (and the judge would have been alert to any such danger) any sort of device to enable the Crown to make an application to put the appellant's previous convictions before the jury. Once the evidence was properly given, within s106(1)(c) the judge would have been entitled to exclude it as a matter of discretion. He was well aware of the need to exercise that discretion. No arguable basis for interfering with his decision has been shown.

39. Accordingly this appeal is dismissed.

Akram

40. This is an appeal against conviction and sentence by Adil Akram. On 18th March 2005 he was convicted of dangerous driving at Burnley Crown Court before Mr Recorder Wright and a jury. On 29th April 2005 he was sentenced to 18 months detention in a Young Offender Institution and disqualified from driving for 3 years and until an extended driving test was passed.

41. The essential facts can be summarised very briefly. On 1st August 2004 Rokab Afzal was driving his car in Nelson, in Lancashire, carrying a passenger, Adnan Khan. They became rather concerned about a potential problem with the steering of the car, so Mr Afzal stopped and got out. While he was there he was approached by a man called Kais Anwar, and they exchanged some unpleasantries. Thereafter a red Peugeot car pulled up on the opposite side of the road, and Kais Anwar went to speak to the driver. After he had done so the red Peugeot revved its engine and drove at the complainant, knocking him over. Fortunately Mr Afzal was not seriously hurt, and he was able to get up and run away into a nearby school. The red Peugeot then drove away from the scene.

42. The prosecution case was that the driver of the red Peugeot was the appellant, recognised both by Mr Afzal and his passenger Mr Khan. The defence case was that the identification was wrong. The appellant had spent the whole of the day, and at the relevant time was at his girlfriend's house. His girlfriend gave evidence to the same effect.

43. The appellant was aware of four specific areas of evidence with which it was proposed to test the evidence of Mr Afzal. The appellant and he had been friends for some time, but eventually a problem arose between them, the precise origins of which depended on which of them was explaining it. From the appellant's point of view he asserted an earlier assault by the complainant in which the complainant counter-asserted that he was the victim. This was described as the 'cricket bat incident.' There was also a falling out over a car stereo or cassette player which went missing from the appellant's car. According to him, either the complainant, or his associates, stole the car stereo in order to exert a measure of self-help to encourage the appellant to pay a debt: that, too was contentious. It was further suggested on the appellant's behalf that on the day when it was alleged that he had been driving the red Peugeot car he was assaulted by associates of Mr Afzal, on his instructions. The final area of contention arose from the fact that Mr Afzal had been charged with an offence of kidnap.

44. The applicable statutory provision is to be found in s100 of the Criminal Justice Act 2003. The Recorder allowed questions to be asked of the complainants about both the cricket bat and car stereo incidents. The allegation of assault on the same day as the offence was not pursued. The Recorder refused the application by the appellant to introduce or cross-examine Mr Afzal about the kidnap charge. This decision forms the basis of complaint before us.

45. It was suggested by the appellant at trial, and before us, that the purpose of this evidence was not to establish that Mr Afzal was a person of 'bad character,' but in order to demonstrate that others, as well as the appellant himself, might have had a motive for attacking him. The jury knew of the 'bad blood' between the two men, and according to the argument by Mr Goldstein, it was essential to the defendant's case to establish that Mr Afzal had other enemies in addition to and beyond the appellant.

46. The problem with this argument is simple. The evidence of 'bad blood' between the complainant and the appellant was introduced by the appellant, after permission had been sought and given for it to be raised. Moreover, at the time when the dangerous driving occurred, the alleged kidnap incident remained some four weeks into the future. Mr Afzal made his complaint, and identified the appellant as the driver of the Peugeot car on the day when the incident happened. On any view, therefore, the dangerous driving cannot have been a response to or some sort of revenge for the kidnap incident. Beyond that, however, even if the kidnap incident had occurred before the dangerous driving, it remains difficult for us to see why, even if the kidnap incident had indeed occurred, the victim of dangerous driving should wrongly attribute responsibility for it to Mr Afzal rather than to the individual who, on this analysis, was falsely accusing Mr Afzal of kidnap. In any event, the best that could be said at this stage of the case was that this was a bare allegation, itself wholly unproved.

47. On these facts, there is no justifiable complaint against the Recorder's decision about the proper application of s 100 of the 2003 Act. The appeal against conviction will be dismissed.

[48. The court dismissed Akram's appeal against sentence.]

Osbourne

49. This is an appeal by Lee Osbourne against his conviction for robbery at Cardiff Crown Court before HHJ Griffith-Williams QC, the Recorder of Cardiff, and a jury.

50. The appellant was jointly charged with Alex Jenkins, whose application for leave to appeal against conviction was abandoned.

51. The essential facts can be briefly summarised. In the early hours of 9th September 2004, the police were called to a public house known as the Grasshopper, following a report that the licensee, Russell Cleverley, had been robbed of £200 in cash from the till. The appellant denied any involvement in robbery, and the defence positively called into question whether a robbery had taken place at all. The appellant, a man with a lengthy list of previous convictions suggested that Mr Cleverley fabricated the complaint of robbery in order to cover up his own misconduct as the licensee at the Grasshopper.

52. The precise details of the incident need no repetition. Mr Cleverley knew the appellant personally. At the end of drinking up time that evening very few people left in the Grasshopper. They included the appellant and Alan Jenkins, who would not leave. After a while Mr Cleverley was threatened by them. Keys to the gaming machines were demanded. The appellant struck him across the left cheek and went with him to the till and demanded money. Mr Cleverley gave him £200 from the till. Jenkins was present at the other side of the bar and told the appellant to take Mr Cleverley upstairs and get the tape. This was a reference to the CCTV tape, which was then removed and destroyed.

53. Mr Cleverley's allegation was supported by a fairly considerable body of additional evidence, but no further narrative of the evidence available to the Crown is required.

54. The material available to the defence extended to four linked areas of alleged misconduct by Mr Cleverley as a licensee. His general conduct and management of the premises produced persistent till shortages. The premises were regularly misused for after hours drinking, free to both staff and late customers, with consequent stock depletion. During these 'parties' drug misuse occurred, condoned if not encouraged by Mr Cleverley who participated in the activity. The fourth criticism was directed to Mr Cleverley's personal use of cocaine on the night of the offence itself.

55. As Mr Cleverley was a non-defendant, the admissibility of any evidence of bad character or misconduct or reprehensible behaviour depended on s100 of the Criminal Justice Act 2003. In brief, to be admissible, such evidence was required to be important explanatory evidence, or evidence with a substantial probative value in the context of the case as a whole. S100 was analysed by the Recorder. He decided that counsel for the appellant was entitled to deploy all the material, with the exception of the generalised allegation of drug misuse during after hours drinking sessions. If true, the allegations of general till shortages and the provision of free drink, and so on, lent support to the allegation that any shortage in the till might be attributed to the landlord's misconduct, rather than an alleged robbery. If Mr Cleverley used cocaine on the night of the offence itself, that might significantly undermine his complaints against the appellant. However, the Recorder was unable to conclude that the drug-taking allegation fell within the rules governing admissibility prescribed by s100.

56. The complaint is that the Recorder's decision was wrong. The excluded material impacted on Mr Cleverley's general credibility but it went further, and served to demonstrate

that he was lying when he claimed that he had been the victim of an offence. Moreover, it was argued, that this material added credibility to the defendant's account to the police in interview.

57. The problem with Mr Jones' fundamental contention can be summarised briefly. The allegation that the premises were misused generally for drug offences did not help to demonstrate why or support the conclusion that Mr Cleverley was or may have been inventing a fictitious crime. In the Recorder's view this allegation therefore lacked the explanatory importance and substantial probative value which was required to be satisfied before evidence of the bad character of a non-defendant could be admitted. These decisions have always to be reached in a particular factual context. We lack what is sometimes described as what is sometimes described as the trial judge's 'feel' for the case. We should therefore hesitate before interfering with his conclusion in a matter of judgment. In our view even if this line of questioning may have had some marginal relevance, given that the Recorder permitted the proper development of lines of questioning which had a direct and significant impact on the issue to be decided by the jury, the prohibition against Mr Jones developing this particular line of cross-examination could have had no bearing on the outcome of the trial. That said, in our judgment the Recorder's decision was right. This particular material did not satisfy the admissibility provisions in s100.

58. A further complaint arising under s 100 is directed against the judge's decision that a defence witness, Welsh, an employee of Mr Cleverley, described by the complainant as a friend, could be cross-examined about his bad character. His evidence purported directly to undermine Mr Cleverley's allegation that he had been the victim of violence on the night in question. In short, he gave evidence which served to support the assertion that Mr Cleverley had indeed invented the claim that he had been robbed.

59. Welsh had as recently as February 2003 been sentenced to two years' detention for an offence of serious violence. The judge agreed with the Crown that he could be cross-examined about it. The evidence of the conviction fell within s 100, particularly germane to the fundamental question whether or not a robbery had taken place. Without knowing of Welsh's character, the jury would have been deprived of important evidence of substantial probative value in relation to the issue of the credibility of Welsh's evidence on the vital question whether Mr Cleverley had fabricated his complaint, or whether in truth he was rightly to be regarded as a victim.

60. We cannot find any principled basis for interfering with the judge's decision. In agreeing that Welsh could be cross-examined about his previous conviction, the judge observed that the jury was entitled to know about Welsh's character. With respect we would suggest that this was an over-parsimonious compliance with the duty of the court under s110(1) of the 2003 Act to give reasons for any rulings made under s100. However, as the decision itself was correct, the absence of detailed reasons does not impinge on the safety of the conviction. Accordingly this appeal will be dismissed.

Razaq and Razaq

61. Ajaz Razaq is the son of Abdul Razaq. On 18th March 2005 in the Crown Court at Isleworth, before Ms Recorder Gupta and a jury, both were convicted of assault occasioning actual bodily harm and affray. Another son of Abdul Razaq, Shabaz Razaq, was similarly

convicted. Each was sentenced to a total of 15 months imprisonment. Ajaz Razaq and Abdul Razaq appeal against conviction with leave of the single judge.

62. An unpleasant incident occurred at about 6 pm in the early evening of 21st December 2003. There was an altercation outside a taxi office run by Perwaz Razaq who was later acquitted of witness intimidation. In the result Tarab Raja sustained a superficial laceration to the left side of his face, some 4 cms long, abrasions and bruising to the front upper chest, soft tissue swellings to the head, abrasions to the elbow and knee, and cuts to his fingers.

63. For ease of reference, and to avoid misunderstanding, we shall throughout the rest of this judgment refer to Ajaz Razaq as Ajaz, Abdul Razaq as Abdul, Shabaz Razaq as Shabaz, Perwaz Razaq as Perwaz and Tarab Raja as Tarab.

64. The case for the Crown was that as a result of a telephone call from Shabaz indicating that he could now collect £100 he was owed, Tarab was tricked into going into the taxi office. He was there set upon by Shabaz and Abdul, who were later joined by Ajaz. The two brothers were armed with knives: the father was wielding a metal pole.

65. The defence was that Tarab was the aggressor. He attacked Shabaz, whose father Abdul, and subsequently whose brother Ajaz intervened to protect him. Neither of these appellants behaved aggressively or violently save to the extent necessary to protect Shabaz.

66. The precise details of the evidence need no further narrative. Although it was virtually impossible to discover the issues from the defence case statement by Ajaz, in reality the jury had to decide whether one or both of these appellants was or may have been acting in what throughout the trial was described as 'self-defence of another.' For resolving that question, the credibility of all the protagonists required close analysis.

67. Two further aspects of the evidence require specific mention. Abdul was a man with previous convictions: so was Shabaz. Ajaz was not. He was a man of good character. The first defendant on the indictment was Abdul: Ajaz came next, then Perwaz, and finally Shabaz. This led, as we shall explain, to some tactical manoeuvrings. In the end, each defendant gave evidence.

68. Tarab, too, had previous convictions. The full information about him was that he was cautioned in April 1997, when he was 15 years old, for assault occasioning actual bodily harm, and cautioned again in September 1998 for theft. We were told that the assault was a very serious incident which resulted in the victim being rendered unconscious in the street. Quite apart from cautions, notwithstanding 'not guilty' pleas, he was convicted in July 2000 of violent disorder, grievous bodily harm with intent, and wounding, and sentenced to a total of 30 months' detention at a Young Offender Institution. These convictions represented two distinct and serious incidents of violence. In addition, in April 2004, he was fined £100 for breach of the peace.

69. This leads to the second general aspect of the evidence, arising in the case of Ajaz. Apart from good character, his evidence-in-chief was exceptionally brief. He simply adopted what he had said in his police interviews. This amounted to a denial of any direct involvement. He had seen a fight between his brother and Tarab. He did not see any metal pole, and he had no weapon himself. He pushed the protagonists apart, and in turn was pushed back onto the floor. Apart from accepting that Ajaz's presence at the incident, as we have already noted, the defence case statement said absolutely nothing of value. It stated that the defendant denied assaulting Tarab and denied using or threatening unlawful

violence by himself or any other person. As to witnesses, he was not accepting the evidence of any prosecution witness which implicated him 'as being responsible for any criminal offence'. If one bothers to read further on, the statement asserts that it 'does not purport to set out every aspect of the defendant's case in detail'. In truth it said virtually nothing which was not fully encompassed in the 'not guilty' plea.

70. We can now come to the issues raised in the appeal.

71. After Tarab had given his evidence-in-chief, counsel for Ajaz, not we emphasise, counsel for Abdul, applied under s100 of the Criminal Justice Act 2003 to cross-examine Tarab about his previous convictions.

72. When the application was made, the Recorder observed that at that stage there was nothing in the defence case statement to suggest that Ajaz was acting in self defence, or indeed that Tarab had initiated the violence. She was concerned that Tarab's conviction for violent disorder had also involved Shabaz when he, too, had been convicted of violent disorder. Thereafter the argument that Tarab's convictions should be admitted was taken up by counsel by Shabaz, although at this stage he did not adopt the argument on his behalf.

73. The Recorder rejected the application on the basis that the defendant who was making it failed to establish for the purposes of s100(1)(b) that Tarab's bad character was of substantial probative value in the case against Ajaz. In reaching her conclusion, she was alert to the contents of Ajaz's interview and the defence case statement. This perhaps distracted her from addressing what was said to be Tarab's 'propensity for violence,' and whether, as was inevitably the case, that his credibility, too, was impugned by conviction after not guilty pleas to three different offences.

74. After this ruling, an application was then specifically made on behalf of Shabaz to introduce the full story of Tarab's previous history. The end result was that permission was given to counsel to cross-examine in general terms that the witness was a violent man, basing it on the previous convictions for violence, and, according to the transcript of the ruling, but not apparently followed up at trial, the caution for assault.

75. In the result Tarab was cross-examined by Abdul and Ajaz without reference to his previous convictions, and then by Shabaz about the convictions for violence and the overall circumstances of each offence, including his 'not guilty' pleas. Neither Abdul nor Ajaz sought leave to further cross-examine, but it is implicit in the arguments that we have heard that the cross-examination on Shabaz's behalf was adopted and later deployed on their behalf. The long-term consequence was that Shabaz's previous convictions also went before the jury. Abdul's did not.

76. The major complaint made by Abdul and Ajaz was that the judge was wrong to reject Ajaz's application to cross-examine Tarab about his previous convictions. We shall assume for present purposes that her ruling limited the cross-examination to the specific incidents of violence represented by the conviction in July 2002. Complaint was made on behalf of Abdul that the full details of both cautions and the subsequent breach of the peace should also have been admitted. Given Tarab's age at the date of the matters which gave rise to the cautions, and assuming that the facts relating to them might also have been admitted, we can see no reason to interfere with the conclusion that this material lacked the substantial probative value required by and did not properly fall within s100(1).

77. Abdul has no legitimate complaint. He never made an application nor sought in any way to introduce Tarab's previous convictions into evidence. We understand the tactical

considerations which may have inhibited his counsel from doing so at trial, but it can only be in exceptional circumstances that a defendant who is unprepared to make or expressly associate himself with an application for leave to cross-examine a prosecution witness may realistically complain at the judge's decision rejecting an application to the same effect by a co-accused. We can see no reason why a defendant has a justifiable complaint if tactical forensic manoeuvres have failed to produce the hoped for result.

78. Ajaz has a sounder basis for complaint. We have some sympathy for the Recorder who was faced with a sparse and deficient defence case statement, and perhaps insufficient focus in argument on the specific allegations made directly against Ajaz by Tarab. Nevertheless, in our judgment insufficient weight was given to the critical importance of Tarab's direct evidence implicating him. In the result, however, Tarab was cross-examined about his critical convictions, and that material, and the character of the complainant making allegations against Ajaz was before the jury.

79. Apart from some generalised unspecific complaint, Mr Cifonelli did not identify any particular prejudice sustained by Ajaz which was not cured by the successful application on behalf of Shabaz. This ground of appeal therefore fails.

80. The Recorder's directions about the use to be made of Tarab's previous convictions are criticised. She had, of course, to exercise a very careful judgment not to direct the jury about Tarab's convictions in such a way to produce an inappropriately adverse reaction to the fact that Shabaz was himself involved in one of those offences.

81. She directed the jury that this material might help them to understand the other evidence in the case, including 'the character of the person who brings these charges and the case as a whole.' She suggested that the jury might be helped to resolve the issue whether Tarab was lying, and pointed out that a person of bad character may be less likely to be telling the truth than someone of good character. Later in the summing up she directed that the previous convictions of Shabaz could be taken into account when deciding whether or not his evidence was truthful, linking it to the case of Tarab, pointing out that a person bad character may be less likely to tell the truth. She completed her summing up observing that the jury had to decide to what extent, if at all, Tarab's 'character helps you when judging his evidence'. She also gave a full good character direction in relation to Ajaz covering credit and propensity.

82. There is force in the complaint that the Recorder did not give any detailed directions about the potential relevance of Tarab's previous convictions for violence to the issue of propensity, and therefore to their possible bearing on the critical question whether or not he may have been the aggressor rather than the victim. It is however difficult to imagine that the jury would have failed to consider and given appropriate weight to those convictions when they considered which of the protagonists was the aggressor. The Recorder had expressly referred to the assistance this evidence might give to help understand 'the case as a whole', and whether Tarab was lying 'about his actions during the incident.' These directions should have been more direct and specific. It needed no more, than perhaps a single clause encompassing words such as, 'may be taken into account by you when considering whether Tarab Raja was the victim or the aggressor.' That said, in our judgment, in the context of this case, the deficiencies we have identified do not undermine the safety of the convictions.

[83. and 84. The court rejected a further ground of appeal, based on an alleged misdirection in relation to the law relating to the use of force in the defence of another.]

85. Having concluded that none of the individual complaints, taken on its own, impugns the safety of these convictions, we reconsidered whether the convictions were rendered unsafe by the cumulative effect of the problems we have identified. Having done so, we have concluded that these convictions are safe. Accordingly the appeals are dismissed.

All appeals dismissed.

R v Weir, Somanathan, Yaxley-Lennon, Manister, Hong and De [2005] EWCA Crim 2866, [2006] 1 CrAppR 19 (303), CA, 11 November 2005; Kennedy LJ, Bell and Dobbs JJ

S. James, R. Kovalevsky QC, P. Mylaganam, A.R.H. Urquart, F. Chamberlain, D. Kapur and
   A. Dalgleish for the appellants
R.Vardon, G. Etherton, N. Lobbenberg, A. Vigars and L. Mabley, for the Crown

Lord Justice Kennedy:

Introduction

1. We heard these five appeals consecutively on 20th and 21st September 2005. They were listed together because they raised points in relation to the Bad Character provisions of the Criminal Justice Act 2003 which have not previously been considered by the Court of Appeal, but the points raised are different in each case. There is no overlap. We therefore deal with the appeals separately in judgments to which all three members of the court have contributed, but it is convenient to begin by setting out those parts of the Act which are relevant in relation to one or more of the appeals.
2. The 2003 Act
[The Court set out sections 98, 99, 100, 101, 102, 103, 104, 110 and part of section 112 of the Act.[6]]

Anthony Albert Weir

3. On 21st March 2005 in the Crown Court at Manchester this 44 year old appellant was convicted of sexual assault by touching a girl under the age of 13, contrary to section 7 of the Sexual Offences Act 2003. He was subsequently sentenced to an extended sentence, the custodial element of which was 15 months imprisonment. As the sentence was in excess of 30 months he is required to comply with the notification provisions of Part 2 of the Act for an indefinite period, not, as stated by the Judge when sentencing, for ten years, but that is not a matter with which have been concerned when considering his appeal.
4. The alleged victim J was a ten year old girl living in the same street as the appellant, who lived with his partner and her children C and T. J and C were friends, and sometimes J slept at C's home. J said that when she did so on Saturday 4th July 2004 the appellant assaulted her

---

6   These are set out in Appendix I above.

by touching her vagina over her night clothes. According to J he had exposed himself to her on four or five previous occasions, and on Sunday 5th July he told her that he used to pay girls £5 to watch him masturbate, and asked her if she wanted to watch. She refused, but on that Sunday when he took the children swimming he peeped into the cubicle when she was naked, and then forced three pounds into her hand. J complained to her mother on the following Sunday, and the police were then informed. When interviewed the appellant denied that anything improper took place. He had not exposed himself to the girl, and on Saturday 4th July his partner was away but his friend Dean Allen was with him, and he had only gone into the children's bedroom to check that all was well. On the Sunday when he took the children swimming he had said nothing about masturbation. He had not spied on J, and although he did give her some money it was only to purchase food from the café. His case in relation to the Saturday evening was supported by Dean Allen, who detected no abnormality.

5. On 16th February 2005, at a plea and directions hearing, the prosecution applied to adduce evidence that on 9th August 2000 the appellant was cautioned for taking an indecent photograph of a child, contrary to section 1 of the Protection of Children Act 1978. The application was granted, and it is that decision which is challenged in this appeal. It is common ground that the relevant statutory provisions are those to be found in the sections 101(1)(d), 103(1)(a), 103(2)(b) and 103(4)(b) of the Criminal Justice Act 2003.

6. On 15th December 2004 the Secretary of State exercised his powers under section 103(4)(b) by making the Criminal Justice Act 2003 (Categories of Offences) Order 2004 which came into force at the same time as sections 98 to 110 of the 2003 Act. Paragraph 2 of the Order provides—

(1) The categories of offences set out in Parts 1 and 2 of the Schedule to this Order are hereby prescribed for the purposes of section 103(4)(b) of the 2003 Act.

(2) Two offences are of the same category as each other if they are included in the same Part of the Schedule.

Part 1 of the Schedule sets out offences in the theft category. Part 2 is headed 'Sexual Offences (Persons under the age of 16) Category'. It includes the section 7 offence with which the appellant was charged before the Crown Court, but contains no reference to the offence in respect of which he had received a caution.

7. Mr James, for the appellant, therefore submits that as the offence in respect of which the caution was administered was not, for the purposes of section 103(2)(b) an offence of the same category as the one with which he was charged the evidence of the caution should not have been admitted. The Order, Mr James submits, is plainly selective. It does not include every possible offence, and unless categorisation is determinative of admissibility (where, as in this case, offences are not of the same description and thus within the ambit of section 103(2)(a)) then what is the point of categorisation? That was an argument which appealed to Mitting J at Preston Crown Court in the unreported case of *O'Neil* 22nd February 2005, but that was a case in which no relevant categorisation Order had been made by the Secretary of State, and it is not clear whether the attention of the judge was drawn to paragraphs 131 to 132[7] of the paper prepared by Professor John Spencer QC for the Judicial Studies Board. As Professor Spencer points out, and as we accept, it is necessary to look

---

[7] §§4.39 and 4.40 in the revised version printed in this book (above pp 67–68).

carefully at the opening words of section 103(2). They show that a defendant's propensity to commit offences of the kind with which he is charged can be proved in ways other than by evidence that he has been convicted of an offence of the same description or an offence of the same category. Unless that approach is adopted no proper weight is given to the use of the word 'may' followed by the words in brackets, and the conclusion makes good sense because it allows for the admission of, for example, the fact that the defendant has previously asked to have taken into consideration offences of the kind with which he is now charged, despite the fact that an offence taken into consideration, like a caution, is not a conviction (see *Nicholson* [1947] 2 All ER 535, (1948) 32 CrAppR 98).

8. Of course if the evidence sought to be adduced is evidence of convictions satisfying the requirements of paragraph (a) or (b) then the task of deciding admissibility is made easier, so the categorisation process does have an effect, and that seems to us to answer the question which Mr James posed.

9. For those reasons, although we do not agree with the trial judge that 'an offence contrary to section 1 of the 1978 Act can properly be regarded (for the purposes of section 103(2)(b) of the Criminal Justice Act 2003) as being within the same category as an offence contrary to section 7 of the 2003 (Sexual Offences) Act' we do agree with the alternative line of reasoning adopted by the judge, and reflected in this judgment. That renders it unnecessary for us to consider the alternative submission put forward by Mr Vardon for the respondent that the evidence of the caution would in any event be admissible pursuant to section 101(1)(g) because the defendant had in effect attacked the character of the complainant. The appeal against conviction therefore fails, and is dismissed.

Romanathan Somanathan

10. On 20th January 2005 in the Crown Court at Croydon this 42 year old appellant was convicted of two offences of rape, and he was subsequently sentenced to nine years imprisonment. In his notice of appeal he seeks an extension of time of approximately four months in which to seek leave to appeal against conviction, and his applications for an extension of time and leave to appeal against conviction were referred to this court by the registrar. During the course of the hearing we granted the necessary extension of time (the delay was attributable to the time required to obtain transcripts) and we granted leave to appeal. We turn now to outline the case.

Outline of the allegations and the trial

11. Mrs WA [the complainant] is now 30 years of age. She came to England from Mauritius in 1996 and married, but her marriage broke down and in 2002 she was buying a new flat. At that time she started to attend the Hindu Temple at Thornton Heath where the appellant was the main priest or Aya. It was the prosecution case that after several conversations, on the telephone and at the Temple, the appellant visited her flat on 11th July 2002 to conduct a poojah (or blessing), and that whilst there he raped her. Thereafter he continued to contact her and she continued to attend the Temple. He visited her flat again in September 2002, ostensibly to give her a gift he had obtained on a religious trip to the Himalayas, and it was the prosecution case that he then raped her for a second time. She became pregnant, she

said by him, and an abortion was performed on 26th November 2002. She said that she made efforts to approach people at the Temple about the appellant, but the community appeared closed to her, and it was not until November 2003 that she complained to the police.

12. The appellant was then interviewed on 11th March 2004 and denied any offending. He said that he did visit the complainant's home in July 2002 to conduct a poojah, but there was no impropriety, and in September 2002 he never even went to her home. He also denied having had any previous problems, in particular when he worked at Tooting. The false allegations made against him were, he said, attributable to members of the Mauritian community who wanted to give his Temple a bad name. In his defence case statement served on 16th August 2004 the appellant relied on his answers given during the course of his interview under caution, and added that the complainant 'is not a witness of truth and has some ulterior motive in making and indeed pursuing this complaint.'

13. At the start of the trial on 11th January 2005 Ms G. Etherton for the prosecution applied to call three witnesses as evidence of bad character, pursuant to Chapter 1 of Part 11 of the Criminal Justice Act 2003. Those witnesses were [Ms IM], [Ms VA] and [Mr S]. The first two were young women who said that at a vulnerable time in their lives they were subjected to sexually charged approaches made by the appellant similar to those which the complainant would say were made to her. The other two women were not visited by the appellant at home because proposed visits were abandoned when he discovered that they would not be alone, and in neither case was there any allegation of rape. Mr S was the founder and chairman of the Board of Trustees of the Temple at Tooting, and he was able to give evidence as to the appellant's behaviour when employed there, and as to the reasons why his employment was brought to an end.

14. The application to call the three witnesses was resisted by Mr Squirrel, who was then appearing for the appellant, and the main argument put forward was that the relevant provisions of the 2003 Act did not apply to this trial because the investigation and the initial criminal proceedings took place before the relevant provisions came into force. As a result of a subsequent decision of this court it is now clear, and before us it has been common ground, that the defence argument was misconceived, and the judge was right to reject it. During the course of his submissions Mr Squirrel was asked by the judge whether if the new Act applied he could argue against the inclusion of evidence of bad character, and he replied 'well, it is going to be difficult, I concede that.' A little later, counsel expressly conceded that the applications fell within section 101(1)(f) and (g) of the 2003 Act, but invited the judge to make use of his power to exclude under section 101(3) of the 2003 Act, and possibly also under section 78 of the Police and Criminal Evidence Act 1984.

15. Having regard to the way in which the application was advanced it is not surprising that the judge, after deciding that the 2003 Act did apply, was succinct in dealing with the requirements of that Act. He found that the application was properly made under section 101(1)(f) and (g) if not under (d) as well and continued—

I have thought hard about my discretionary power under subsection 3 to exclude the evidence, but do not do so. Much of this proposed evidence would have been admissible under the old law in any event.

The trial then began, and on the following day, 12th January 2005, Miss Etherton sought a ruling that the statement of VA should be read pursuant to section 23 of the Criminal

Justice Act 1988. Evidence was called as to the circumstances under which her statement was obtained, and as to the steps taken to secure her attendance at court. They were conceded to have been appropriate steps, but it was nevertheless submitted, principally by reference to section 26 of the 1988 Act, that the statement should not be read because the evidence was important and could not be challenged. As to that the judge said—

> There is no doubt that this witness is an important and significant one. She gives evidence of similar fact to the extent of the grooming process that this defendant allegedly employed to wear down the resistance of those that he targeted. However, in my judgment, Mr Squirrel falls into error in saying that the evidence cannot be challenged. The defendant has challenged her account in interview, and, moreover, the defence is as able to controvert the evidence in the statement as ever it was . . . And I have come to the conclusion that, having thought about the matter carefully, that the statement ought to be read in the interests of justice, and so doing will not cause an unfairness within the meaning of this section or section 78 of the Police and Criminal Evidence Act, and consequently I allow Miss Etherton's application.

16. The jury then heard the rest of the evidence of the complainant and they heard evidence from two witnesses to whom she complained in June or July and in November 2002. They also heard from IM and the statement of VA was read. They heard from Mr S (of Tooting Temple) and they heard from Professor Lipner, professor of Hinduism at Cambridge University [part of whose expert evidence was then described].

The prosecution case concluded with evidence in relation to the interview with the appellant on 11th March 2004, and there were also schedules in relation to telephone contacts between the complainant and the appellant.

17. The appellant gave evidence on his own behalf, but the defence which he advanced was not as foreshadowed in his interviews and in his Defence Case Statement. He said that he fell out with Mr S at Tooting because Mr S was running the Temple as a business. He thought Mr S was worried that the appellant was too popular, and he added that by the end he was unhappy and 'my contract was not renewed by agreement.' As to the complainant he gave details of his dealings with her, maintaining that she attempted to seduce him, and said—

> [the complainant] has lied because she was obsessed with me and I rejected her—three times she tried to get me and failed. I accept I didn't mention this in interview; only afterwards did I learn about things.

Referring to IM and VA as well as the complainant the appellant said—

> All three women have collaborated and told lies about me.

At this stage it is unnecessary for us to refer to the summing-up. We will deal with specific criticisms made in relation to it later in this judgment.

Issues on appeal

18. Having set the scene we can now summarise the issues raised in this appeal. They are as follows—

(a) That the judge was wrong to admit the bad character evidence (ie the evidence of IM, VA and Mr S) because none of it was admissible under section 101(d)(f) or (g) of the 2003 Act.

(b) That the judge gave inadequate reasons for admitting the evidence, a point only taken during the course of submissions to us.

(c) That the judge's directions to the jury in relation to bad character evidence were inadequate.

(d) That the evidence of Professor Lipner as to the likelihood of a woman making an allegation against a Hindu priest was inadmissible and prejudicial.

(e) That the judge should not have permitted the statement of VA to be read, and failed to give adequate directions in relation to it, and—

(f) That each of the convictions is thus rendered unsafe.'

For the purposes of this appeal it was common ground that the convictions stand or fall together.

Relevant legislation

19. In this appeal the following sections of the 2003 Act are relevant, and the relevant parts of those sections are to be found set out in our introduction to all five appeals—

Section 99(1)
Section 101(1)(d), (f) and (g)
Section 101(3)
Section 103(1)(a) and (b)
Section 105(6)
Section 110

It will also be necessary to refer in due course to sections 23 to 26 of the Criminal Justice Act 1988, and to section 78 of the Police and Criminal Evidence Act 1984.

Chronology

20. For certain purposes it is important in this case to bear in mind the sequence of events as disclosed by the evidence, so we summarise the chronology.

21. In 1998 the appellant ceased to work at Tooting Temple after being there for two years, and moved to Hendon. In November 2001 he left Hendon to open his own Temple at Thornton Heath.

22. In about June 2002 the appellant was consulted by the complainant. She says that he went to her home to perform a poojah on 11th July 2002 and that was when the first rape took place. The complainant had intended her friend [Ms P] to be present for the poojah but she was unable to attend. However, according to the complainant, very soon after the rape she spoke to [Ms P] and to another friend [Ms EL] about what had occurred, and EL gave evidence of that conversation at the trial. She said that in about June or July 2002 she was at Manchester University when telephoned by the complainant in distress. She said that her priest had come to her house, didn't want to leave, and had bolted the door. He had pinned her to the floor and she struggled. She couldn't fight him off. He said they should be

together. She said no several times, but afterwards she felt weak and dirty. She said he forced her, she didn't want to, and EL understood she meant something sexual.

23. In August/September 2002 the appellant was in India with his family and, according to the complainant, it was in September 2002, soon after his return, that he visited her home with a gift and raped her for the second time. She then became pregnant and consulted a Marie Stopes Clinic with a view to an abortion. She told DB, a nurse at the clinic, that the putative father was the priest at the Temple, and DB gave evidence to that effect. The abortion on 26th November 2002 was preceded by a scan on 22nd November 2002, which showed the foetus to be just over seven weeks old, indicating that conception took place early in October.

24. In about February or March 2003 VA was planning a fast, and consulted the appellant. According to her sexual approaches then began which she initially terminated by threatening to tell his wife what he was doing. He then, in about March 2003, offered to do prayers at her house and she agreed because she wanted the house blessed. When he telephoned to say he was on his way she said that her brother was with her and looking forward to meeting him. The appellant then cancelled his visit, saying that he was getting late for the Temple. Later he rang to say that she must be alone for the blessing, which VA did not accept, pointing out that her father was a priest. According to her the appellant then became offensive, and she terminated the conversation and changed her telephone number.

25. It was at about the same time, in March 2003, that IM, who is the sister-in-law of VA, consulted the appellant, and according to her suggestive conduct of which she complained continued until July 2003.

26. Meanwhile the complainant was still in contact with the appellant and taking part in ceremonies at the Temple. In April 2003 she says that she went to Windsor with her son to visit Legoland, and stayed in a family room at an hotel. According to the appellant she asked him to perform a poojah at Windsor, and provided him with a railway ticket. When he got there she took him to her hotel bedroom where she made advances to him, which he rejected, and he then left. The complainant accepted that under pressure she told the appellant of her proposed visit to the hotel and was scared that he might follow her, but he did not do so.

27. On 6th May 2003 the complainant paid £150 to the appellant for a poojah. She was about to have an operation and, according to her, wanted a poojah in another Temple with people around, but the appellant found out and insisted that he would do it.

28. In July 2003 the appellant was to perform a service at the home of IM, who arranged for her sister-in-law VA to be present, although the appellant had told her that she should not have any family member present. About two hours before the proposed service, at a time when the appellant knew that VA was to be present, the appellant telephoned to cancel the service, saying, according to IM, that he had to have an eye operation. When she saw him a couple of days later there was no sign of any operation, and he said that his eyes had recovered. According to the appellant he did not cancel services at the homes of either VA or IM when he knew that they would not be alone, nor did he say anything to IM about an eye operation. He was due to meet a priest from India, and simply told her that he had another appointment.

29. The appellant stated that on 11th September 2003, after a summer visit to India, he took a gift to the complainant at her home which she rejected. That, he said, was dis-

respectful, and although she subsequently visited the Temple he ignored her because she had been disrespectful.

30. The appellant asserted that in October 2003 he finally rejected the complainant, and the last recorded telephone call between them was in that month.

31. In November 2003 the complainant went to the police. They then obtained statements from the complainant, VA and IM, whose name was given to the police by VA, and, as we have already said, on 11th March 2004 the appellant was interviewed by the police.

Issue 1—Admissibility of bad character evidence

32. We turn now to the first of the issues which arise in this appeal, reminding ourselves that at the outset in the court below it was accepted that the criteria set out in section 101(1)(d) (f) and (g) were satisfied. Had that not been the case no doubt a distinction would have been drawn between the evidence of IM and VA on the one hand and the evidence of Mr S on the other. His evidence would also have been divided into two parts—the first relating to the reasons for the appellant's departure from Tooting, and the second relating to what the witness saw or heard relating to the appellant's behaviour whilst at Tooting.

33. Mr Kovalevsky QC, for the appellant, submitted to us that none of the bad character evidence (ie none of the evidence of IM, VA or Mr S) should have been admitted under section 101(1)(d) because none of it was relevant to any important matter in issue between the defendant and the prosecution. As Miss Etherton, for the respondent, pointed out, section 101(1)(d) does have to be read in the light of section 103(1), which makes it clear that for the purposes of section 101(1)(d) matters in issue include a propensity to commit offences of the kind charged, and a propensity to be untruthful.

34. Mr Kovalevsky submitted, correctly, that the sole issue was whether the complainant's account was true, and he went on to submit, again correctly, that before the implementation of the 2003 Act the evidence of IM and VA, if not that of Mr S, would only have been admitted if it satisfied the requirements of similar fact evidence, as set out in *DPP v P* [1991] 2 AC 447. Mr Kovalevsky then submitted, contentiously, that the coming into force of the 2003 Act has not significantly altered the test for admissibility of similar fact evidence. In support of that proposition he relied upon certain passages from the speech of Lord Phillips in *O'Brien v Chief Constable of South Wales Police* [2005] 2 AC 354, and upon the reference made to those passages in *Edwards and others* [2005] EWCA Crim 1813 (**p 169 above**).

35. As Mr Kovalevsky recognised, *O'Brien* was not a criminal case, and we remind ourselves that section 99(1) of the 2003 Act expressly provides that—

The common law rules governing the admissibility of evidence of bad character *in criminal proceedings* are abolished (our emphasis).

At paragraph 12 of his speech in *O'Brien* Lord Phillips said—

Where a defendant to a criminal charge has a criminal record, his propensity to commit crime will normally have some relevance to the question of whether he committed the offence with which he is charged. As a general rule such evidence has nonetheless been held to be inadmissible on the ground that its prejudicial effect is likely to outweigh its probative value. Exceptions have, however, been made to this general exclusion. The nature and extent of those exceptions have proved a frequent preoccupation of the appellate courts and, on at least four occasions, of your Lordships' House. They are now to be found codified in sections 101 to 106 of the Criminal Justice Act 2003, which were brought into effect in December last year.

We consider that passage, which is not an essential part of the reasoning in *O'Brien*, to be capable of being misunderstood. The 2003 Act completely reverses the pre-existing general rule. Evidence of bad character is now admissible if it satisfies certain criteria (see section 101(1)), and the approach is no longer one of inadmissibility subject to exceptions (see also the Explanatory Notes to the Act Paragraph 358 and the observations of Professor John Spencer QC in his paper for the Judicial Studies Board at paragraphs 37 and 143).[8]

36. In paragraph 33 of his speech Lord Phillips said—

> The test of admissibility advanced by Lord Mackay in *Director of Public Prosecutions v P* still requires similar fact evidence to have an enhanced relevance or substantial probative value before it is admissible against a defendant in a criminal trial. This is because such evidence usually shows that the defendant is a person of bad character and thus risks prejudicing a jury against the defendant in a manner that English law regards as unfair. Instead of applying Lord Mackay's simple test, the trial judge now has to apply his mind to the matters set out in sections 101 to 106 of the 2003 Act. These preserve, however, by rules of some complexity, the requirement that the similar fact evidence should have an enhanced probative value.

That is also reflected in paragraph 52 of the speech. The Act does not say anything about 'enhanced probative value' or 'enhanced relevance' (the words used in *Edwards and others*). Paragraph 363 of the Explanatory Notes does refer to an 'enhanced relevance test' but only in relation to section 100 of the Act. The terms of that section clearly impose a higher test in respect of the introduction of a non-defendant's bad character than the test for the introduction of a defendant's bad character. If the evidence of a defendant's bad character is relevant to an important issue between the prosecution and the defence (section 101(1)(d)), then, unless there is an application to exclude the evidence, it is admissible. Leave is not required. So the pre-existing one stage test which balanced probative value against prejudicial effect is obsolete (see also section 99(1)).

37. In the context of this case we are satisfied that all of the bad character evidence which the prosecution sought to adduce satisfied the requirements of section 101(1)(d). In substance it was the case for the prosecution that over a prolonged period, beginning when she was emotionally vulnerable, the complainant was subjected by the appellant to sexually charged behaviour which on two occasions culminated in rape. The defendant's response was one of complete denial. He did not simply say that there was never any rape. He denied that he had behaved improperly at any time. It was therefore plainly relevant to an important matter in issue between the parties, namely the credibility of the complainant on the one hand and the defendant on the other, for the prosecution to show that the behaviour to which the complainant said that she had been subjected (other than the actual offences of rape) followed a pattern used by the defendant in relation to two other women who

---

[8] § 35 of the original text appears as §1.50 in the revised text printed in this book (at p 18 above); §147 of the original text has been deleted.

attended the Temple at Thornton Heath, that his behaviour towards women at Tooting gave cause for concern, and that, contrary to his assertion in interview that he had no problems at Tooting, he left his post there because of his behaviour and because he was untruthful, thus exhibiting a propensity to be untruthful (see section 103(1)(b)).

38. That brings us to the second stage of the procedure required by the statute, namely the application of section 101(3). In this case counsel for the defendant did apply to exclude the evidence, and bearing in mind the provisions of Article 6 of the European Convention, we consider it important that a judge should if necessary encourage the making of such an application whenever it appears that the admission of the evidence may have such a adverse effect on the fairness of the proceedings that the court ought not to admit it. As Miss Etherton accepts, section 101(3) does require the judge to perform a balancing exercise, and that exercise does require the judge to look carefully at the evidence sought to be adduced.

39. In our judgment the probative force of the evidence of IM and VA was considerable because, if accepted, it lent powerful support to what the complainant said about the appellant's technique. Without going into detail the evidence of each woman showed that the appellant sought to strike up a relationship with them when they were at a low ebb in their lives. He belittled their former or intended partners, he admired their clothes, and suggested what colours they should wear, he acquired telephone numbers and addresses and then telephoned regularly, often late at night. He spoke of dreaming of them, of being married to them in a past life, and of the Gods now sending them to him. He offered gifts and did things to their hands and hair in the Temple which were inappropriate because they were only done when a girl became a woman or by her husband. Finally he sought to visit each of them at home when they were alone, and only in the case of the complainant did he succeed. There was no significant indication of collusion although, as we have noted, IM and VA were related by marriage, and one gave the name of the other to the police. The admission of that highly relevant evidence could not in our judgment, have such an adverse on the fairness of the proceedings that the court ought not to have admitted it, not least because the appellant knew precisely who the witnesses were, and what they would say, so he would be able where appropriate to challenge what they had said, and to adduce evidence to the opposite effect.

40. Turning to the evidence of Mr S, we take a similar view of his evidence as to the reasons why the appellant ceased to work at Tooting. The appellant had told the police officers that he had no trouble there, and it was highly probative to show that he had been dismissed because he lied to Mr S and because of behaviour which Mr S had witnessed, or put to the appellant. With all of that the appellant could be expected to deal. If Mr S had been allowed to give evidence about complaints made in relation to the appellant's behaviour which he received from unidentified third parties and which were not put to the appellant such evidence by its nature would have been very difficult for the appellant to meet, and should therefore in fairness to the appellant have been excluded pursuant to section 101(3), but there was no such evidence tendered in this case. Mr S was quite clear that his concerns, arising from what he saw and heard, were put to the appellant. For example he was asked—

Q. Did you speak to him about the concerns that were being raised or coming to your attention about his attitude to some women?

A. Yes on several occasions I have spoken to him, even spoken about his dress.

41. Similarly in relation to the lies which, according to Mr S, the appellant told about his contact with a French family, even to the extent of swearing on God. It is quite clear from the evidence that what mattered to Mr S was the appellant's response to him and the appellant was well able to deal with that.

42. We therefore conclude that the judge was right to admit all of the evidence pursuant to section 101(1)(d) having given consideration to the application made under section 101(3).

43. Our conclusions in relation to section 101(1)(d) make it possible for us to deal more succinctly with the other gateway provisions. We accept that a simple denial of the offence or offences alleged cannot, for the purposes of section 101(1)(f), be treated as a false impression given by the defendant. But that was not the situation in this case. The appellant put himself forward as a man who not only had no previous convictions but also enjoyed a good reputation as a priest, particularly at Tooting, where he had previously been employed, and was the victim of a conspiracy hatched up by members of the Mauritian community at Thornton Heath. That, as Mr Kovalevsky accepted, opened the gateway for the admission of evidence as to what happened at Tooting, but he invited our attention to section 105(6) which states that evidence is admissible under section 101(1)(f) 'only if it goes no further than is necessary to correct the false impression.' We accept that is a statutory reversal of the previous common law position that character is indivisible (*Winfield* [1939] 27 CrAppR 139), but we do not accept Mr Kovalevsky's submission that all that was required in this case to correct the false impression was for Mr S to state that decisions had been taken not to renew the appellant's contract because of complaints that had been received. The gateway having been opened the prosecution was entitled to adduce a full account of what, according to their witness, brought the Tooting contract to an end. A slightly more difficult question is whether the evidence of IM and VA would be admissible to correct a false impression given by the appellant. Miss Etherton submitted that it was because of the appellant's allegations in interview about a conspiracy. We prefer to put it slightly differently. In our judgment the evidence of the two women was admissible under section 101(1)(f) because part of the false impression given by the appellant in interview and, as it turned out later by calling seven character witnesses, was that he was a priest who had never behaved inappropriately towards female worshippers at his Temple.

44. We note that the provisions of section 101(3) do not apply to subsection (1)(f), and we see no reason to doubt that section 78 of the 1984 Act should be considered where section 101(1)(f) is relied upon (see the judgment of Lord Woolf CJ in *Highton and others* [2005] EWCA Crim 1895 (**p 153 above**) at paragraph 13, and the views of Professor Spencer at paragraph 21 of the paper to which we have already referred[9]). In this case for the reasons which we have already given when dealing with the application of section 101(3) to section 101(1)(d) we do not see any way in which, in relation to subsection (1)(f), section 78 would assist the appellant.

45. We turn now to the final gateway provision relied upon, namely that the appellant at interview and thereafter made an attack on the complainant's character (section 101(1)(g)). Mr Kovalevsky accepts that he did so, but he submitted that the opening of that gateway should not be regarded as rendering all available evidence of bad character admis-

---

[9] This paragraph appears as §1.24 in the revised text of the commentary printed in this book (at p 10 above).

sible. That is a somewhat difficult submission because in the first place it must be noted that section 105(6) has no application to section 101(1)(g), and, secondly, it is clear from the decision in *Highton* that once this gateway is open the evidence admitted may be used not only in relation to credibility but also in relation to propensity. In our judgment the attack on the character of the complainant clearly opens the door to all of the evidence on which the prosecution sought to rely, subject to the requirements of section 101(3), which we have already considered in relation to section 101(1)(d).

Issue 2—The judge's reasons

46. We accept that the judge's reasons for deciding as he did were brief, but they have to be considered in the light of the argument advanced before him. The principal issue was whether the 2003 Act applied. He was right about that. It was accepted by the defence that the gateway provisions were satisfied, so the only other issue was the application of section 101(3) of the 2003 Act or section 78 of the 1984 Act. The significant difference between those provisions is to be found in the mandatory opening words of section 101(3), but they do not apply until the court reaches its conclusion as to whether the admission of the evidence would have such an adverse effect on the fairness of the proceedings that the court ought not to admit it. In other words the first step is for the judge to perform the balancing act, and it is clear to us that is what the judge did. That is what he was referring to when he spoke of his discretionary power under subsection (3) to exclude evidence. We accept that he could have expressed himself better, but we do not regard infelicity of expression as an effective ground of appeal.

Issue 3—Directions to the jury

47. Mr Kovalevsky submits that the judge failed to direct the jury properly as to the use that could be made of the bad character evidence of IM, VA and Mr S. In particular it is said that the judge failed to refer to the possibility of collusion or innocent contamination as required by *H* [1995] 2 AC 596 and, secondly, he did not invite the jury to consider the similarities between the accounts.

48. Collusion was never raised as an issue in this case but the possibility of innocent contamination was put to and rejected by IM. During the course of the evidence the judge did caution the jury about the way in which they should approach evidence of bad character, and he returned to the topic in his summing-up, saying at page 38G of the transcript in relation to VA—

> Bear in mind the direction I gave you about that, but consider both her account and that of [IM]. In the absence of collaboration and putting minds together and fabricating these allegations that they make, is it likely that these women have separately invented these incidents?
>
> You heard from Mr S, the owner of the Tooting Temple. I referred to his evidence when I gave you a direction about character generally. His evidence is admissible to counter the defendant's assertion in interview that there was never any problem at Tooting, and also the defendant has made an attack on the truthfulness of [the complainant] .

That, as it seems to us, in the context of this case, satisfied the requirements of *H*, and earlier in his summing-up the judge had referred to the evidence of VA and IM as evidence capable of supporting the complainant. He said—

> Now, these incidents and aspects of their evidence, if you accept them, are capable of supporting [the complainant's] account of the defendant's course of conduct or course of behaviour towards her, and the prosecution say that together they show a picture of the targeting of vulnerable women at uncertain times in their lives and a purposeful course of grooming towards a situation from which he could take advantage. Now, that is a matter for your judgment.

The judge went on to deal with the evidence in detail. In our judgment he cannot be criticised for failing to spell out similarities between the accounts, and indeed had he done so he would have been assisting the prosecution rather than the defence.

Issue 4—Professor Lipner

[49. The court held that Professor Lipner's evidence was properly admitted.]

Issue 5—The statement of VA

50. VA made her statement on 1st March 2004 but later indicated that she did not wish to attend to give evidence, and the judge heard evidence from which he was able to conclude that all reasonable efforts had been made to locate her. That is not disputed. He then had to consider whether her statement could be read, having regard to the factors set out in section 26 of the Criminal Justice Act 1988, namely (1) the contents of the statement; (2) the risk of unfairness to the accused having particular regard to whether it was likely to be possible for the accused to controvert the statement, and (3) any other circumstances that appeared to the court to be relevant. The judge considered those statutory provisions and in a ruling set out earlier in this judgment decided that the statement could be read. Mr Kovalevsky submitted that his conclusion was wrong because the witness was important and if she could not be produced and cross-examined her evidence should not be adduced at all. In our judgment that cannot be accepted, not least because it would frustrate one important purpose of the statute, which was to prevent a prosecution from being hampered by intimidation of witnesses. The reality was, as we have already indicated, that the appellant was well able to deal with the statement of VA and, as Miss Etherton points out, his counsel was able to put his case not only to the complainant but also to IM. We consider that the judge's carefully considered decision to allow the statement to be read cannot be faulted.

51. Then it is said that the judge failed properly to direct the jury in relation to the statement which had been read. When the statement was read the judge warned the jury to bear in mind that because the witness did not attend they were deprived of the opportunity to hear her cross-examined, and he repeated that warning in his summing-up, saying at page 8G of the transcript—

> Remember that Mr Squirrel was deprived of the opportunity to cross-examine her and challenge her evidence, and take that into account when you assess how much weight to

put upon what that witness says, bearing in mind that it was a statement made to a police officer in contemplation of criminal proceedings. So tread carefully, and bear in mind Mr Squirrel was not able to put his case to her in the way that he did, for example, to [IM].

52. Mr Kovalevsky submitted that the direction was inadequate because the witness was important, and drew our attention to the decision of this court in *McCoy* 10th December 1999, unreported save in [2000] 6 Archbold News 2. In that case the statement read was that of the victim of what was alleged to be a wounding with intent to do grievous bodily harm who identified his attacker. His evidence was, as this court found, 'wholly crucial to the case.' It was not entirely clear why he did not attend, and the judge was precipitate in allowing his statement to be read before giving sufficient time to exhaust the possibility of his being brought to court. It was in that context that Laws LJ said at paragraph 25 of the transcript—

> If a statement of a critical witness is to be read to a jury, perhaps especially in an alibi case where identification is the true issue, it must be incumbent on the trial judge to ensure that the jury realise the drawbacks which are imposed on the defence if the prosecution statement is read to them. It is not enough simply to say that counsel has not had the opportunity of cross-examining. A lay jury may not appreciate the significance of that fact. The judge must at least explain that it means that they may feel quite unable to attach anything like as much weight to the evidence in the statement as they might if it was tested in cross-examination; and where appropriate it would be necessary, certainly desirable, for the judge also to indicate to the jury by way of illustration the sort of matters that might well be put in cross-examination in the particular case.

53. In the present case the evidence of VA was important, but it was not crucial, and the judge in his direction drew attention not only to the lack of opportunity to cross-examine but also to the question of how much weight should be put on what the witness said. He also illustrated what might have been put to her had she attended by referring to the cross-examination of IM. In those circumstances it seems to us that he did all that was required of him in this case, where the situation was different to that which arose in the case of *McCoy*.

Conclusion

54. Thus we conclude that the appellant has failed to substantiate any of his grounds of appeal, and accordingly this appeal against conviction is dismissed.

Stephen Yaxley-Lennon

The Background

55. On 18th April 2005, in the Luton Crown Court, this appellant was convicted by a majority of 11–1 of assault occasioning actual bodily harm (Count One) and by a majority of 10–2 of assault with intent to resist arrest (Count Two). He was sentenced to 12 months imprisonment on Count One and 3 months imprisonment concurrent on Count Two. He appeals by way of leave of the single judge.

The prosecution case

56. The incident in question took place in Luton at around 3am on 4th July 2004. The victim was an off duty police officer called Dalton. He and his neighbours Mr and Mrs Bye were woken by an argument in the street between the appellant and his girlfriend Jenna Vowles. Although living in the same street, Dalton and the Byes did not know each other. Concerned by the screaming and raised voices, the three of them went into the street from their homes.

57. The appellant was described as being 'on a short fuse' and that 'something had riled him'. Miss Vowles was sobbing and hysterical wanting nothing to do with him. Dalton, concerned for Miss Vowles, told the appellant that he should let her go home alone. He indicated that he was a police officer and showed the appellant his warrant card. He tried to bring the appellant to the ground. Both men fell to the ground. The appellant managed to get to his feet and kicked Mr Dalton in the head. Dalton had thrown no punches. Dalton then stood up and told the appellant that he was arresting him for assaulting a police officer. It was subsequently decided that such an arrest would not be prudent and that the Byes, who had witnessed the whole incident, would ascertain the appellant's address.

The defence case

58. In interview and in evidence, the appellant said that he had been out clubbing. He had drunk one bottle of Smirnoff Vodka. He and Jenna Vowles had an argument. She had dropped her mobile phone and was on her hands and knees trying to pick it up. The eye witnesses must have assumed that he was the aggressor. Dalton came up to him. He asked the appellant what he was doing. His breath smelled of alcohol. Jenna was not sobbing or crying. Dalton told him he was not going home and pushed him around, pushing him in the face and pulled his legs from under him. He did not produce a warrant card or say he was a police officer. The appellant did not kick him. It was only at the end when Dalton was threatening him that he indicated he was a police officer. The appellant did not believe him. He suggested that Mr Bye knew Dalton as he addressed Dalton by his Christian name, telling him to leave it and go home. The appellant and Jenna then ran home.

59. Jenna Vowles gave evidence along the same lines of the appellant, describing the argument as a tiff, but that they were happily going home when the incident broke out.

Background to the judge's ruling

60. During evidence in chief of Jenna Vowles, counsel for the appellant asked her whether she or the appellant had taken any drugs that evening. She replied 'No.'

61. In cross examination, counsel for the Crown asked her the following questions:

Q. You were asked questions by Mr Urquhart about what you had been drinking. Yes?
A. Yeah.

Q. An you say you had had four drinks and you were a bit tipsy. Correct?
A. Yeah.

Q. And then he asked you about whether you had taken any drugs. Correct?
A. Yeah.

Q. Just tell about drugs please for a moment. What do you want to tell us about drugs?
A. I don't take drugs.

Q. Never taken drugs?
A. No.

Q. Never possessed drugs?
A. Yes.

Q. Yes. Tell the jury about that.
A. I was cautioned in November for possession of drugs.

Q. Which drug?
A. It was cocaine.

Q. Cocaine.
A. It was in my possession. There were two empty bags which I was clearing out my house. I put them in my bag so my parents wouldn't find them.

It was at this point that the judge asked the jury to retire. There then followed discussions between counsel and court.

62. The Crown whilst conceding that they should have made an application to introduce the caution, said that they would not have raised the issue had the witness not been asked about drugs in evidence in chief. They submitted that the evidence was relevant to the question of credibility.

63. The defence having taken instructions made an application for the discharge of the jury on the basis that the wording of section 100(1)(b) could not include issues relating to credibility and thus the evidence did not relate to a matter in issue in the proceedings. The judge said that it was premature to discharge the jury at that point without more and that he may have to re-visit the decision at a later point.

64. It was agreed between the parties and the court that the witness should be asked further questions about her caution. The witness was then called and questions were put to her in the absence of the jury. Following the voir dire, defence counsel submitted that the evidence could not fall under section 100 (1)(a) or (b).

65. The judge ruled that Jenna Vowles caution for possession of cocaine had substantial probative value to her credibility, which was an important issue in the case. It had been put that she was lying to support her boyfriend's case and there was a stark difference between the Crown and Defence accounts. He gave leave for the Crown to ask further questions to the witness in front of the jury, but indicated that he was going to direct the jury that so far as credit is concerned they should ignore the evidence completely, as it could not really help the prosecution prove that she had been lying about what happened in relation to the events of the incident, given that she did not lie in relation to the caution. In the light of the judge's comments, counsel for the crown did not cross examine further on the matter in the presence of the jury. Counsel for the appellant re-examined the witness on the background facts leading to the caution.

Direction in summing up

66. When summing up to the jury, the learned judge gave a strongly worded direction to the jury, as follows:

One exchange between Mr Heimler and her (Vowles) concerned this question of cocaine. I need to deal with it. You have heard about it. Can I ask you to disregard it completely? It has got about as much to do with this case as the price of tomatoes. First of all the caution took place well after this incident itself occurred. . . . Secondly—and it is important—although her credibility is in issue, clearly just as much as all the witnesses credibility is in issue, the effect of drugs on that is unknown. It has got really no issue, no bearing on any issue in this case. . . . . I am directing you to disregard her previous caution completely because it cannot help you decide what happened in the street that night. . . . In fairness please just disregard that completely.

Grounds of appeal

67. The ground of appeal is that the judge erred in holding that the evidence of the caution was admissible and rejecting the defendant's application to discharge the jury.

68. The appellant's submissions are put on two bases: Firstly, that the evidence did not relate to a matter in issue in the proceedings as the section does not encompass matters of credibility. Second that even if credibility is encompassed by the section, the evidence did not pass the test of admissibility as it had no *substantial* probative value in relation to the question of credibility and was not of substantial importance in the context of the case as a whole. It was submitted that the evidence had very little value in relation to credibility and no relevance at all to the offence in question because (a) the caution did not relate to an offence of dishonesty or showing evidence of untruthfulness; (b) it related to an incident after the events in issue; (c) the witness by agreeing to be cautioned had accepted her guilt; (d) the witness was frank about her caution in evidence; and (e) there was no suggestion that she was under the influence of drugs during the incident itself.

69. The appellant also submits that the conviction is unsafe in the light of the majority verdicts on each count on the basis that the evidence could have adversely affected their view of the witness despite the judge's strong warning.

70. On behalf of the respondent, it is submitted that Section 100(1) must cover the issue of credibility, for were it not to do so, unfairness would ensue. It was submitted that the evidence of the caution was relevant to credibility, but it was conceded that it was difficult to suggest that the evidence had substantial probative value in relation to credibility in the light of the witnesses' answers.

71. Their primary submission therefore is that the conviction was safe and that the strong warning given by the judge corrected any harm done by the introduction of the evidence.

Judgment

72. We now deal with the submissions and the questions arising therefrom.

Does section 100 (1) cover issues of credibility?

73. Although couched in different terms from the provisions relating to the introduction of the defendants bad character, in our view, section 100(1) does cover matters of credibility. To find otherwise would mean that there was a significant lacuna in the legislation with the potential for unfairness. In any event, it is clear from paragraph 362 of the Explanatory Notes that the issue of credibility falls within the section.

Did the judge err in coming to the conclusion that the evidence of the caution had substantial probative value in relation to the witness's credibility?

74. In our view he did err for a number of reasons, including those which were put forward by the judge himself when directing the jury to ignore the evidence of the caution. It follows, therefore, that we find that the evidence of the caution was inadmissible under section 100.

Is the verdict unsafe as a result of the inadmissible evidence being in front of the jury?

75. Mr Urquhart conceded that had the judge found the evidence to be inadmissible but nevertheless declined to discharge the jury, he would have difficulty persuading the court that the judge had exercised his discretion wrongly. Although the exercise of discretion was not the basis upon which the judge declined to discharge the jury, the practical effect is still the same. We have to take a view therefore whether in the light of the admission of the evidence of the caution, the conviction is unsafe. We have considered the evidence as a whole and in particular the very strong warning given to the jury and come to the conclusion that the verdicts in this case, despite being majority verdicts are not unsafe. This appeal against conviction is therefore dismissed.

Simon Charles Manister

76. On 15 April 2005 in the Crown Court at Bristol, this appellant was convicted of three offences of indecent assault contrary to section 14(1) of the Sexual Offences Act 1956.

77. A, the complainant in each case, was born on 12 March 1990 so she was thirteen at the time of the alleged offences; the appellant was thirty-nine. He was a friend of the girl's father and he moved into the family home on 23 July 2003 and stayed there until December 2003.

78. A alleged that the appellant touched her sexually on a number of occasions, but the allegations which led to the three counts in the indictment were: Count 1, placing his hand between her legs in the region of her vagina, then on her breasts, both over her clothes, in December 2003 soon after he left her family home; Count 2 (an allegation of rape of which he was found not guilty but guilty of indecent assault), full sexual intercourse in mid February 2004; and Count 3, forcibly kissing her, touching the outside of her leg and her bottom and then between her legs in the area of her vagina, all over her clothes, before putting his hand under her upper clothing and bra and touching her breast, on 27 February 2004. All the offences were alleged to have been committed in his car.

79. A did not make any allegation against the appellant until just over a week after the last, alleged incident, when she was arrested for shoplifting. She was interviewed on three occasions, and the video recordings of the interviews stood as her evidence in chief. In the first interview on 9 March 2004 she spoke of the appellant's relationship with her family and her sympathy for him because he said he had cancer, although it turned out to be a swollen gland in his throat. She spoke of the appellant touching her up on occasions and gave her account of events which led to Counts 1 and 3. At the end of the interview she asked what she should do if she later remembered something else. The interviewing officer said A could come back and speak on tape, and asked her if she had told as much as she could. She said, 'Yes.'

80. The second interview was on 19 May 2004. A spoke slowly and it was difficult for the officer to get much out of her. She said that on an occasion in about mid February the appellant had spoken about paying her for sex, which disgusted her, and he tried to kiss her. She spoke of an earlier occasion just before Christmas when she was in his house and he came down naked after a shower. She spoke of him threatening to kill himself on 27 February 2004. She was asked if there was anything else she wanted to say, and she answered 'No.'

81. On 28 June 2004 she was interviewed for a third time because she had more to say, and she spoke of the appellant kissing her, pulling her jeans and thong down to her ankles and having sexual intercourse with her in his car on the occasion in mid February 2004. He had ejaculated onto the seat. She had not spoken about it before because she thought people would be mad at her, and she was embarrassed.

82. The appellant had no previous convictions. His case, when interviewed by the police and in his evidence at trial, was that nothing of a sexual nature had occurred between him and A. None of the allegations upon which the indictment was based were true. In interview he said that he and A had a friendship; he gave her a little bit of confidence; he never thought that she thought there was more to their friendship, and he told her 'just be mates.' In his evidence, he said that his relationship with A was just a friendship where he wanted to help a friend, a teenager. He was someone who was just there, a sounding board, someone to talk to. He accepted that, looking back, it was an emotionally unhealthy relationship, but he had not done any of the improper things that A said he had done.

83. The prosecution relied on various matters in support of the allegations. Semen with the appellant's DNA was found on his car seat. It could not be related to A or any particular woman, and the appellant said it was the result of unprotected sex with other, adult women.

84. There were records of a large number of mobile telephone calls between the appellant and A. He had sent her a card with the message, 'Be mine as I miss you lots,' which A had hidden under her mattress where it was found by her sisters.

85. The judge ruled that evidence of an earlier sexual relationship with another girl was admissible in evidence, as a result of which the appellant formally admitted, as agreed facts, that from October 1998 to September 2001 he had had a sexual relationship with B, a girl who was sixteen at the start of the relationship, when the appellant was thirty-four.

86. The judge also ruled admissible the evidence of C, a sister of A, and fifteen at the material time, that after going to the gym with the appellant he had told her, 'Why do you think I'm still single? If only you were a bit older and I a bit younger.' The appellant denied saying that; it was put to C in cross-examination that she had made it up.

87. The verdict of not guilty of rape but guilty of indecent assault on Count 2 must mean that the jury was sure of sexual intercourse, unlawful because of A's age, in mid February 2004, but not sure that A did not consent, or not sure that the appellant was reckless as to whether she consented. In those circumstances, the prosecution does not seek to uphold the appellant's conviction for indecent assault on Count 2 in the light of the decisions of the House of Lords in *J* [2004] UKHL 42, [2005] 1 AC 562 and of this court in *WR* [2005] EWCA Crim 1907.

88. The appellant was never charged with unlawful sexual intercourse, and the effect of those decisions is that on 15 April 2005 when Count 2 was left to the jury, it was too late to prosecute the appellant under section 6(1) of the Sexual Offences Act 1956 for having unlawful sexual intercourse as an alternative to the allegation of rape, because section 37(2) of, and

paragraph 10(a) of Schedule 2 to, the 1956 Act provided that no such prosecution could be commenced more than twelve months after the alleged sexual intercourse in mid-February 2004. In accordance with *J* and *WR*, the alternative of indecent assault could not be left to the jury either. A prosecution for unlawful sexual intercourse could not be commenced, so it was also impermissible to commence a prosecution for indecent assault by leaving it to the jury as an alternative to rape. In those circumstances the appeal against conviction on Count 2 must succeed and the conviction for indecent assault on that count is quashed.

89. The remaining appeal against the convictions for indecent assault on Counts 1 and 3 is based on a number of grounds, but primarily on the contention that the judge was wrong to rule the evidence of B and C admissible.

90. The relevant sections in Part 11, Chapter 1, of the Criminal Justice Act 2003 are sections 98, 99(1), 101(1)(3) and (4), 102, 103(1) and 112(1).

91. So far as the potential evidence of an earlier sexual relationship between the appellant and B was concerned, the trial judge concluded that for a man of thirty-four to institute a sexual relationship with a girl of sixteen was properly to be described as reprehensible behaviour, and that this brought the relationship within 'gateway' (d) of section 101(1). It showed a propensity to be attracted to girls of an age which was inappropriate for persons of the appellant's age. Since this was the context of the evidence, the passage of five or six years since the earlier relationship was not of significance for the purposes of section 101(4). Having formed a clear view in respect of gateway (d), the judge did not think it necessary to form a view on the additional gateway (f), to correct a false impression, argued by the Crown; he thought it more difficult, but he would not shut it out.

92. The judge ruled that the potential evidence of what the appellant was alleged to have said to A's sister, C, was admissible as 'part of the background as to what is going on in this family, involving the defendant, that the jury was entitled to hear and which, if they accept the evidence, may be useful to them.'

93. Mr Chamberlain challenged both rulings, as he resisted them at the trial. In respect of the sexual relationship with B, he contended that a perfectly legal relationship could not involve the commission of an offence, which we accept; nor could it, being countenanced by the law, amount to 'reprehensible behaviour.' There was no exploration of the details of the relationship. What if the appellant had married B? It could not, therefore, amount to misconduct or a disposition towards misconduct. The disputed evidence of what the appellant said to C indicated restraint on his part.

94. In our combined view, the judge was wrong to conclude that the sexual relationship between the appellant and B, without more, amounted to 'evidence of, or of a disposition towards, misconduct on his part' and therefore evidence of 'bad character' for the purposes of section 98, and therefore sections 101, 102 and 103 of the Act. The definition of 'misconduct' in section 112(1) is very wide. It makes it clear that behaviour may be reprehensible, and therefore misconduct, though not amounting to the commission of an offence. The appellant was significantly older than B. But there was no evidence, or none that the Crown put forward and the judge ruled admissible, of grooming of B by the appellant before she was sixteen, or that her parents disapproved and communicated their disapproval to the appellant, or that B was intellectually, emotionally or physically immature for her age, or that there was some other feature of the lawful relationship which might make it 'reprehensible.' Indeed it might be inferred from the simple agreed facts

that the relationship with B was a serious one, with some real emotional attachment, because it lasted some time.

95. However, once it is decided that evidence of the appellant's sexual relationship with B did not amount to 'evidence of bad character', the abolition of the common law rules governing the admissibility of 'evidence of bad character' by section 99(1) did not apply. We have no doubt that evidence of the relationship was admissible at common law, in the particular circumstances of this case, because it was relevant to the issue of whether the appellant had a sexual interest in A. It was capable of demonstrating a sexual interest in early or mid-teenage girls, much younger than the appellant, and therefore bore on the truth of his case of a purely supportive, asexual interest in A. It was not in our judgment unfair to admit the evidence (see section 78 of the Police and Criminal Evidence Act 1984).

96. Although the judge came to his conclusion as to the admissibility of the appellant's relationship with B by a different route, his direction to the jury as to its possible relevance was fair and accurate. He directed them that it was for the jury to decide whether it had any relevance. He reminded them that the age of consent was sixteen. 'It is something that you can take into account in deciding whether he might have been attracted to [A]. It does not mean that he would have behaved as she says that he behaved; that is assaulting her sexually. To state the obvious, you can be attracted to someone without assaulting them'.

97. So far as C's evidence was concerned, the judge did not expressly rule on whether it amounted to evidence of 'bad character' for the purposes of the Act, or was simply relevant as part of the background as to what was going on in the sister's family, involving the appellant. Unattractive as the alleged conversation was, we do not consider that it could safely be judged to amount to reprehensible conduct on the appellant's part. But his words, with their implied admission of sexual attraction to fifteen year old C, were again, in our view, clearly relevant to the issue of whether the appellant was sexually attracted to A, and therefore admissible for the same reasons which applied to the sexual relationship with B. It was not unfair to admit C's evidence.

98. The judge did not direct the jury as to the potential relevance of C's evidence, but it must have been plain that it fell in the same category as the admission in respect of B, namely something which the jury could take into account in deciding whether the appellant was sexually attracted to A.

99. We therefore reject the challenge to the admissibility of the appellant's conduct in respect of B and C.

100. Mr Chamberlain challenged the judge's direction in respect of the appellant's character. Having indicated in the summing-up that he would give a full 'good character direction' he did so in the terms of the standard direction suggested by the Judicial Studies Board which, accordingly, concluded by telling the jury that they were entitled to take into account all that they had heard about the appellant. This, Mr Chamberlain contended, was likely to be understood by the jury to refer to his earlier relationship with B, and, therefore, to qualify the terms of the good character direction as a whole. We cannot accept this. The relevance of the appellant's lack of convictions, to be taken into account in his favour both as to his credibility and the lesser likelihood of committing the offences of which he was accused, was clearly described to the jury who, nevertheless, had to take account of all they had heard. We see no mischief in that.

101. It was contended that the judge should have given the jury a specific warning to exercise caution in relation to A's evidence in the light of what Mr Chamberlain suggested were weaknesses or implausibilities in her evidence. In particular she told the police in her first two interviews that nothing else had happened, before alleging sexual intercourse, amounting on the face of it to rape, in the third. But the case of *Makanjuola* [1995] 1 WLR 1348, to which we were referred simply says that a judge 'may' give a special warning, and we can not fault the judge's decision not to do so in this case. The judge pointed up the possible weaknesses or implausibilities as he reminded the jury of relevant evidence and issues.

102. It was argued that the judge made comments which might have suggested that A's shoplifting was caused by the appellant's behaviour towards her, when he should have directed them that the reprimand for shoplifting was central to her credibility; and that he raised matters which were not canvassed by counsel on either side, including the possibility that A was attracted to the appellant and may have consented to what happened. But the jury was clearly reminded of her shoplifting and the judge's comments all related to questions which would have come to the minds of worldly members of the jury, and were fairly balanced. We reject the final, and associated submission that the summing-up was 'overly favourable' to the Crown's case.

103. For all these reasons we reject the challenges to the conduct of the appellant's trial. His convictions on Counts1 and 3 were safe and his appeals against those convictions are dismissed.

[104. and 105. The court dismissed the defendant's appeal against sentence.]

Hong Qiang He and De Qun He

106. On 10 March 2005, in the Crown Court at Southwark, these appellants were convicted of violent disorder (Count 1), contrary to section 2(1) of the Public Order Act, 1986. Each now appeals against his conviction.

107. A co-defendant, Feng He, was convicted of the same count of violent disorder. A further co-defendant, Pin Shuen Chan was acquitted of the count of violent disorder on the judge's direction, but convicted of wounding with intent to cause grievous bodily harm (Count 2).

108. The counts arose out of a running fight between two groups of young men in Chinatown in west central London on the evening of 9 September 2004. Various weapons including knives and baseball bats were used. Parts of the concluding events were captured on CCTV in Shaftesbury Avenue.

109. The CCTV film was alleged to show the appellant De Qun He ('De') being struck on the head after which he ran away up Shaftesbury Avenue. A group was seen fighting and moving in the direction taken by Hong Qiang He ('Hong'). Hong was said to have used a baseball bat before falling to the ground. Pin Shuenn Chan ('Chan') was said to have walked towards the group and then run to where Hong was lying, before bending over and stabbing him twice in the leg. De was seen to return, pick up an advertising board, and wave it in a threatening manner towards the group fighting over Hong. Hong was helped to his feet and his friends moved up the street and around the corner. Two of the friends were carrying baseball bats. De put down the advertising board and went with them. They turned into Gerrard Place where some got into a car in which some of the weapons were deposited. Feng He drove the car away. Two got out of the car in King William IV Street, including Hong

who was bleeding badly from leg wounds. The car was driven off but soon stopped by police. The driver and the one remaining occupant, De, were arrested. Metal bars wrapped in cellophane, lawn edge cutters and a hammer were found in the boot.

110. Hong, De and Feng He were alleged to belong to one group, and Chan, who was arrested in Shaftesbury Avenue, to the other.

111. When interviewed, Hong said he went to the scene to calm the situation. He did not know if he went to Shaftsbury Avenue. He was hit on the head and stabbed twice, and taken away in a car.

112. De was not interviewed.

113. Chan said he armed himself with a knife, fearing that he would be attacked. He was set upon by others who were armed with knives. He denied using the knife to stab someone, but he was not very clear and did not remember.

114. None of the defendants gave evidence. They put their characters in. Feng He and Chan had no previous convictions. Hong had a caution and De a Conditional Discharge. The judge gave a good character direction in respect of all.

115. The issues in the case of each defendant were his involvement in events and whether he might have been acting in lawful defence of himself or another.

116. The appeals revolve around the admission of evidence, adduced on behalf of Chan, that the appellants were known to the police from previous incidents. On 19 November 2002 they had been the victims of a knife attack but had refused to provide statements. On 6 June 2004 they had been arrested on suspicion of committing a serious assault but had been released without charge after the alleged victims refused to provide statements.

117. Counsel for Chan submitted that evidence of both incidents was admissible by virtue of section 101(1)(e) of the Act which provides that:

In criminal proceedings evidence of the defendant's bad character is admissible if, but only if . . .

(e) it has substantial probative value in relation to an important matter in issue between the defendant and a co-defendant.

118. The judge rejected this submission, rightly in our view, because he did not consider that being the subject of the conduct of others on 19 November 2002, and failing to make witness statements, demonstrated 'reprehensible behaviour', still less the commission of an offence; nor did the mere fact of arrest on 6 June 2004, without evidence to support a charge against either appellant. So neither previous matter could amount to 'misconduct' as defined in section 112(1) or, therefore 'bad character', as defined in section 98 for the purpose of section 101(1)(e).

119. However, the judge concluded that the fact that evidence of the previous matters was not admissible as 'bad character' did not exclude its relevance. He took the view that

it is potentially relevant to Mr Chan's defence, namely that he was attacked. In this regard the position between defendants on the one hand and the prosecution and defendants on the other is quite different. In short a greater latitude is allowed to a defendant and if there is evidence that some defendants are to be found at or about the scene of disturbances such as the one with which we are concerned then it may assist the jury in deciding whom to believe. This is not necessarily one and the same thing as bad character.

There is no conduct reprehensible or otherwise necessarily inherent in the circumstances by which someone may be surrounded, but equally the repetition of such circumstances may be relevant . . . in the light of the defence actually advanced by Mr Chan . . . I make this ruling, of course, under the common law.

120. No doubt there are cases where previous conduct of a defendant is of probative value and therefore relevant to a matter in issue between him and the prosecution or him and a co-defendant, yet the 'bad character' provisions of Chapter 1 of Part 11 of the Act relating to the defendant's 'misconduct' do not apply. In such cases, section 99(1) of the Act whereby the common law rules governing the admissibility of evidence of 'bad character' in criminal proceedings are abolished does not exclude the relevant material because it does not amount to 'evidence of bad character.' But this was not such a case. The evidence of events on 19 November 2002 and 6 June 2004 could only be relevant if it might show that either appellant had a propensity to violent conduct and therefore bear on Chan's case of self-defence. To show such a propensity it had to amount to 'reprehensible behaviour', 'misconduct' and, therefore 'bad character.' By the same measure as events on 19 November 2002 and 6 June 2004 could not amount to reprehensible behaviour, misconduct or, therefore bad character, they could not bear on Chan's case. There was no room for relaxing this approach simply because it was a defendant, Chan, who sought to introduce the evidence, rather than the prosecution.

121. On the face of the CCTV evidence, interpreted by police officers who knew the appellants, and unchallenged by evidence at trial from the appellants, there was a strong case against each appellant on Count 1, but the admission of the earlier incidents may have poisoned the well so far as their own case of self-defence were concerned, making their convictions unsafe. Their appeals against conviction are accordingly allowed.

122. It is not therefore necessary to consider Hong's second ground of appeal, but we do so for completeness. The prosecution relied on two alleged lies by Hong, in his police interview. Mr Kapur argued that the judge erred when directing the jury: 'You must first decide whether the defendant did, in fact, deliberately tell these lies.' Those words, Mr Kapur contended, removed from the jury the decision as to whether the statements were lies at all, which was contested. However, that argument depends on a partial reading of the summing-up. The judge had hitherto referred to the 'alleged lie', it being 'alleged that he lied,' and to 'the lies alleged' and 'the alleged lies.' The jury must have understood that it was for them to decide whether either statement by Hong was in fact a deliberate untruth. The remainder of the judge's direction on the topic was fair and accurate. We see no merit in this ground of appeal.

Weir's and Somonathan's appeals against conviction dismissed.
Manister's appeal against conviction allowed in part; appeal against sentence dismissed.
Hong's and De's convictions quashed.

R v Edwards and Rowlands; R v McLean; R v Smith; R v Enright and Gray [2005] EWCA Crim 3244, CA, 21 December 2005; Scott Baker LJ, Gross and Ramsey JJ

K Davey, M Roochove, J Stanniland, T Moores and I Wade for the appellants
A Shaw, L Matthews, S Foster and J Weeks for the Crown.

Lord Justice Scott Baker:

1. We heard these appeals consecutively on 25 November 2005. Since each of the conviction appeals raises issues relating to the bad character provisions in sections 98 to 112 of the Criminal Justice Act 2003 we are giving one judgment dealing with all four cases. Before turning to the individual cases we wish to make one or two general observations that have occurred to us when considering these appeals.

(i) Often the first enquiry is whether it is necessary to go through the 'bad character' gateways at all. In this regard, section 98 is not to be overlooked. It excludes from the definition of bad character evidence which 'has to do with the alleged facts of the offence' or evidence 'of misconduct in connection with the investigation or prosecution of that offence.' While difficult questions can arise as to whether evidence of background or motive falls to be admitted under those exclusions in section 98 or requires consideration under section 101(1)(c), it does not follow that merely because the evidence fails to come within the section 101 gateways it will be inadmissible. Where the exclusions in section 98 are applicable the evidence will be admissible without more ado.

(ii) Applications to admit bad character evidence may well arise at an early stage giving rise to real difficulty for the trial judge. Some applications e.g. under section 101(1)(b) cannot be refused; others, for instance brought under section 101(1)(e) may well be difficult to refuse (of which more in a moment). The parties would be well advised to reflect, at the time of the application, as to the use to which such evidence is likely to be put and be in a position to assist the judge in this regard. There can be difficulties for the judge in summing up when bad character evidence that has been admitted turns out, for whatever reason, to have only marginal relevance to the issues before the jury.

(iii) Under the new regime it is apparent that Parliament intended that evidence of bad character would be put before juries more frequently than had hitherto been the case. The judge's role is to determine *admissibility* under the statutory gateways and any questions of exclusion, for example under sections 101(3), 103(3) or section 78 of the Police and Criminal Evidence Act 1984. Once evidence of bad character is admitted (and not excluded) questions of *weight* are for the jury, subject to: (a) the judge's powers under 107 (stopping the case where the evidence is contaminated) and (b) the judge's direction as to relevance and to other matters, as to which see *Hanson* [2005] 2 CrAppR 21 (**p 153 above**) para 18 and *Highton* [2005] 1 WLR 3472 (**p 183 above**) para 11.

(iv) Where evidence of bad character is admitted, the judge's direction is likely to be of the first importance. It will need to cover the matters canvassed in *Hanson* and *Highton*. It may also need to pull threads together on an issue where the ground may have shifted considerably since the evidence was admitted. In an appropriate case, the judge's direction may need to underline that given the course taken by the trial, the evidence of bad character is by then of very little weight indeed.

(v) Simply because an application to admit evidence of bad character is made by a co-defendant, the judge is not bound to admit it. The gateway in section 101(1)(e) must be gone through. Sections 101(1)(d) and (e) give rise to different considerations. In determining an application under 101(1)(e) analysis with a fine tooth comb is unlikely to be helpful; it is the context of the case as a whole that matters. Section 112 makes this clear by its definition of what amounts to an important matter in issue.

(vi) There are a number of other points about the position of co-defendants:

(a) the gateways under sections 101(1)(d), (f) and (g) are not open to them as only prose-cution evidence, as defined in section 112, is admissible: see sections 103(6), 105(7) and 106(3).
(b) section 104(1) is not exhaustive of the scope of section 101(1)(e). It limits evidence rele-vant to a defendant's propensity to be untruthful.
(c) whether a defendant's stance amounts to no more than a denial of participation (see *Varley* 75 CrAppR 24), or gives rise to an important matter in issue between a defendant and a co-defendant will inevitably turn on the facts of the individual case.

(vii) Whilst we note the observation of the Vice-President in *Bovell* [2005] 2 CrAppR 27 para 21 that the court entertained considerable doubt whether the mere making of an allegation is capable of being evidence within 100(1), we are persuaded that it so capable, at any rate when considering the effect of section 109 in relation to an issue under section 101(1)(d). This is an area, however, in which it is important to guard against satellite liti-gation (see *Bovell* para 22). Further, it is appropriate to proceed with caution and with due regard to the judge's discretion to exclude evidence.

(viii) Finally we reiterate two points that have been made in the previous decisions of this court but which we think are worth repetition:

(a) 'admissibility' and 'use' give rise to different questions;
(b) the 'feel' of the trial judge is very important and this court will only interfere where the conviction is unsafe.

Edwards and Rowlands

2. In this appeal the following sections of the Criminal Justice Act 2003 are referred to: sections 98, 101(1)(e), 101(1)(g), 101(3), 101(4), 104(1), 106.

3. On 15 April 2005 both these appellants were convicted in the Crown Court at Ipswich before Judge Newton and a jury of conspiracy to supply a class A drug, ecstasy, and sen-tenced to ten years imprisonment. A charge of possessing ammunition without a certificate against Rowlands was severed from the indictment. A co-defendant, Mitchell, was found not guilty of conspiracy under section 17 of the Criminal Justice Act 1967.

4. Rowlands appeals against conviction with the leave of the single judge, but leave was only given on one ground rather than all three. Both Edwards and Rowlands renew their applications for leave to appeal against sentence after refusal by the single judge. As Rowlands' grounds of appeal against conviction are to an extent interlinked, we have granted leave on the remaining grounds.

5. The facts of the case are as follows. At 12.45pm on 16 September 2004 Rowlands was observed by the police as he arrived at Edwards' home address at 25 Collingwood Fields, East Bergholt appearing to remove something from the boot of his car. A few minutes later officers entered the house to execute a search warrant. Edwards, who was wheelchair-bound following a serious road accident 6 weeks earlier, and his brother-in-law Rowlands, were both present at the house. Officers took possession of a vacuum sealed package which was found on top of a black bin liner on the cooker. A second similar sized package was recovered from Edwards' bed in the lounge. The packages were found to contain a total of 10,190 ecstasy tablets. One of the packages contained Edwards' fingerprints. Latex gloves, containing Edwards' DNA and traces of ecstasy were also recovered along with £2,830 in cash.

6. During the police search of the property a young man called Stewart Mitchell (the co-defendant who was found not guilty) entered the property and was arrested. A struggle ensued after he tried to grab the money and run away.

7. It was the prosecution case that between 31 August and 16 September 2004 Rowlands and Edwards had participated in a conspiracy together and with unknown persons to supply ecstasy to another. In the alternative it was alleged that Edwards had the ecstasy in his possession with intent to supply it to another.

[8.–15. The court detailed the defendants' evidence, in the course of which each one cast the blame upon the other.]

16. This was therefore a cut-throat defence. If the drugs did not belong to both Edwards and Rowlands they must have belonged to one or other of them. Edwards case was that his brother-in-law, a trusted friend, came to his house and without warning produced a large quantity of ecstasy. He pulled a package out and said, 'look at this'. Edwards told him to remove it.

17. Prior to the start of his cross-examination, counsel for Edwards sought to ask Rowlands about his bad character. This was supported by the Crown. He wished to cross-examine Rowlands about three matters:

(i)   his previous convictions;
(ii) the live cartridge found at his home; and
(iii) the antique firearm which, so it appears, was perfectly lawfully held by him.

18. The judge's ruling was that he allowed cross-examination about the previous convictions and the cartridge. He said he did not prevent questioning on the firearm, but that it was a matter for counsel to deal with in the way they thought fit. Rowlands appeals on the following grounds.

(i)   the judge was wrong to allow a co-defendant to cross examine him on his previous convictions pursuant to section 101(1)(e), as his defence did not undermine his co-defendant and his conviction for handling could not properly be regarded as evidence relevant to his propensity for truth.

(ii) He was also wrong to allow cross-examination pursuant to section 101(1)(g) as only prosecution evidence is admissible under this gateway. Alternatively, the judge failed to exercise his discretion under sections 101(3) and 101(4) in respect of the length of time between the previous convictions and the offence for which he was being tried.

(iii) The judge was wrong to rule that the cartridge and firearm found at his house was evidence of bad character as defined by section 98 and permit questioning thereon. The cartridge was the subject of a severed count and should therefore be properly regarded as evidence in connection with the alleged offence and or evidence of misconduct in connect with the investigation. The possession of an antique firearm is not a criminal offence and cannot be regarded as either evidence of disposition or misconduct. Alternatively, the cross-examination about the cartridge and firearm was more prejudicial then probative.

The single judge gave leave on the third ground, but refused leave on the first two.

19. Rowlands previous convictions comprised the following:

— criminal damage in 1983, for which he was fined;
— handling in 1992, for which he was fined £50;
— criminal damage in 1993 for which he was conditionally discharged for 12 months;
— religiously aggravated harassment in 2004 for which he was fined.

20. All Rowlands' previous convictions were put before the jury by his co-defendant in cross-examination. He was not cross-examined on them by the Crown. It is difficult to see how any of them could possibly have had any relevance in the case except possibly the handling to which we shall return in a moment.

21. The position about the gun and the cartridge was that Rowlands admitted possession of them. They were in a shoe box. He said he had found them when digging in the garden. This was not disputed by the Crown.

22. We take first ground 3. Section 98 provides:

References in this Chapter to evidence of a person's 'bad character' are to evidence of, or a disposition towards, misconduct on his part, other than evidence which—

(a) has to do with the alleged facts of the offence with which the defendant is charged, or—

(b) is evidence of misconduct in connection with the investigation or prosecution of that defence.

23. It is difficult to see how evidence of lawful possession of an antique firearm can amount to evidence of, or a disposition towards, misconduct. The judge did not prevent questioning on it, but doubted its relevance. In our view it was not evidence of bad character and therefore no question of admissibility under section 101 arose. As to the cartridge, Mr Roochove, for Rowlands, submits that it comes within either subsection 98(a) or (b) and thus does not fall for consideration under section 101. As Ramsey J pointed out in argument, material falling within section 98(a) or (b) could very well be brought into the trial quite apart from through the provisions of Chapter I of Part II of the Criminal Justice Act 2003. The words in section 98(a) 'has to do with the alleged facts of the offence' are quite widely drawn and it seems to us are wide enough to cover the cartridge in this case, which had originally been the subject matter of the count joined in the same indictment, albeit subsequently severed. It is irrelevant for the purposes of the present issue whether there was a single cartridge or an arsenal of weapons. In the light of the explanation of Mr Rowlands, apparently accepted by the Crown, it is difficult to see what relevance the cartridge had, in the event, to the jury's verdict.

24. As to the previous convictions, it is now conceded that the judge was in error to admit the evidence under section 101(1)(g)—the defendant has made an attack on another person's character. It was a co-defendant, not the Crown, who made the application. This gateway is not concerned with issues between co-defendants (see section 106 and particularly 106(3) which provides, that only prosecution evidence is admissible under section 101(1)(g)). (See also *Hanson* para 5).

25. That leaves section 101(1)(e). Here the evidence is admissible only if it has substantial probative value in relation to an important matter in issue between a defendant and a co-defendant. Mr Roochove's submission is that Rowlands' defence was no more than a denial of participation (see *Varley*). His co-defendant had accepted by way of admission under section 10 of the Criminal Justice Act 1967 that:

— cash found on the premises was his;
— his fingerprints were found on the package containing the drugs;
— his fingerprint was discovered on a latex glove that contained traces of ecstasy.

However, we do not think that these admitted facts take this case outside section 101(1)(e). This was in reality a cut-throat defence. The judge was entitled, indeed required, to look at the whole picture.

26. It should be borne in mind that the judge's discretion not to admit evidence in sections 101(3) and (4) does not apply to the gateway in section 101(1)(e). However, the passage of time between a previous conviction and the offence charged referred to in section 101(4) may be a very relevant matter to which the judge should draw attention when he sums up to the jury.

Our attention was also drawn to section 104(1) which provides:

Evidence which is relevant to the question whether the defendant has a propensity to be untruthful is admissible on that basis under section 101(1)(e) only if the nature or conduct of his defence is such as to undermine the co-defendant's defence.

27. But the judge still had to be satisfied that the evidence had substantial probative value before it was admissible through the gateway in section 101(1)(e). This question is ultimately a question for the judge on his 'feel' of the case. It is not clear from his ruling that he fully considered this issue. We are very doubtful whether, had we been in the same position as the judge, we would have concluded that the evidence crossed this threshold. Once admitted however, what weight the jury was to attach to the evidence was an entirely different matter. The Vice-President gave this warning in *Hanson* at paragraph 18:

Our final general observation is that, in any case in which evidence of bad character is admitted to show propensity, whether to commit offences or to be untruthful the judge in summing up should warn the jury clearly against placing undue reliance on previous convictions. Evidence of bad character cannot be used simply to bolster a weak case, or to prejudice the minds of a jury against a defendant. In particular, the jury should be directed; that they should not conclude that the defendant is guilty or untruthful merely because he has these convictions. That, although the convictions may show a propensity, this does not mean that he has committed this offence or been untruthful in this case;

that whether they in fact show a propensity is for them to decide; that they must take into account what the defendant has said about his previous convictions; and that, although they are entitled, if they find propensity as shown, to take this into account when determining guilt, propensity is only one relevant factor and they must assess its significance in the light of all the other evidence in the case.

28. We come then to the judge's summing up. He said this:

During the course of this trial you have heard evidence that both defendants have previous matters recorded against them, but you will recall those previous convictions, as they are called, are of a dissimilar nature and are, for the most part, some considerable time ago. You may think that they are of little or no relevance to this trial.

He continued a little later:

Both defendants have given evidence and you may therefore think that it is right to take all those matters into account when deciding whether or not the defendant's evidence to you was truthful. The defendants, of course, argue that in making a clean breast before you and relying on the positive character evidence that each of them is more likely to be telling the truth. You must decide because the facts are for you, to what extent, if at all, the character of each of them helps you in deciding whether you believe their evidence.

29. This seems to us to be very close to advising the jury to ignore the previous convictions. The judge gave no direction about the cartridge or the antique firearm. This is hardly surprising as they had faded into insignificance in the case. The prosecution had said nothing about them in their final speech; nor had they sought to rely on Rowlands' previous convictions.

30. The handling offence was committed 13 years before the trial. The jury was not made aware of its circumstances and, it seems to us, that it can have had only the most marginal relevance to the question whether Rowlands was telling the truth about the drug offences with which he was charged. That apart, none of the previous convictions can have had any relevance either to propensity to truthfulness or the commission of drug related offences.

31. At page 35 the judge, when dealing with Rowlands evidence, reminded the jury that he had earlier given them a direction about his convictions and also that there was an admission about the gun and the cartridge.

32. There was a strong case against Rowlands who was, in effect, caught red handed. Each defendant blamed the other for the considerable quantity of drugs that was found in the house where they were. The introduction of the previous convictions of Rowlands by his co-defendant was admitted by the judge. They were, however, insignificant in relation to the real issue in the case. The judge effectively told the jury to ignore them and in our view the conviction is safe.

33. [The court dismissed the appeal against sentence.]

McLean

34. The sections of the Criminal Justice Act 2003 referred to in this appeal are sections 101(1)(d), 101(1)(e), 101(3), 104(1) and 112.

35. On 5 July 2005 in the Crown Court at Taunton McLean was convicted of two counts of section 18 wounding with intent before Judge Hume Jones and a jury. Because the

appellant had a qualifying previous conviction he was given an automatic life sentence. The determinate sentence was 5 years on each count concurrently. A co-defendant called Saunders was acquitted of one offence of wounding with intent.

36. McLean's application for leave to appeal against conviction has been referred to the full court by the registrar. We grant leave.

37. By count 1 McLean and Saunders were jointly charged with wounding Julian O'Toole with intent to cause grievous bodily harm. By count 2 McLean alone was charged with wounding Adrian Green with like intent.

38. The Crown's case was on the following lines. On 8 July 2004 O'Toole (the victim in count 1) received a phone call from Saunders suggesting he went to 5 Regal Court to collect some money he was owed. At the flat were three men, the appellant, Saunders and a man called Johnny.

39. When O'Toole and his brother Adrian Green (the victim in count 2) arrived at the flat they were invited into the living room where McLean was present. Johnny appeared at the door and went to attack O'Toole with a baton, with Saunders saying, 'hit him, hit him.' McLean produced a knife from under a cushion and struck out at O'Toole's head. Green tried to stop this. O'Toole saw Saunders with a knife and he was pushed into the kitchen by Saunders and Johnny. Saunders tried to stab O'Toole. Johnny was wielding the baton. Meanwhile McLean turned on Green and struck him on the head. Green managed to get out and slipped down the stairs. At the bottom of the stairs he was attacked by McLean with a knife, which Green held onto in order to try and defend himself. McLean then went back upstairs to join Saunders in the attack on O'Toole.

40. McLean's case was that he had no involvement in the attack whatever. O'Toole was attacked by two men; one of them must have been Saunders. As to count two, Green produced a knife. He only responded in self defence, possibly kicking Green in the face and then punching him and banging his hand to try to make him release the weapon.

41. Saunders' case was that he was not a party to a plan or the attack on O'Toole. The injuries to both victims were caused by McLean and Johnny. Also, McLean had a propensity for violence which made it more likely he would have fought with O'Toole and Green.

42. When interviewed, McLean said he was not present at the time of the attack. Saunders said he had played a minor role in the attack. He threw a single punch and then retreated to another room from which he heard the attack. In evidence, Saunders said he took no part in the attack at all. Johnny hit O'Toole and Green with a butt and McLean attacked O'Toole and Green with a knife.

43. The Crown sought to adduce during the prosecution case evidence of McLean's previous convictions under sections 101(1)(d) as relevant to an important matter in issue between the defendant and the prosecution namely whether the defendant had a propensity to commit offences of violence. The offences were, wounding with intent using a knife in May 1998, two offences of battery in July 2001 and affray in May 2004. The judge rejected the application.

44. However, the following day the co-defendant Saunders sought to adduce evidence of McLean's bad character under section 101(1)(e) on the ground that it had substantial probative value in relation to an important matter in issue between the defendant and the co-defendant.

45. The judge ruled that the separate versions put forward by the two defendants was an important matter in issue between McLean and his co-defendant and that McLean's bad character had substantial probative value.

The grounds of appeal are:

(i) The judge erred in granting the application of the co-accused to produce evidence of the (McLean's) bad character under section 101(1)(e) of the Criminal Justice Act 2003 when the judge had hitherto refused the Crown's application for leave to adduce the same evidence under section 101(1)(d) of the Criminal Justice Act 2003 on substantially the same grounds.

(ii) It was perverse of the judge to resolve the same arguments differently on the second application where the arguments in the case were so similar under section 101(1)(d) on the Crown's application and under section 101(1)(e) on the application of the co-accused.

(iii) The bad character evidence of (McLean) neither had 'substantial probative value' nor went to 'an important matter in issue between the defendant and a co-defendant.'

46. The judge in admitting the evidence ruled as follows:

There is therefore an issue set up between these two defendants, it may not be what is customarily called a cut-throat defence in that the one is not making the affirmative allegation that the other was responsible for the crime or crimes, but there is an issue between the defendants, their separate versions create an issue between the defendants. Is that an important issue, matter in issue? It seems to me that it must be an important matter in issue. The next question I have to ask myself is whether or not the co-defendant that is Mr McLean's bad character has substantial probative value in relation to that important issue. It seems to me that it must be right that if one defendant who is saying he was not involved in violence and the other one is saying he was not involved in the violence, but one has got previous convictions of violence it seems to me that on the basis of *Regina v Price* there must be, it must be relevant, sorry, it must have substantial probative value in relation to the issue between the two defendants and so I find this gateway is open and therefore it must be right that Mr Warren can adduce the evidence of bad character, of Mr McLean's bad character. So far as the position is concerned in relation to my ruling of yesterday, it seems it has been said it must follow that if I rule it out yesterday, I should rule it out today. It seems to me that there are different considerations between an application made by the Crown to adduce evidence of bad character and evidence, applications between defendants to adduce bad character. It seems only common sense to me there must be different considerations when one is considering the position between two defendants as opposed to the applications made by the Crown and it seems to me that therefore because I ruled against the Crown yesterday I am not bound to rule against Mr Warren today.

47. No complaint is made of the summing up which seems to us to have dealt appropriately with the issues in the case. The sole complaint is that the judge should not have admitted evidence of McLean's previous convictions as relevant to propensity to commit offences of violence.

48. The first two grounds of appeal are both directed to the point that the judge rejected the Crown's application to adduce evidence of McLean's previous convictions under section

101(1)(d) on 28 June 2005, yet very soon afterwards on the next day acceded to the co-defendant's application under section 101(1)(e) on substantially the same grounds and argument. In our view the defence may have been somewhat fortunate to have resisted successfully the Crown's application under section 101(1)(d). The main reason for the judge's decision appears to have been that McLean's earlier violence was in response to longstanding problems that he had been unable to resolve and that this was distinguishable from the violence in the charges. When the judge rejected the Crown's application he said, 'there is no propensity here shown to such an extent that it would be relevant and, in any event, it seems a bit unfair.'

49. Different considerations applied to the co-defendant's application which was made under a different provision, namely section 101(1)(e). The question for this court is whether the judge properly applied the relevant provisions on this application; it matters not that he may previously have been in error on the Crown's application, even if his factual conclusions on that application appear, to an extent, in conflict with his later conclusions.

50. The judge correctly directed himself that he first had to decide whether there was an important matter in issue between the two defendants and secondly whether the bad character had a substantial prohibitive value. He referred to *Price* [2005] EWCA Crim 1359 as illustrating that the propensity to violence of D1 may be relevant as making it less likely that the offender was D2. It was important which of McLean or Saunders was more likely to have been O'Toole's assailant and the fact of McLean's section 18 conviction was of substantial probative value. See *Weir and others* [2005] EWCA Crim 2866 (**p 206 above**) para 120.

51. The judge concluded that although this was not perhaps a cut-throat defence in the classic sense, their separate versions of what had occurred created an important issue between them. This seems to us to be plainly correct. Each individual tells an entirely different story as to what went on. Mr Stanniland, for McLean, sought valiantly to distinguish between important issues and ancillary issues, his argument really coming to this, that although there was a series of ancillary issues between the defendants there was no important issue. We remind ourselves that 'important matter' is defined in section 112 as a matter of substantial importance in the case as a whole and this, as Sir Igor Judge P pointed out in *Renda and others* [2005] EWCA Crim 2826 (**p 193 above**) para 3, is very much a matter for the 'feel' of the judge. The judge went on to consider whether the previous convictions of McLean had substantial probative value to the issue between the defendants. He said it seemed to him that if each defendant was saying he was not involved in the violence and one has previous convictions for violence that must have substantial probative value on the issue between them.

52. Mr Stanniland argued that the judge's ruling against him was even more perverse when one took into account that section 101(1)(e) provided a more stringent test than section 101(1)(d) and yet he had admitted the evidence under the former but not the latter. We are not, however, persuaded by any of Mr Stanniland's grounds. The judge applied the correct test and, contrary to Mr Stanniland's third ground of appeal, the bad character evidence did, in our view, have substantial probative value. The appeal is accordingly dismissed.

53. Before leaving this case we make two further comments. It was not a case where the judge had any discretion to refuse to admit the evidence under section 101(3) and, in fairness, it was never suggested that he had. Once the section 101(1)(e) gateway was open the evidence was in. Nor did section 104(1) apply because the issue was propensity to violence not a propensity to untruthfulness.

Smith

54. The sections of the Criminal Justice Act 2003 referred to in this appeal are sections 98, 100, 101(1)(c), 101(1)(d), 101(3), 101(4), 103(1) and 109(1).

55. On 17 June 2005 in the Crown Court at Newport, Isle of Wight sitting at Portsmouth before Judge Hetherington and a jury this appellant, aged 62, was convicted of five counts of gross indecency with a child (counts 3–7) and sentenced to 21 months imprisonment on each count concurrently. He was acquitted of rape, count 9. Further counts of rape, count 1, indecency with a child, count 2, and indecent assault on a female, count 8, had been stayed as an abuse of process before the trial. He appeals against conviction by leave of the single judge.

56. There were three complainants: TAM who was born on 17 October 1976, her sister DB who was born on 18 November 1979 and SR who was born on 21 June 1988.

57. The three counts that were stayed as abuse of process were count 1, rape, on TAM between October 1989 and October 1993 when she was aged between 13 and 17; count 2 gross indecency with a child on DB between November 1988 and November 1991 when she was aged between 9 and 10; and count 8 indecent assault on TAM on the 3 February 1998 when she was aged 21.

58. The remaining counts on which Smith was tried and convicted related to SR. The 9th count, on which Smith was acquitted, alleged that he had raped TAM in October 1992. The counts on which he was convicted alleged sexual abuse of SR over the period of June 1993 to June 1995, when she was in the age range 5 to 7.

59. The reason why counts 1, 2 and 8 were stayed as an abuse of process was that the Hampshire Police had written to Smith in June 2 1998 saying no further action would be taken against him in respect of these matters.

60. The application to stay was resisted by the Crown and the judge made his ruling on 14 April 2005. The judge indicated when ruling on the stay that the Crown might wish to apply to adduce the evidence that underlay these counts as evidence of bad character under the Criminal Justice Acts 2003. The Crown duly made such an application and the judge ruled in its favour on 10 May 2005. The terms of the application were to adduce the following evidence:

A. Allegations by TAM:

(i)   That the defendant raped TAM when she was about nine years old.
(ii) That the defendant indecently assaulted TAM between the ages of five to nine.
(iii) That on 3 February 1998 the defendant indecently assaulted TAM.
(iv) That on 9 February 1998 the defendant told TAM to 'drop the case'.
(v)   Supporting evidence of the above: [three persons named]

B. Allegation by DB:
That the defendant indecently assaulted DB when she was aged about nine or ten on several occasions.

61. The underlying question on this appeal is whether the judge was right to admit the evidence in the light of section 101(3). Section 101(3) provides:

The court must not admit evidence under subsection (1)(d) or (g) if, on an application by the defendant to exclude it, it appears to the court that the admission of the evidence would have such an adverse effect on the fairness of the proceedings that the court ought not to admit it.

And section 101(4):

On an application to exclude evidence under subsection (3) the court must have regard, in particular, to the length of time between the matters to which the evidence relates and the matters which form the subject of the offence charged.

62. The facts are these. Smith was arrested in March 1998 following an alleged indecent assault on TAM. The police were then investigating three matters. The first was a complaint by TAM that sometime between 1989 and 1991 Smith had given her a lift in a van, driven her somewhere and raped her. He denied giving her a lift in any vehicle. That became count 1, the first of the stayed counts. Next, DB claimed he had committed an act of gross indecency with her in his garden shed at Coronation Gardens between 1988 and 1991 where he lives. He denied ever allowing DB into his shed. That became count 2, the second of the stayed ccounts. Third was TAM complaint that Smith gave her a lift in his van to a different location on 3 February 1998 and indecently assaulted her. This became count 8, the third of the stayed counts. As is apparent, the third of the three events took place shortly before Smith was arrested, the other two some years before.

63. On 2 June 1998 the Hampshire Constabulary wrote to Smith in these terms:

On the 9th of March 1998 you were arrested and detained by Detective Constable Hardy in connection with an allegation of attempted rape and indecent assault. A full report has now been submitted by the investigator to myself. This in turn has been forwarded to the Crown Prosecution Service for their advice. After careful consideration, it has been decided that no further action will be taken against you in relation to these alleged offences.

64. The judge said in his ruling that the letter would have been intended by the prosecution and understood by the defendant as an unequivocal statement that no further action would be taken. He said he did not think it would have been interpreted by the defendant, nor should it have been, as meaning that in the event no further complaint came forward or further evidence emerged that the decision might be revisited and the prosecution might be launched.

65. The position was indeed as set out in that letter for a period of about five years, but then fresh allegations against Smith emerged and these eventually came to form the subject matter of counts 3–7 and count 9 of the indictment.

66. We should add that we were told that nowadays letters are no longer written in such unqualified terms as the letter of 2 of June 1998. There is usually now a qualification in terms such as, 'unless new evidence emerges.'

67. Smith and his family moved to 11 Parsonage Road, Sandown on 21 November 1988. The third complaint SR, lived at 6 Parsonage Road with her family. In 2002 she alleged that in 1993 to 1995 when she was aged between five and seven, Smith committed a number of acts of indecency with her in his garden shed. TAM made a further statement to the police in February 2004 in which she alleged that she had been raped on her way home in October 1992 when she was about sixteen years old. That was count 9 on which the jury acquitted.

68. SR's evidence relating to count 3–7 was as follows. She used to go to Smith's house and play with his son Matt. She said that there was a wooden garden shed at the bottom of the garden on the right hand side. She said that when Matt went into the house Smith would invite her into the shed. She said that she would go inside the shed thinking that he wanted to show her his tools. Smith would undo his trousers and make her touch his penis. She said he would tell her it was a natural thing to do and there was nothing wrong with it. She said he would pretend to be tightening his belt; he would then take out his penis and would start touching himself and demonstrate how he put his hand around it. She said he would then tell her it was her turn. She did not tell her mother as she was too scared and she also thought there was nothing wrong. She said she did not know why she kept going back to the house. On the final occasion she refused to touch him and he said, 'just do it.' She said that by this stage she had realised what she was doing was wrong. In cross-examination she said she had bonded with Smith and that he made her feel loved. He was friendly towards her and she was friends with him as she did not really get on well with her mother. She accepted that in 2003 she made an allegation that somebody at a party had been punched and held by the throat. She said that she later withdrew this allegation because she had problems at the time and did not wish to take the matter to court. She described her relationships with other members of her family in 2002 and 2003 as volatile and that at times she was depressed and had attempted to take her own life. She did not recall TAM or DB although she had heard of the latter.

69. In re-examination she said that the first people she told about the allegations were her father and Tina Dempsey in 2003. She did not wish to pursue the allegations as she was friends with Smith's son Matt and she did not want it to appear as if she did not wish to go to his house.

70. Smith categorically denied the allegations in interview. When he gave evidence he said that there was a shed at Parsonage Road but that it was a home made wooden lean-to adjacent to the side entrance to the house. He used it for welding and small engine work. He never dealt with fish or lobsters in the shed. He said the shed was less then 3ft wide and he did not allow children anywhere near the electric welder. He did not recall SR ever being in the shed and he denied ever touching her.

71. The evidence that the judge was invited to admit was the evidence of TAM and DB that would have supported the stayed counts and also some more general allegations of TAM that she had made in her witness statement of February 1988 about what happened to her between the ages of five and nine. This was a series of indecent assaults and being shut in the lobster pot in the shed, on Shanklin beach when she was sixteen that she referred to in her March 2004 statement and other incidents in the garden shed when Smith tried to make her touch his penis. Thus in summary the Crown was seeking the admission of evidence from TAM that (a) supported the stayed charges 1 and 8 and (b) went to other indecency by Smith towards her and also evidence from DB that supported charge 2.

72. The judge in a conspicuously clear and careful ruling started with section 98 noting that references to bad character in Part II of the 2003 Act are to evidence of, or to a disposition towards misconduct on Smith's part. The description, therefore, was widely drawn.

73. The judge in our view rightly rejected the submission that the evidence was admissible through gateway 101(1)(c) as important explanatory evidence. He turned then to section 101(1)(d) and concluded that the question for him was whether the evidence was

capable of establishing a propensity on the part of the defendant to commit the offences charged. By section 103(1) matters in issue between defendant and the prosecution include whether the defendant has propensity to commit offences of the kind with which he is charged. Whether it did or not, i.e. the weight to be attached to it would be a matter for the jury. He referred to para 18 of the judgment of the Vice-President in *Hanson* to which we have already referred in paragraph 27. The judge rightly observed that this was a case of misconduct or disposition towards it rather than convictions, and secondly that the number and pattern of incidents could be important as more indicative of a propensity than a single incident. He also reminded himself of para 9 of the judgment in *Hanson* observing that what had to be looked at was probative force. He then went on to say:

> I note that all incidents in this case involve young girls, or young women aged 21 at a maximum, all known to the defendant and I make no findings as to how well known, they were not strangers. Secondly, there are strong connections made by the garden shed, references made to it at respective houses in Coronation Gardens by DB, at Parsonage Row by SR and at Coronation Gardens by TAM. Thirdly, it seems to me that there is a discernable pattern to the abuse allegedly taking place in the shed with fishing tackle and the smell of fish. I do not overlook the fact of course that there are some obvious differences as well.

And a little later:

> I conclude that there is ample evidence to conclude that the defendant did have a propensity. The material sought to be produced to that issue is relevant to and probative of that propensity.'

He accordingly concluded that the section 101(1)(d) gateway was open.

74. He then went on to consider section 101(3) he noted that the material was old and that by analogy with the observations in *Hanson* about old convictions it ought only to be admitted if it showed continuing propensity. He observed that the counts had been stayed not because the defendant would not receive a fair trial but because it would be unfair to try him. There was some prejudice which he said went to the fairness of being tried and the possibility of being convicted. It was fairly minimal and could be dealt with by telling the jury the reason why they were no longer trying the stayed counts. As to the defence contention that the evidence was being introduced to bolster a very weak case, he said that it was not for a court to judge the witnesses in advance and evidence should not be excluded on this ground. Any issues about collusion and contamination were for the jury.

75. The court's discretion in section 101(3) is widely phrased and the test is whether the court thinks the admission of the evidence would have such an adverse effect on the fairness of the proceedings that the court ought not to admit it. Provided in exercising his discretion the judge has in mind the time factor in section 101(4) (which the judge did in this case) this court will not ordinarily interfere with the decision unless there has been some error in principle.

76. Absent some error of principle in the present case, it is difficult to find any justifiable basis for concluding that the judge erred in the exercise of his discretion. Did he err in principle? Here the argument is that it is quite simply wrong for someone who has been told he will not be prosecuted in respect of certain allegations to find himself facing the selfsame allegations, not as charges but as prosecution evidence, in a criminal trial.

77. The relevant underlying principle seems to us to be this. Prima facie all evidence that is relevant to the question whether the accused is guilty or innocent of the offence charged is admissible. In *Z* [2000] 2 AC 483 it was accepted by the defendant that the evidence of the three complainants in respect of whose complaints he had been acquitted was relevant to the question whether he was guilty of the offence of rape with which he had been charged. The issue was not whether the defendant was guilty of having raped the three other complainants; he was not being put on trial again for those offences. The only issue was whether he was guilty of the fresh allegation of rape. Lord Hope said at p.487 that the guiding principle was that prima facie all evidence which is relevant to the question whether the accused is guilty or innocent of the offence charged is admissible. He said that the objection to the admissibility of the evidence was based on Lord MacDermortt's statement in *Sambasivam v Public Prosecutor, Federation of Malaya* [1950] AC 458, 479 that the effect of the verdict of acquittal pronounced by a competent court after a lawful trial is not restricted to the fact that the person acquitted cannot be tried again for the same offence. He said that it is binding and conclusive in all subsequent proceedings between the parties of the adjudication. Lord Hope went on:

> But I agree with my noble and learned friend Lord Hutton that the observation which is contained in the second of these two statements is in need of qualification in order to confine its application to its proper context. The principle which underlines both statements is that of double jeopardy. It is obvious this principle is infringed if the accused is put on trial again for the offence of which he has been acquitted. It is also infringed if any other steps are taken by the prosecutor which may result in the punishment of the accused on some other ground for the same offence. But it is not infringed if what the prosecutor seeks to do is to lead evidence which was led at the previous trial, not for the purpose of punishing the accused in any way for the offence of which he has been acquitted, but in order to prove that the defendant is guilty of a subsequent offence which was not before the court in the previous trial.

78. If evidence of previous allegations is in principle admissible notwithstanding that the accused was acquitted of charges based on those allegations in a previous trial, it is difficult to see why in principle evidence relating to allegations that have never been tried (i.e. because of a stay for abuse of process) should not be admissible. The defendant's protection comes through the judge's discretion under section 101(3) or, in an appropriate case, through section 78 of the Police and Criminal Act 1984.

79. Mr Moores, who has appeared before us for Smith as he did in the court below, submits that Smith was in effect tried on the charges that were stayed. We cannot accept this. The jury was not required to return any verdict; it simply heard evidence that the Crown claimed on the basis of propensity supported the charges that were before the jury. In this regard it should be noted that Smith was acquitted of the only remaining offence in respect of which either TAM or her sister were complainants.

80. There is one other point with which we wish to deal. The judge correctly identified at paragraph 14 of his ruling that what he had to decide was whether the evidence had the capacity to establish propensity to commit the offences charged. Whether it actually did so was a matter for the jury. As Kennedy LJ pointed out in *Weir and others* [2005] EWCA Crim 2866 (**p 206 above**) para 7 a defendant's propensity to commit offences of the kind charged

can be proved in ways other than by evidence that he has been convicted of an offence of the same description or an offence of the same category.

81. Mr Moores questions whether an allegation that is untested by a judicial or quasi-judicial finding is *evidence* of a defendant's bad character within the opening words of section 101. He refers to *Bovell* para 21 where the Vice-President expressed considerable doubt as to whether the mere making of an allegation is capable of being evidence within section 100(1). That was said in the context of an allegation of wounding with intent made and withdrawn by the victim against the complainant. As the Vice-President said, if the allegation was to be admitted there would have to be an investigation of relevant-matters. Section 100 is dealing with a non-defendant's bad character, whereas section 101 is dealing with a defendant's bad character. We are persuaded that the allegations in the present case are capable of constituting evidence under section 101, particularly in the light of section 109(1) which provides that:

> Subject to subsection (2), a reference in this Chapter to the relevance or probative value of evidence is a reference to its relevance or probative value on the assumption that it is true.

Accordingly we do not have any difficulty with the fact that the evidence admitted by the judge was in the category of allegations rather than convictions. Whether or not the allegations were true was a matter for the jury.

82. Mr Moores submitted that the protection of section 101(3) was illusory if the judge did not conduct an assessment of the weight of the evidence sought to be admitted. We note the similarity in wording between section 101(3) and section 78 of the Police and Criminal Evidence Act 1984. Each section requires the judge to exercise a discretion based on the particular circumstances of the case and an assessment of the adverse effect, if any, on the fairness of the proceedings of the introduction of the evidence. Whilst the judge in exercising that discretion will have regard to the potential weight of that evidence it is not his job to usurp the jury's function of deciding what evidence is accepted and what rejected. But obviously if, for example, it is inherently incredible that would be likely to be a strong factor against admitting it. We wish to emphasise the broad nature of the judge's discretion under this subsection. The judge's job is to police the gateway not to embark on the jury's job of evaluating the evidence. We reiterate the cautionary words of the Vice-President in *Bovell* about the undesirability of descending into satellite litigation. We have considered carefully the judge's exercise of discretion in the present case and we are unable to find any fault with it.

83. A peripheral point taken by Mr Moores is that item A(iv) in the Crown's application that on 9 February 1998 Smith told TAM to drop the case was not evidence of bad character as defined in section 98. Even if that is correct, it makes no difference as the evidence was admissible anyway.

84. There is a second ground of appeal that the court should allow the appeal on the 'lurking doubt' basis referred to in *Cooper* [1969] 1 QB 267. This submission seems to us to come very close to saying that if the relevant provisions of the Criminal Justice Acts 2003 are applied as the judge, in our view correctly applied them, an unsafe conviction and therefore an unjust result necessarily follows. We do not agree. No complaint whatsoever was made about the way in which the judge summed up this case and we are unpersuaded that the conviction is unsafe.

85. Our conclusion in this appeal is as follows. There could have been no justifiable complaint about the admission of the 'bad character' evidence but for the letter and following it the stay previously ordered by the judge. That stay does not, in principle render the evidence inadmissible. The judge's exercise of discretion under section 101(3) cannot be faulted as *Wednesbury* unreasonable as submitted by Mr Moores and the appeal must be dismissed.

86. We understand the Crown's desire to put the whole picture with regard to TAM and DB's evidence before the jury in this case. We do, however, give a word of caution for the future about the general undesirability of the jury being required to explore satellite issues one stage removed from the charges they are trying unless this is really necessary. Prosecutors should keep this in mind.

Enright and Gray

87. The sections of the Criminal Justice Act 2003 referred to in this appeal are sections 98 and 101(1)(b).

88. On 10 February 2005 in the Crown Court at Luton before Judge Foster and a jury Kevin Enright and Rosalind Gray were both convicted possessing a class A drug, ecstasy, with intent to supply (count 1); possessing a class B drug, amphetamine, with intent to supply (count 3); and possessing another class B drug, cannabis resin, with intent to supply (count 5). Earlier on 26 July 2004 Gray had pleaded guilty to possession of cocaine. Each received concurrent sentences of four year's imprisonment. Enright appeals against conviction by leave of the single judge. Gray renews her application for leave to appeal against sentence after refusal by the single judge.

89. The facts of the case are as follows. On 31 October 2003 police officers attended 59 Pelham Court in Hemel Hempstead with a search warrant. Upon entering the property they found Enright and Gray in bed together. The officers began to search the bedroom and found capsules containing white powder on Enright's side of the bed. Enright was then arrested. The search continued and a bag containing a resinous substance and some paper wraps was found on Gray's side of the bed. Two bags containing tablets were also found on Gray's side of the bed. Gray was arrested and then taken into the bathroom in order to be strip searched. Gray took off her dressing gown and leant forwards into the laundry basket. A police officer then found a large lump of cannabis resin in the basket and four clear plastic bags containing a hard brown substance in her dressing gown pocket. Pills, hollow pills, electronic scales and a penknife were later found in the living room and a small lump of resin and four self-seal bags were found in the kitchen. Enright and Gray were both taken to Hemel Hempstead Police Station. A forensic scientist later confirmed that all the substances seized from the flat were controlled drugs. In total 84.5 ecstasy tablets, 19 capsules containing a total of 7.63 grams of amphetamine and just over 200 grams of cannabis resin were seized.

90. The prosecution case was that Enright and Gray were running a small scale drug dealing business together from their flat. This could safely be assumed from the volume of drugs and the positions of the drugs found in the flat coupled with the electronic scales, the knife, the re-sealable bags and the hollow capsules which were also found in the flat. Enright's case was that he knew nothing at all about the presence of the drugs; they were nothing to do with him.

91. The issue for the jury was whether Enright was aware of the presence of the drugs in the flat and if so, whether he and Gray were in possession of those drugs with the intention of supplying them to others.

92. Included in the Crown's witnesses was John McCawley, who was Gray's former husband. They had been divorced for over 10 years but Gray had stayed with him on a short term basis. He said he saw her taking crack cocaine almost everyday and he saw her with a large amount of cannabis resin. Gray had packets of cocaine, some of which were for her own use. People were contacting Gray on her mobile phone although he said he did not hear her 'setting up anything'. Gray told him she was not dealing in drugs. On 20 October 2003 he asked Gray to leave and then went to work. When he returned Gray had gone but she had stolen some items from the house. He contacted the police two days later as she had neither apologised nor returned any of the items to him.

93. The Crown made a successful application to adduce the convictions of Gray in the light of her counsel's cross-examination of McCawley. Enright's counsel elected to cross-examine the police officer and lead evidence of his convictions. He said he had a catalogue of convictions, some for theft going back to the 1970s and 80s. More recently most were drink related including assaults, criminal damage, driving offences and assaulting a police officer. In 2003 he was convicted of possession of a small amount of amphetamine (1 gram).

94. One reason why Enright's counsel took this course was to minimise the potentially prejudicial effect of evidence that when the police raided the flat and arrested him he was handcuffed.

95. Enright's sole complaint on the character issue relates to the direction the judge gave the jury. His grounds of appeal read:

> The judge erred and/or misdirected the jury by directing them that they were entitled to regard the appellant's previous convictions, admitted by the appellant voluntarily under s101(1)(b) Criminal Justice Act 2003, as evidence upon which they could find that he was either more likely to have committed the disputed offences or that he was not truthful.

In other words the judge should not have allowed the jury to treat Enright's previous convictions as being relevant to propensity or untruthfulness.

96. The judge's direction to the jury begins at page 34 line 17. He said:

> In this case you have heard evidence that both defendants have bad character in the sense that they have criminal convictions. It is important that you should understand why you have heard this evidence, and how you may use it. As I will explain in more detail later, you must not convict only because a defendant has bad character.

He then dealt with Gray before going on to deal with Enright. He said:

> You also have heard about Mr Enright's extensive criminal record, as well as his explanation for it. You have heard about this because of the questions by his barrister to PC Guinan, the officer in the case, as well as, of course, Mr Enright told you about it himself when he gave evidence.
>
> You may use the evidence of either defendant in this regard . . . of either of the defendants' bad character in the following ways: if you think it right, you may take it into account when deciding whether a particular defendant's evidence to you was truthful. A person with a bad character may be less likely to tell the truth, but it does not follow that

he, or she, is incapable of doing so. You must decide to what extent, if at all, his character, or the character, helps you when judging each defendant's evidence.

If you think it right, you may also take it into account when you are deciding whether or not either defendant has committed the offences for which they are now charged. You must decide to what extent, if at all, character helps you when you are considering whether or not he, or she, is guilty. But bear in mind that bad character cannot by itself prove guilt. It would therefore be wrong to jump to the conclusion that he, or she, is guilty just because of bad character.

You have heard about Mr Enright's one conviction for simple possession of amphetamine and Miss Gray's one conviction for the simple possession of cocaine. You may feel that the other offences, of a completely different type (Mr Enright's convictions for assault, driving matters, criminal damage; Ms Gray's conviction for theft) have no bearing whatsoever upon the likelihood of these defendants having committed these drugs offences now.

As regards Mr Enright's convictions for theft and other offences of dishonesty, bear in mind that these are old and stale and occurred when he was a much younger man.

You must also bear in mind what either defendant has said about those convictions.

97. The thrust of the submissions of Mr Wade, who appeared before us for Enright as he did in the court below, was originally this. The use to which evidence of bad character can be put depends entirely on the gateway through which it has been admitted. The law does not authorise the use of bad character evidence for the purpose of establishing propensity to commit the offence or propensity to be untruthful unless it was admitted for that purpose under section 101(1)(d) ie relevant to an important matter in issue between the defendant and the prosecution. Here it was adduced under section 101(1)(b) at the defendant's instigation. Section 101(1)(b) provides:

The evidence is adduced by the defendant himself or is given in answer to a question asked by him in cross-examination and intended to elicit it.

98. It was allowed in, submits Mr Wade, only for whatever purpose the defendant required it. Thus it could not be used either as evidence of propensity to commit the offence or as evidence of propensity to be untruthful.

99. In our view section 101(1) deals merely with the issue of admissibility. It does not deal with the relevance of the evidence once admitted, any more than it deals with the weight to be attached to it.

100. Bad character in section 98 is broadly defined. Its relevance will vary from case to case. Once admitted (no matter through which gateway) it can be used for any purpose for which it is relevant. The Lord Chief Justice made this clear in *Highton*.

101. Mr Wade, appreciating that what the Lord Chief Justice said in *Highton* has taken the rug from under his feet on his specific point, has directed his argument more generally to what the judge said in his summing up. The judge told the jury that Enright's bad character might mean he was less likely to tell the truth and that his one previous drug offence might have some bearing on his having committed the drug offences with which he was charged. But he pointed out:

— all the other offences were of a completely different kind;
— his dishonesty offences were old and stale and committed when he was much younger;

— he had no history of drug dealing;
— he volunteered his convictions;
— what the jury made of the evidence and whether it helped was a matter for them;
— a person of bad character is not necessarily incapable of telling the truth;
— they could not convict just because of a defendant's bad character.

102. The case was tried very soon after the relevant provisions in Part II of the Criminal Justice Act 2003 came into force. The judge did not have the help that subsequent authorities from this court have given. He did his best and followed the Judicial Studies Board Specimen Direction. In truth, however, the evidence of the appellant's bad character had very little, if any, probative value. Enright's previous convictions played no part in prosecuting counsel's final speech. Ms Weeks, for the prosecution, accepts that the judge should have given the jury a clearer and stronger direction. In submissions to the judge before he summed up she submitted that the convictions had no relevance to propensity and she accepted before us that the convictions cannot show a propensity for untruthfulness when the circumstances relating to them were never explored. There were in any event ancient.

103. There are one or two passages in the part of the summing up to which we have referred that are potentially unfavourable to Enright, for example that a person of bad character may be less likely to tell the truth. But viewed as a whole the summing up came close to advising the jury that Enright's convictions had little bearing on the issues they had to decide.

104. In our judgment the judge should have given a clearer direction to the jury that the evidence of his bad character did not assist the Crown on either untruthfulness or propensity. The drug offence was at best of marginal relevance and the dishonesty convictions were never explored to see whether they showed propensity for untruthfulness. But, when all is said and done the evidence against Enright was strong. When the police arrived they found drugs and drugs paraphernalia all over the flat.

105. There is a second ground of appeal that the judge should not have prohibited the jury from returning verdicts on the alternative counts of possession just because they had convicted of possession with intent to supply. Mr Wade's reasoning appears to be that the evidence shows that there were different sources and different amounts of drugs found in different places in the flat and the jury was deprived of the opportunity of finding that Enright was not involved with all of the drugs. In our view this argument is hopeless. Having found Enright guilty of the more serious offences it was inappropriate for the jury to go on to consider alternatives.

106. Enright's appeal against conviction is accordingly dismissed.

107. Gray did not appear before us and was not represented. Her case did, however, appear in our list as a non-counsel renewed application for leave to appeal against sentence. It appears from correspondence with the Criminal Appeal office that counsel was prepared to appear on a pro bono basis on her behalf that he would have done had he been made aware of the listing date. There appears to have been some confusion within the office. It is unnecessary to explore where any fault lies. In the circumstances we adjourn Gray's application to be heard by a different court on another day.

Appeals of Edwards, Rowlands, McLean, Smith and Enright dismissed.
Gray's appeal adjourned.

INDEX

*References in **bold** are to the page numbers of Appendix V. Otherwise references are to paragraph numbers in the commentary.*